C&H
$7.50

JUL 30 '88 Surratt   61-13707

FRANKLIN AND NATURE'S GOD

ALFRED OWEN ALDRIDGE

BENJAMIN FRANKLIN AND NATURE'S GOD

To lead a virtuous Life, my Friends,
and get to Heaven in Season,
You've just so much more Need of Faith,
as you have less of Reason.
POOR RICHARD *(February, 1748)*

Atheism is unknown there; Infidelity rare
and secret; so that persons may live to a
great Age in that Country, without having
their Piety shocked by meeting with either
an Atheist or an Infidel.
INFORMATION TO THOSE WHO WOULD
REMOVE TO AMERICA *(1782)*

DUKE UNIVERSITY PRESS
DURHAM, N. CAROLINA 1967

© 1967, Duke University Press

Library of Congress Catalogue card no. 67–13409

PRINTED IN THE UNITED STATES OF AMERICA
BY KINGSPORT PRESS, INC., KINGSPORT, TENN.

PREFACE

THIS book grew out of a lecture which I gave several years ago at the University of Georgia under the auspices of the philosophy department and more recently at the University of California in Berkeley under the auspices of the history department.

I am grateful to the General Research Board of the University of Maryland for two grants which enabled further research. Also I am indebted to the Library of Congress and the libraries of the University of Maryland, the American Philosophical Society, and Yale University as well as to the past and present editors of the Franklin *Papers*.

CONTENTS

ONE. RELIGION AND NATURE ~*3*

TWO. "AN INFIDEL OR ATHEIST" ~*12*

THREE. OF GOD AND GODS ~*25*

FOUR. SCIENTIFIC DEIST ~*34*

FIVE. PRACTICAL MORALIST ~*47*

SIX. THEORETICAL MORALIST ~*58*

SEVEN. RELUCTANT METAPHYSICIAN ~*75*

EIGHT. "WE ZEALOUS PRESBYTERIANS" ~*82*

NINE. WHITEFIELD AND METHODISM ~*103*

TEN. MORE FAITH AND WORKS ~*124*

ELEVEN. RELIGION BY HOAX ~*133*

TWELVE. SECTARIAN CONTACTS ~*144*

THIRTEEN. A PROFESSING "PROTESTANT OF THE CHURCH OF ENGLAND" ~*158*

FOURTEEN. THE CHURCH OF AMERICA ~*180*

FIFTEEN. THE JUDAIC TRADITION ~*195*

SIXTEEN. UNITARIANS AND DEISTS ~*207*

SEVENTEEN. FRENCH CATHOLICS ~*222*

EIGHTEEN. AMERICAN CATHOLICS AND A SPANISH SERMON ~*235*

NINETEEN. LAST THOUGHTS ~*250*

TWENTY. LAST WORDS ~*260*

INDEX ~*273*

FRANKLIN AND NATURE'S GOD

RELIGION AND NATURE

THE first sentence of the American Declaration of Independence affirms that the final authority upon which all human relationships rest consists in "the laws of nature and nature's God." Although Benjamin Franklin was not the author of this declaration, he was a member of the committee which worked with its framer, Thomas Jefferson, and he suggested certain verbal changes. More important, he and most of the members of the Continental Congress subscribed to this propostion and to the related ones that divine wisdom and divine decrees are revealed in nature and that any human contact with God must come through the channels of natural law.

Dozens of popular books of theology and ethics published throughout the eighteenth century attest to the tendency in English thought to couple religion and nature. Some of the most important of these volumes are: William Wollaston, *The Religion of Nature Delineated* (1722); Mathew Tindal, *Christianity as Old as the Creation; or, the Gospel a Republication of the Religion of Nature* (1730); Joseph Butler, *The Analogy of Religion, Natural and Revealed, to the Constitution and Course of Nature* (1736); and Thomas Chubb, *An Enquiry into the Ground and Foundation of Religion, Wherein is shewn, that Religion is founded in Nature* (1740).

Some of these books taught that the laws of nature and the Christian Scriptures provide identical truth or may at least be reconciled with each other. Others taught that nature and the Scriptures are incompatible. The first view was called Christian deism; the second, deism alone. And it was to the latter religious system that Franklin and Jefferson adhered.

Many attempts have been made to explain the essence of deism by studying such works as Thomas Paine's *The Age of Reason* or by dealing with a whole group of deistical texts at once. The present study will follow a contrary method—biographical rather than analytic—attempting to understand the complex of ideas involved in deism as they developed in the thought of one man. We shall look first at Franklin; second at the ideas he held and upheld.

In our day, deism has fallen out of vogue, and many critics adopt a supercilious tone in treating it. Those who are antagonistic toward deism are likely to be antagonistic toward Franklin as well, condemning him for metaphysics allegedly superficial and ethics allegedly materialistic. The following comparison with Jonathan Edwards illustrates this condescending attitude.

> Franklin started us on the road which has led to a gadgeteers' paradise. But now that it is becoming startlingly clear that gadgets can't save us, and may all too readily destroy us; now that thoughtful members of this mechanistic age are seriously asking the question which the Philippian jailer, trembling, put to Paul and Silas, 'Sirs, what must I do to be saved?'; now that Dr. Franklin's lightning rod begins to look, from one viewpoint, like a pathetic symbol of human pride and inadequacy, while Edwards' soul-probings seem more searching to this generation of readers perhaps than they have ever seemed before, it is possible that Edwards will yet emerge, is already emerging, as the more useful, the more truly helpful, of the two.[1]

Another of Edwards' modern apologists, considering Franklin as at best an apostle of utilitarianism, assumes that empirical philosophy is by definition inferior to a system of metaphysical rigidity.

> Does one become a disciple of experience by obliterating nice speculations and subtle distinctions, thus abandoning himself to a fancied freedom which amounts to treating one's neighbors in an assuming manner and to answering the question of questions, in a universe where solidity itself means inexorable gravity, with an "I am not able to reconcile my Free-will to God's Foreknowledge"? Others might accept such intellectual bankruptcy; Franklin did, most Americans would, but Jonathan Edwards could not.[2]

1. Randall Stewart, approvingly quoted by Douglas J. Elwood, *The Philosophical Theology of Jonathan Edwards* (New York, 1960), p. 2.
2. Perry Miller, *Jonathan Edwards* (New York, 1959), p. 117.

This tirade seems to suggest that philosophical depth is based on "nice speculation and subtle distinctions." Despite the assumption that only Edwards among eighteenth-century Americans came to grips with the issue of free will and determinism, we shall see that a good deal of evidence exists to indicate that Franklin also faced the problem in all its complexities.

The question is—does it make more sense to begin with nature and to reason therefrom to nature's God (the method of Franklin and Jefferson), or to begin with God, a metaphysical assumption, and to reason therefrom to God's nature (the method of Edwards)?

We must not forget that both Franklin and Edwards lived in the intellectual period known as the Enlightenment, a period which assumed that human reason represented the best agency for the solving of philosophical and social problems. Edwards' best-known work, his *Freedom of the Will,* is praised by his disciples as a masterpiece of logical reasoning —and it is in this regard at least a reflection of the Enlightenment. Yet there can be no question that Franklin, more than Edwards, epitomized its true spirit and ideals. The philosophy of the Enlightenment has been splendidly defined by the abbé André Morellet, one of Franklin's friends and admirers: "It is this ardor for knowledge, this activity of mind which does not wish to leave an effect without seeking the cause, a phenomenon without explanation, an assertion without proof, an objection without a reply, an error without combating it, an evil without seeking the remedy, a possible good without seeking to attain it; it is this general movement of minds which has marked the eighteenth century and which will constitute its glory forever."[3]

To be sure, God is notably absent from this rhapsodical portrayal of Enlightenment thinking, and quoting it certainly does not prove anything at all about Franklin's reli-

3. "Eloge de Marmontel," translated from A. O. Aldridge, "Benjamin Franklin and the *philosophes,*" *Studies on Voltaire and the Eighteenth Century,* XXIV (1963), 43.

gion. It is merely intended to show that Franklin may be judged by a quite different scheme of values from that usually applied to Edwards.

There is no doubt that Franklin became a deist from the moment he began to think rationally on the subject of religion, but he also had direct contact with every other religious belief which was prevalent in his society. In his autobiography he remarked that "This is the age of experiments," and he applied the experimental method to his attempt to unravel the secrets of divinity and morality. No other subject occupied more of his time and reflection.

Furthermore, Franklin's spiritual quest has in our day lost none of its significance or vitality. His electrical experiments are antiquated in the atomic age—even his political theories have been superseded. But his religious ideas are as valid now as they were in the eighteenth century. Religion, which deals with eternal truth, does not seem to be susceptible to progress. Both deists, to whom Franklin most closely approached, and orthodox Christians, who claim him as a kindred spirit, deny that the passage of time brings any increase of religious knowledge. Orthodox Christianity rests on the revelation of the Old and New Testaments, and deism assumes that nature communicates directly to all men in all periods of time everything that is necessary to be known about God.

Any man's religion, including Franklin's, may be viewed in terms of two major perspectives. First, we may study his credo: in other words, his moral and metaphysical notions and their connection with his private system of worship. We may investigate his opinion of such metaphysical matters as the freedom of the will, the essence of the universe (whether it be matter or spirit), and the problem of evil. We may examine also his views on such ethical considerations as the nature of virtue and the motives for adhering to it in daily life. And we may consider his feelings about immortality, the function of prayer, and the authenticity of revelation (the

Old and New Testaments). Second, we may trace his relations with organized religious groups or formal sects. Regardless of his private beliefs, a man may have close ties with one or more church denominations or with sectarian leaders whose views may be either similar to his own or highly divergent. In the following pages, we shall study in detail the development of Franklin's credo as well as his direct personal contacts with the major religious currents of the eighteenth century.

Reared in the New England Congregationalist tradition, he led a theological rebellion in the Presbyterian church of Philadelphia. He collaborated with an English friend in abridging the Book of Common Prayer of the Church of England and fostered the development of cordial relations between English bishops and the American Episcopal church. He helped to create a deistical center of worship in London as well as to establish the first Unitarian chapel. As a diplomat, he carried on discussions with the papal nuncio which led to the organization of the Roman Catholic church in America after the Revolution. Even more important, he directly contributed to the downfall of the Spanish Inquisition. A criticism, of the Inquisition which he made to a Spanish priest in Philadelphia led this priest to deliver a sermon in the local Catholic church attacking the institution; it was the first Spanish sermon in Philadelphia. Later, in the session of the Cortes of Madrid which terminated the Inquisition, this priest repeated the substance of his Philadelphia sermon and acknowledged that Franklin had instigated it.

As a man of letters, Franklin advocated a new translation of the Bible into modern idiom and prepared sample passages. He also wrote a new version of the Lord's Prayer, criticizing both the style and theology of the old. The symbols of Christianity were ingrained in Franklin's mental processes, and he used scriptural language with the ease and familiarity of a Puritan divine.

7

The paradox in Franklin's religious life is that he completely disbelieved Christianity; yet he was attracted by it as a system of worship, and he enjoyed the company of clergymen of all faiths. Unlike such militant deists as Lord Shaftesbury and Thomas Paine, Franklin did not attempt to wither Christianity by ridicule or bludgeon it to death by argument. Instead he was irresistibly drawn to external manifestations of Christian fellowship. Intellectually he had little more faith in orthodox doctrine than in witchcraft or astrology; yet he sympathized with the church as a social institution and supported it so loyally that many sectarians identified him with their causes. As John Adams remarked in great disgust, "The Catholics thought him almost a Catholic. The Church of England claimed him as one of them. The Presbyterians thought him half a Presbyterian, and the Friends believed him a wet Quaker."[4]

The central problem in studying Franklin's religion is to distinguish between those notions about which he was merely curious or to which he gave only temporary or perfunctory assent, and those which he postulated as firm articles of belief.

During his very long life, Franklin's attitudes toward religion as well as other subjects changed and varied with the years. It is exceedingly misleading to assume that all the statements in his writings accurately reflect his inner convictions. In his personal relations Franklin was exceedingly friendly and sociable, and he ordinarily tried to harmonize his views with those of his associates and correspondents. Some of the pious or orthodox sentiments which he expressed in letters to strict religionists may need to be discounted.

Franklin's religious life is the record of an incessant attempt to reconcile and combine private notions with a series of orthodox systems of worship. He failed in this endeavor because his fundamental concepts frequently changed. If he

4. C. F. Adams (ed.), *Works of John Adams* (Boston, 1851), I, 661.

cannot be compared to John of the Cross or to Calvin, it is not because he lacked an all-consuming devotion to a higher power but because he could never be certain about the nature of that power. When Franklin thought of God, as he often did, there was little of reverence; and when he felt compelled to a spirit of reverence, as he often was, there was little of God. Yet the persistence of his quest reveals that he was much more than "a great pagan" who lapsed now and then into pseudo-religious platitudes.

In the popular mind Abraham Lincoln is considered to be a more religious man than Franklin. His gaunt profile and his memorable speeches in Biblical language have created the image of an Old Testament patriarch. A few episodes from his life and selected passages from his letters have served as inspiration for hundreds of sermons. Scholars have sifted Lincoln's works from beginning to end looking for evidence of religious faith, and his commentators have treated each of his references to God or morality with a reverence bordering on that due to Scripture. Yet the concrete result of all this searching is not impressive. Although there is no question that Lincoln believed in destiny, his god is a nebulous, abstract, and impersonal figure. It is not surprising then that the free-thinkers have tried to claim him—just as they have made a few half-hearted and unsuccessful attempts to claim Franklin.

The contrasts between Lincoln's religion and Franklin's are enormous, and all the concrete manifestations of a religious spirit are on Franklin's side. Lincoln was never baptized or otherwise affiliated with any denomination. He never belonged to a church and "never subscribed to any particular ritual or liturgy." Although called a "Christian without a creed," his lack of a creed was more apparent than his Christianity.[5]

Franklin, on the other hand, was formally baptized; he

5. For a treatment of Lincoln's theology, see William J. Wolf, *The Almost Chosen People. A Study of the Religion of Abraham Lincoln* (New York, 1959).

joined several congregations, subscribed to credos, devised some himself, wrote or collaborated in the composing of various liturgies and rituals, and constantly identified himself with formal associations for public worship. Briefly stated, these circumstances may suggest that Franklin was a trimmer or opportunist in religion, but nothing could be further from the truth. If Franklin ever gleaned practical benefit from his religious affiliations, he did so incidentally. Indeed, his acknowledged deism probably harmed his public career.

More important than his ecclesiastical associations are the metaphysical and theological problems which he formulated and discussed as such in his own writings. To him, religion was of primary, not incidental, importance. Franklin found many virtues in religion. To him, discovering the nature of God was the fundamental problem of philosophy, and in his younger years especially he devoted himself earnestly to this intellectual quest. Much of his metaphysical speculation was far removed from the realities of this world and from the conventions of human association.

Also, Franklin needed a religious faith in order to attain inner tranquillity. Emotionally he was driven to recognize a superior force in nature and to respond with expressions of adoration and gratitude. Out of this spiritual need grew the various systems of individual and group worship which he devised.

But on the surface Franklin was a pragmatist, advocating beliefs and practices because of their salutary effect upon society. He constantly taught that the primary function of religion was to promote external welfare. For this reason he was profoundly disturbed when he encountered examples of human behavior at variance with religious belief or profession. In his autobiography Franklin wrote that "the most acceptable service of God is doing good to man," and he affirmed this doctrine endlessly throughout his life.

By and large the issues of right and wrong which interested

Franklin have little to do with so-called personal morality. In the section of his autobiography devoted to the Art of Virtue, he discussed such generally admired forms of restraint as moderation, temperance, and chastity but defined them in a broad sense. Of chastity, he said, for example, "Rarely use Venery but for Health or Offspring; Never to Dulness, Weakness, or the Injury of your own or another's Peace or Reputation."[6] This is hardly an imperative to rigorous self-denial. Indeed, in many editions of the autobiography this passage has been expurgated as shocking immorality. Although Franklin professed to accept the adage "that *our Sins and our Debts are always more than we take them to be,*"[7] he followed hedonistic principles in the conduct of life and "considered neither wine, women, nor good cheer any hindrance to his experiments in electricity, cardinal politics, and noble charity."[8]

Shunning dogmatism and sectarianism, Franklin carried on a continuous quest for religious truth at the same time that he devoted himself to social reform and humanitarian projects. We might even say that in addition to his deistical presuppositions, tolerance and humanitarianism were the only continuous and unchanging dogmas in his creed.

John Selden in the seventeenth century compared religion to the knowledge which men receive at school. "Some men forget all they learned, others spend upon the stock, and some improve it."[9] Franklin belongs to the latter group. His superb intellectual talents and experimental method kept his religious spirit always alive.

6. Leonard W. Labaree *et al.* (eds.), *Autobiography of Benjamin Franklin* (New Haven, 1964), p. 150.

7. Albert Henry Smyth (ed.), *Writings of Benjamin Franklin* (10 vols., New York, 1905–1907), VI, 203.

8. Charles J. Ingersoll, *Recollections* (Philadelphia, 1861), p. 59.

9. Robert Waters (ed.), *John Selden and His Table Talk* (New York, 1899), p. 187.

CHAPTER TWO

"AN INFIDEL OR ATHEIST"

FRANKLIN's parents were God-fearing and Bible-reading tradespeople (candle-makers, to be exact), who brought him up to respect hard work and rigid morality. His father, an English nonconformist, had emigrated to America because in England conventicles (associations for independent worship) had been forbidden by law. Originally he intended Benjamin "as the tithe of his sons" for the church, but before Benjamin had completed his first year at grammar school the cautious parent changed his mind because of the expense of a theological education and the low income of those who succeeded in obtaining it.

Franklin was precocious and his rearing orthodox. By the age of five, he had already begun to read the Bible. His uncle was so impressed with this timely piety that he wrote, "If the Buds are so precious what may we expect when the fruit is ripe?"[1] Franklin's parents guided him through "Childhood piously in the Dissenting Way," exposing him regularly to Presbyterian dogmas such as "the Eternal Decrees of God, Election, Reprobation," which he found at first unintelligible and later unbelievable.[2] His father's library was mainly theological, consisting chiefly of polemical divinity, a circumstance upon which Franklin later blamed his own disputatious tendency.

His reaction against Puritan rigor began early. He was scarcely fifteen "when, after doubting by turns" several doctrinal points as he found them disputed in various books, he "began to doubt of Revelation it self."[3] Some books against deism fell into his hands; "they were said to be the Substance of Sermons preached at Boyle's Lectures"—a series of annual discourses in England designed to curb deism and

1. F. B. Dexter (ed.), *Literary Diary of Ezra Stiles* (New York, 1901), II, 375–376.
2. Leonard W. Labaree *et al.* (eds.), *Autobiography of Benjamin Franklin* (New Haven, 1964), p. 145. Hereinafter cited as Labaree (ed.), *Autobiography*.
3. *Ibid.*, p. 113.

atheism. These books wrought upon Franklin, as upon many others, an effect "quite contrary to what was intended by them: For the Arguments of the Deists, which were quoted to be refuted, appeared . . . much stronger than the Refutations." In short, Franklin "soon became a thorough Deist." While reading other books in an effort to improve his literary style, he encountered Shaftesbury's *Characteristics,* the most influential deistical work published in England before Paine's *Age of Reason.* At the same time he fell upon even more outspoken attacks on orthodoxy by Shaftesbury's disciple, Anthony Collins. These books finished the process of turning Franklin into "a real Doubter."

Because of his precocious skepticism and also because of a program of self-education he had undertaken at an early age, Franklin evaded as much as he could "the common Attendance on publick Worship," Sunday being his studying day. He rebelled also against domestic observances, particularly the interminable prayers and blessings which his father was accustomed to recite. One day Franklin noticed him salting a barrel of meat for the winter. "Father," he said, "you ought to say grace over this barrel of meat once and for all; it would be a great saving of time."[4]

In his twelfth year, Franklin was apprenticed as a printer to his brother James, publisher of one of the oldest newspapers in Boston, the *New England Courant,* an organ receptive to the grumblings of Episcopalians and hidden deists against the ruling Puritan hierarchy of New England. After four years in his brother's shop, Franklin, then sixteen, contributed anonymously to the *Courant* a series of essays known as the *Dogood Letters.* In one of these he ridiculed the ministerial profession, that to which he had himself at one time been destined (May 7–14, 1722).[5] By means of allegorical symbols he suggested that few students at Har-

4. J. P. Brissot de Warville, *New Travels in the United States of America,* ed. Durand Echeverria (Cambridge, Mass., 1964), p. 184.
5. L. W. Labaree *et al.* (eds.), *Papers of Benjamin Franklin,* I (New Haven, 1959), 14–18. Hereinafter cited as Labaree (ed.), *Papers.*

vard College attained a competent knowledge of the ancient languages although the majority tried to pass themselves off as linguistic experts. Divinity students, he suggested, were willing to undergo their laborious and painful studies because they hungered after pecuniary rewards—and they sometimes resorted to doctoring their sermons with plagiarized passages from famous English divines.

In a subsequent essay (July 16–23, 1722) Franklin raised the question "Whether a Commonwealth suffers more by hypocritical Pretenders to Religion, or by the openly Profane?" and decided that the hypocrite is the more dangerous.[6]

In the fall of the year, the rector of Yale College, Timothy Cutler, and two college tutors shocked the people of New England by announcing that they had been converted from Congregationalism to the Church of England. They solemnly declared that only bishops had the power of ordaining other clergy and that, therefore, the ministerial orders of the New England Congregationalists were invalid. Jonathan Edwards, then a prudent Yale undergraduate, made no statements on the controversy which have survived, but Franklin immediately seized the occasion to publish an essay on the theme that there existed "too many blind Zealots among every Denomination of Christians."[7]

This essay, written at the age of sixteen, is important as Franklin's first extended statement on the doctrinal phase of religion. Since he was writing for publication in conservative Boston, he was kept from an open expression of deistical concepts, but he was able at least to suggest two related themes, the absurdity of sectarian differences in Christianity and the importance of humanitarian ethics.

"An indiscreet Zeal for spreading an Opinion," he argued, "hurts the Cause of the Zealot. . . . He that propagates the Gospel among *Rakes* and *Beaus* without reforming them in their Morals, is every whit as ridiculous and impolitick as a

6. *Ibid.*, p. 30.   7. *Ibid.*, pp. 43–45.

Statesman who makes Tools of Ideots and Tale-Bearers."
When Franklin was almost seventy years old, he similarly
reminded a young Anglican clergyman that the only valid
purpose of pulpit eloquence was to lead his congregation to
righteousness. "Without that effect," he insisted, "the
Preacher or the Priest, in my Opinion, is not merely sound-
ing Brass or a tinkling Cymbal, which are innocent Things;
he is rather like the Cunning Man in the Old Baily, who
conjures and tells Fools their Fortunes to cheat them out of
their Money."[8]

Franklin's remarks in his early essay on changes in religious outlook foreshadow the frequent shifts in his own external observances of religion. His experimental changes seldom came violently or suddenly, however, nor did he parade
arguments to invalidate his former practices—the form of
ostentatious conversion against which he addressed his essay.
"In Matters of Religion," he declared, "he that alters his
Opinion on a *religious Account,* must certainly go thro'
much Reading, hear many Arguments on both Sides, and
undergo many Struggles in his Conscience, before he can
come to a full Resolution."[9] Despite his incessant searching,
Franklin never obtained absolute conviction of the truth of
a particular sect and thus escaped bigotry and narrowness
throughout his entire life.

Franklin's precocious comments on clerical matters in
New England now seem circumspect rather than rebellious,
but they indicate the underlying deism which Franklin tells
us in his autobiography he had already acquired. Indeed, he
left Boston the next year at the age of seventeen in part
because his "indiscrete Disputations about Religion" had
caused good people to point at him with horror "as an Infidel
or Atheist."[10]

As everyone knows, he soon found his way to Philadelphia,

8. Albert Henry Smyth (ed.), *Writings of Benjamin Franklin* (10 vols.,
New York, 1905–1907), VI, 233.
9. Labaree (ed.), *Papers,* I, 43.
10. Labaree (ed.), *Autobiography,* p. 71.

15

where almost his first activity was attendance at a Quaker meeting. After reaching the city by boat early on a Sunday morning he joined a crowd of clean, neatly-dressed people, who led him into the principal Quaker meeting house. He "sat down among them, and after looking round a while and hearing nothing said, being very drowzy thro' Labour and want of Rest the preceding Night, . . . fell fast asleep, and continu'd so till the Meeting broke up," when he was awakened by a kind neighbor.[11] As Franklin observed in his autobiography, this was the first house he entered or slept in in Philadelphia.

Franklin eventually found employment with an eccentric printer, Samuel Keimer, an individualist like Franklin in religious matters. Disinclined to conform to any of the orthodox sects of the city, both felt the need for adherence to a shared religious creed, and accordingly they adopted a covenant based upon a combination of their private doctrines.

Keimer had earlier been one of the French prophets ridiculed by Shaftesbury in his *Letter concerning Enthusiasm* and "could act their enthusiastic Agitations." At the time he associated with Franklin, "he did not profess any particular Religion, but something of all on occasion." Keimer was both naïve and knavish. He kept the seventh day Sabbath and "wore his Beard at full Length, because somewhere in the Mosaic Law it is said, *thou shalt not mar the Corners of thy Beard.*"[12] Franklin disliked both points but agreed to accept them if Keimer would conform to his own principle of eating nothing but vegetable food. This notion Franklin had adopted from reading Thomas Tryon's *The Way to Health, Long Life and Happiness,* a seventeenth-century combination of religion and hygiene. The two experimental sectarians followed their joint regime until one day Keimer, a great glutton, invited Franklin and two women friends to dinner and thereupon succumbed to the flesh-pots of Egypt. Franklin soon after gave up his own vegetarianism under the

11. *Ibid.,* p. 76.   12. *Ibid.,* p. 88.

twin influence of the smell of codfish hot out of the frying pan and the accommodating ease of his own reason. Recollecting that he had seen small fish taken out of the stomachs of larger ones, he argued, "if you eat one another, I don't see why we mayn't eat you."

Along with his vegetarianism, Franklin probably gave up the remaining vestiges of any Puritan metaphysics which had survived from his Boston background as well as the positive side of the deism which he had absorbed from his reading. The young are traditionally radical—and many religious leaders go through a stage of spiritual doubt at an early age. Franklin was no exception. The next stage in his intellectual career was atheism.

At the age of nineteen, he abandoned his friends and career in Philadelphia to seek a greater arena for his talents in London, where he had been led to expect patronage. But disappointed in his great expectations, he fell back on his printing trade, securing employment at Palmer's, a well-established printing house. Here he set type for the 1725 edition of a famous deistical work, William Wollaston's *The Religion of Nature Delineated*. Finding Wollaston's reasoning too tame, Franklin wrote a refutation, which he entitled *A Dissertation on Liberty and Necessity, Pleasure and Pain,* and printed an edition of one hundred copies.

In treating this pamphlet in his autobiography, Franklin made the same confusion between deism and atheism which was then common to many orthodox Christians.[13] He lumped them together as forms of free-thinking which lead to the obliteration of the distinction between virtue and vice. Actually, deism insists upon high standards of moral conduct, and Franklin himself remarked elsewhere that it is as different from atheism as chalk is from charcoal. Franklin's pamphlet does indeed deny moral distinctions—but it is atheistic rather than deistic in its metaphysics as well as in its ethical overtones. When Franklin says in his autobiography that he

13. *Ibid.*, p. 114.

later renounced the metaphysical conclusions of his pamphlet because of practical reasons—because he "grew convinc'd that *Truth, Sincerity and Integrity* in Dealings between Man and Man, were of the utmost Importance to the Felicity of Life"—he was giving up his own form of atheism, not deism.

To be sure, Franklin in his pamphlet assumes the existence of a benevolent god, but this divine force is so impersonal that it is inseparable from natural law. Franklin's scheme is pure materialism. He argues that man is a machine, denies the distinction between virtue and vice, demonstrates that man is not immortal, and proposes a novel theory that all men experience equal degrees of pleasure and pain. All this he does while presumably correcting the faults of Wollaston's scheme of ethics—no mean achievement for a teenager. Franklin's employer, Palmer, expostulated with him upon these principles, considering them abominable. Franklin later considered his printing of the pamphlet one of the major errors of his life.

In the first step of his argument, Franklin assigned to God direct responsibility for every occurrence in the universe.[14] If God is omnipotent, he reasoned, nothing may exist or act without his consent. Franklin would not accept a distinction maintained by many theologians: that some activities in the universe are initiated and directly controlled by God and others are initiated independently by his agents. Such a distinction between what God himself does and what he permits, Franklin charged, is a tacit admission "that many Things in the Universe exist in such a Manner as is not for the best" and is a loophole to exempt God from responsibility. Franklin refused to admit of any abridgments of divine power and control. "If God permits an Action to be done, it is because He wants either *Power* or *Inclination* to

14. The pamphlet is published in Labaree (ed.), *Papers*, I, 57–71. Further background information may be found in A. O. Aldridge, "Benjamin Franklin and Philosophical Necessity," *Modern Language Quarterly*, XII (1951), 292–309.

hinder it; in saying He wants *Power,* we deny Him to be *almighty;* and if we say He wants *Inclination* or *Will,* it must be, either because He is not Good, or the Action is not *evil."*

We are much better off as controlled beings, Franklin continued, than we would be as free agents. If we were left to make our own choices, we should never know what is best to be done. Since the infinite possibilities and intricate consequences of every action are incomprehensible to any but an all-knowing power, we should ordinarily have but one chance in ten thousand to blunder on the right action. Hence we should be grateful that all our actions are governed by necessity and that we are spared decisions. "Man is a Part of this great Machine, the Universe, his regular Acting is requisite to the regular moving of the whole." The moral world demands the same flawless regularity and order which govern the constellations and the plant and animal creations.

Franklin compared a world inhabited by free agents to an intricate machine containing many smoothly functioning interdependent moving parts mixed in with other parts endued with independent powers of motion. The unco-ordinated wheels of this hit-or-miss contraption would every now and then move wrong, disorder the true movement, and make continual work for the mender. Far superior, he argued, is the prevailing necessitarian system in which all parts are interdependent and harnessed to a central controlling force. Since man in this system has been reduced to a part of a gigantic machine, he is obviously nothing but a machine himself.

Franklin was trying to build for himself the reputation of a bright young man, and was more concerned to shock than to convince his readers. In the second part of his treatise, therefore, he developed a novel psychological theory to support the concept of divine benevolence—the notion that every human being experiences an exact balance of pleasure and pain. According to this view, pain is necessary to the world order as the motivating force behind all living things: an organism is a machine set in motion by pain and continually seeking release from pain. Franklin's reasoning was simple: since uneasiness causes desire, the satisfaction of desire produces pleasure, great or small, in exact proportion to the desire. Pleasure and pain are, therefore, inseparable. As many degrees as one descends or ascends on the scale, the other moves in the opposite direction. The pleasure from eating is proportionate to the pain of hunger, or the pleasure from liberty is proportionate to the pain of confinement.

This brings us to Franklin's central principle that all men are equally used by the Creator in experiencing pleasure and pain in amounts exactly equal to each other. All men do not receive the same quantity of pleasure and pain, but since each man's total experience of either pleasure or pain is always in exact proportion to the opposite sensation, the net result is equality for all mankind. A sensitive person, for example, may experience sixty degrees of pleasure and sixty degrees of pain, and a piece of matter zero degrees of both. According to Franklin's account, both are on an equal footing. This psychological system gave Franklin the occasion for the only comment which he ever made on space travel. "The Accomplishment of a long and difficult Journey yields a great *Pleasure*," he affirmed, "but if we could take a Trip to the Moon and back again, as frequently and with as much Ease as we can go and come from Market, the Satisfaction would be just the same."[15]

Franklin's conclusion serves to undermine a favorite doctrine of many theologians: the view that there must be a future state in order that the inequities of this life may be

15. Of all the thinkers of the Enlightenment who have devoted their minds to religious speculation, Franklin comes closest to the twentieth century in its obsession for penetrating outer space. The stellar system occupied a position of major importance in his theology. He continually exercised his imagination with the hypothesis that the other stars are inhabited, and he weighed the implications of their being controlled by the god of this world or by other gods.

adjusted—the guilty punished, the virtuous rewarded, and the sufferings of the innocent compensated. If Franklin's theory were true that all men experience a balance of pleasure and pain in this life, there would be no inequities to adjust in a future state.

Not content with refuting the ethical necessity of a future life, Franklin even denied its metaphysical possibility. He gratuitously added a refutation of a current argument in favor of immortality, that of the immateriality of the soul. Even though we grant that the soul is not material, he argued, it is still capable of cessation of thought, the condition which exists during sleep or stupor. And this is the state which may prevail after death—the soul existing without any power of action. Following Locke, Franklin asserted that our ideas, all of which are admitted by the senses and imprinted on the brain, are the only subjects upon which the soul may act. Thinking depends upon memory or the ideas impressed upon the brain. The soul is merely a power of contemplating and comparing these ideas. After death, which entails the destruction of the body and consequently of the brain, the soul, lacking the necessary equipment, must cease to think or to act. "And to cease to *think* is but little different from *ceasing to be.*" Franklin admitted the possibility that after death the soul may be attached to a new body but pointed out that since the new body would acquire an entirely different set of ideas, the identity of the soul would be lost. This would not be immortality, but the coming into existence of an entirely new being.

The two parts of Franklin's treatise are thus two independent demonstrations that all men are equally used by the Creator and represent two different approaches to the problem of evil. In one he asserted that evil does not exist, and in the other that pleasure and pain balance each other. Franklin freely admitted the existence of pain, sickness, and want in the universe but asserted that they are not "in reality *Evils, Ills,* or *Defects* in the Order of the Universe." He realized that this contention implies "that *God permits evil Actions to be done, for* wise *Ends and Purposes*" and tried to dispose of the objection, but he was not very successful. According to his answer, "whatever an infinitely good God hath wise Ends in suffering to *be,* must be good, is thereby made good, and cannot be otherwise." Since he had granted that sickness, want, pain, and murder exist, his explanation (little more than a quibble) does not exempt him from being charged with justifying the means by the end.

Franklin's materialistic depiction of mankind has much in common with a widespread notion in seventeenth-century French philosophy that likened animals to machines. Franklin probably did not know enough French at this time to read in the original language, but he may have heard his tavern companions debating the concept. His own extension of the notion to human beings anticipated a notorious French book published later in the eighteenth century by Julien de La Mettrie entitled *The Man Machine.* A recent scholar in analyzing La Mettrie's mechanistic theory has come to the conclusion that there exists "an underlying inter-action between *volupté* and materialism, with the result that scientific and erotic curiosity seem . . . to function together in a sort of alliance, each serving to strengthen and stimulate the other."[16] The same parallel may be observed in Franklin. Throughout his life, erotic references abound in his works in both private letters and surreptitious pieces. At the time Franklin was writing his necessitarian pamphlet, he was also engaging in "foolish Intrigues with low Women," which because of the expense, he commented, "were rather more prejudicial to me than to them."[17]

Although Franklin's youthful treatise was virtually un-known until late in the nineteenth century, he had earlier been accused of atheism on other grounds. The French free-

16. Aram Vartanian, *La Mettrie's L'Homme Machine: A Study in the Origins of an Idea* (Princeton, 1960) , pp. 32–33.
17. Labaree (ed.) , *Autobiography,* p. 115.

thinker Ernest Renan, familiar with little else in Franklin
except his emphasis on thrift and industry in such works as
The Way to Wealth, argued that he was a gross materialist
with no understanding of spiritual values. According to
Renan's reasoning, the real atheists are those who cherish
dead formulas, who mumble religious catch-words devoid of
feeling or sentiment. "Men of the type of Franklin," he
wrote, "worldly materialistic men (beyond whom there are
none in the world more atheistic), are often the most nar-
rowly attached to formulas."[18]

Such an indictment is based on an inadequate knowledge
of Franklin's life and writings. We shall see in subsequent
pages that Franklin developed an individual system of ethics
and worship, designed primarily to satisfy his spiritual rest-
lessness. It is true that Franklin was attached to formulas and
that he exalted prudence in daily life, but his religious
thought and practice went far beyond material concerns.

In both style and philosophy, Franklin's *Dissertation*
shows the influence of the blunt and cynical Dutch physician, Bernard Mandeville, who in his notorious *Fable of the
Bees* had merrily gone about to expose the corruption of
human nature. Mandeville's purpose seemed to be to destroy
all illusions concerning the existence of virtue, honor, or
social feeling in mankind. And Franklin, who had been
Mandeville's drinking companion in London taverns, mir-
rored this iconoclastic attitude, particularly in his conclusion:

> I am sensible that the Doctrine here advanc'd, if it were to
> be publish'd, would meet with but an indifferent Reception.
> Mankind naturally and generally love to be flatter'd: What-
> ever sooths our Pride, and tends to exalt our Species above
> the rest of the Creation, we are pleas'd with and easily
> believe, when ungrateful Truths shall be with the utmost
> Indignation rejected. "What! bring ourselves down to an
> Equality with the Beasts of the Field! with the *meanest* part
> of the Creation! 'Tis insufferable!" But, (to use a Piece of

18. Translated from Henriette Pschari (ed.), *Œuvres complètes* (Paris,
n.d.), II, 981.

23

common Sense) our *Geese* are but *Geese* tho' we may think
'em *Swans;* and Truth will be Truth tho' it sometimes prove
mortifying and distasteful.

But neither this cynical view of human nature nor the bland
materialism of his metaphysical propositions satisfied Franklin for very long. Shortly after printing his pamphlet he
rejected it on both moral and metaphysical grounds and
burned most of the remaining copies, "as conceiving it might
have an ill tendency." Although he drew away from Mandeville in later life to adopt the moral theory of Shaftesbury, he
never found an answer to the problem of evil which he could
propound with the easy confidence revealed in the necessitarian theories of his *Dissertation*. In his autobiography he
preserved a remnant of his determinism, however, arguing
that the instances of immorality and injustice he had been
guilty of in his salad years "had something of *Necessity* in
them, from . . . Youth, Inexperience, and the Knavery of
others."[19]

19. Labaree (ed.) , *Autobiography,* p. 115.

CHAPTER THREE

OF GOD AND GODS

FRANKLIN remained in London less than two years, and his atheism did not even survive the return voyage to Philadelphia. From the virtual denial of the existence of any god at all, he shifted to a fanciful faith in a plurality of gods. Perhaps disillusioned in some sense with human conduct—his own or that of certain companions in London—he aspired to associate himself with a superior power. Instead of finding his absolute of perfection in the person of the founder of Christianity, he sought it in several superior beings—in a complete hierarchy of gods.

In November, 1728, Franklin prepared for his own use a system of private worship or "little liturgy" to which he gave the title "Articles of Belief and Acts of Religion." Here he set forth his personal creed and a pattern of devotions, including prayers and forms for petition and thanksgiving.

His creed, which he called "First Principles," reveals a richness of imagination, a daring range of speculative inquiry, completely absent from the stream of propositions and syllogisms of his atheistic dissertation.

I BELIEVE there is one Supreme most perfect Being, Author and Father of the Gods themselves.

For I believe that Man is not the most perfect Being but One, rather that as there are many Degrees of Beings his Inferiors, so there are many Degrees of Beings superior to him.

Also, when I stretch my Imagination thro' and beyond our System of Planets, beyond the visible fix'd Stars themselves, into that Space that is every Way infinite, and conceive it fill'd with Suns like ours, each with a Chorus of Worlds for ever moving round him, then this little Ball on which we move, seems, even in my narrow Imagination, to be almost Nothing, and my self less than nothing, and of no sort of Consequence.

When I think thus, I imagine it great Vanity in me to suppose, that the *Supremely Perfect,* does in the least regard such an inconsiderable Nothing as Man. More especially, since it is impossible for me to have any positive clear Idea of that which is infinite and incomprehensible, I cannot conceive otherwise, than that He, *the Infinite Father,* expects or requires no Worship or Praise from us, but that he is even INFINITELY ABOVE IT.

But since there is in all Men something like a natural Principle which enclines them to DEVOTION or the Worship of some unseen Power;

And since Men are endued with Reason superior to all other Animals that we are in our World acquainted with;

Therefore I think it seems required of me, and my Duty, as a Man, to pay Divine Regards to SOMETHING.

I CONCEIVE then, that the INFINITE has created many Beings or Gods, vastly superior to Man, who can better conceive his Perfections than we, and return him a more rational and glorious Praise. As among Men, the Praise of the Ignorant or of Children, is not regarded by the ingenious Painter or Architect, who is rather honour'd and pleas'd with the Approbation of Wise men and Artists.

It may be that these created Gods, are immortal, or it may be that after many Ages, they are changed, and Others supply their Places.

Howbeit, I conceive that each of these is exceedingly wise, and good, and very powerful; and that Each has made for himself, one glorious Sun, attended with a beautiful and admirable System of Planets.

It is that particular wise and good God, who is the Author and Owner of our System, that I propose for the Object of my Praise and Adoration.

For I conceive that he has in himself some of those Passions he has planted in us, and that, since he has given us Reason whereby we are capable of observing his Wisdom in the Creation, he is not above caring for us, being pleas'd with our Praise, and offended when we slight Him, or neglect his Glory.

I conceive for many Reasons that he is a *good Being,* and as I should be happy to have so wise, good and powerful a Being my Friend, let me consider in what Manner I shall make myself most acceptable to him.

Next to the Praise resulting from his Wisdom, I believe he is pleased and delights in the Happiness of those he has created; and since without Virtue Man can have no Happiness in this World, I firmly believe he delights to see me Virtuous, because he is pleas'd when he sees me Happy.

And since he has created many Things which seem purely design'd for the Delight of Man, I believe he is not offended when he sees his Children solace themselves in any manner of pleasant Exercises and innocent Delights, and I think no Pleasure innocent that is to Man hurtful.

I *love* him therefore for his Goodness and I *adore* him for his Wisdom.

Let me then not fail to praise my God continually, for it is his Due, and it is all I can return for his many Favours and great Goodness to me; and let me resolve to be virtuous, that I may be happy, that I may please Him, who is delighted to see me happy. Amen.[1]

Least familiar to twentieth-century church-goers in this rhapsodic system may be Franklin's belief that man is not the most perfect being next to God, but that he exists as an intermediate being between ranks of superior and inferior creatures. This notion may seem revolutionary and extravagant even for the space age, but in the eighteenth century it was commonplace. It belongs to a complex of ideas originating in ancient Greece known as the Great Chain of Being. Believers in the chain assumed that God's perfection and benevolence required him to share the blessings of existence. His perfect love could be satisfied only when he had given life to every type of being which could possibly exist. The result was a chain composed of every possible form of living creature arranged in a continuous gradation from highest to lowest. The concept was featured in Locke's *Essay concerning Human Understanding* and is most widely known in English literature through a passage in Pope's *An Essay on Man,* written shortly after Franklin's "Articles of Belief."

> See, thro' this air, this ocean, and this earth,
> All matter quick, and bursting into birth.
> Above, how high, progressive life may go!
> Around, how wide! how deep extend below!
> Vast chain of Being! which from God began,
> Natures aethereal, human, angel, man,
> Beast, bird, fish, insect, what no eye can see,
> No glass can reach; from Infinite to thee,
> From thee to Nothing.

Franklin's contemporaries would also have seen nothing unusual in the notion of a plurality of inhabited worlds. This

1. L. W. Labaree *et al.* (eds.), *Papers of Benjamin Franklin,* I (New Haven, 1959), 102–104.

was a concept widely discussed by both Catholic and Protestant theologians.

One of the inevitable results of the deists' concentration upon the law and order in the universe—the mechanical efficiency with which the physical and organic worlds performed jointly and separately—was to remove God to a position of remoteness from mankind. The complete rejection of supernatural revelation (the Old and New Testaments as well as any individual visions or annunciations) further shut off the deists from all sense of personal contact with God. This is the main reason that deism never became a vital religion. When God is removed from human affairs, contemplation of his power engenders scant emotional satisfaction, provides no reason for group worship, and offers no dynamic for the conversion of others. Franklin resolved this dilemma by conceiving of one supreme, infinite, and aloof god and a number of inferior gods with passions resembling those of human beings. His subordinate divinities governed the worlds under their control with all the personal concern of magistrates and patriarchs. By assuming these intermediate deities, Franklin could repeat the conventional rhapsodies of the deists over the mechanical perfection of the universe while retaining the personal bond between God and man which supplies the bulwark of orthodox Christianity.

As a conventional deist, Franklin rebuked the vanity of human beings in supposing that "the *Supremely Perfect* does in the least regard such an inconsiderable Nothing as Man." Franklin could not "conceive otherwise, than that He, *the Infinite Father,* expects or requires no Worship or Praise from us, but that he is even INFINITELY ABOVE IT." Paraphrasing a passage from Shaftesbury's *Characteristics,* Franklin compared the Supremely Perfect to a great artist who is not flattered by the praise of ignorant men who fail to understand the true beauty of his creation. But Franklin needed more than this deistical logic and imperturbability.

As a wondering, self-conscious creature, burning with the same desire for personal contact with God which besets evangelicals like John Bunyan or George Whitefield, Franklin felt within himself, as in all men, "something like a natural Principle, which enclines . . . to DEVOTION or the Worship of some unseen Power." Conceiving that this power was a good being, Franklin aspired to have him as a friend. And since it was his duty as a man to pay divine worship to something, it became his primary object to consider how to make himself most acceptable to this unseen power. Emotionally, this deity appeared to Franklin as the fountain of wisdom and goodness. Intellectually, he appeared merely as one of a number of inferior gods created by the Father of All. As Franklin conceived the universe, the god of our world, like his fellow gods, has created a system of sun and planets which he rules over for his own pleasure. He has some of the same passions as human beings—for he is not above being pleased by praise and hurt by neglect. Franklin was not even sure of the immortality of the god of our world. He and his fellow secondary gods may endure forever, "or it may be that after many Ages, they are changed, and Others supply their Places."

This type of polytheism was an amplification of the concept of the Great Chain of Being which had not occurred to any previous writer. It remained a strong and abiding idea with Franklin, not merely a juvenile notion, for he repeated it in subsequent periods of his life. James Parton has suggested that Franklin's notion of subordinate gods has scientific ramifications based upon Newtonian theories, and I. Bernard Cohen in his comprehensive study *Franklin and Newton* also accepts polytheism as one of the links between the two men. In March, 1725, when Franklin himself was in London, Newton in a conversation with John Conduitt, his nephew by marriage, "seemed to doubt whether there were not intelligent beings superior to us who superintended those revolutions of the heavenly bodies by the direction of the Supreme Being."[2]

Even though most of the notions in Franklin's creed, like that of a plurality of gods, were highly speculative and imaginative, his orderly mind led him to codify them as articles of belief. He sought similar precision in the second part of his system of worship, a formal liturgy neatly divided into sections for adoration, petition, and thanksgiving.[3] The first section he opened with the self-admonition that before addressing the deity, his soul "ought to be calm and Serene, free from Passion and Perturbation" and "otherwise elevated with Rational Joy and Pleasure." The section devoted to requests or "Petition," Franklin predicated on the principle that men cannot be sure which of the things they desire would actually prove to be good for them if they were to be granted. He presumed, therefore, to ask only to be given aid in "eschewing Vice and embracing Virtue." His detailed requests for this divine aid were essentially enumerations and descriptions of vices and virtues. The first of these is especially significant in view of his London pamphlet: "That I may be preserved from Atheism and Infidelity, Impiety and Profaneness, and in my Addresses to Thee carefully avoid Irreverence and Ostentation, Formality and odious Hypocrisy, Help me, O Father." Since "Ingratitude is one of the most odious of Vices," Franklin closed his liturgy with grateful acknowledgment of the favors of heaven. His precise and detailed enumeration furnishes evidence of the solid and simple comforts which Franklin prized and enjoyed: "Peace and Liberty, . . . Food and Raiment, . . . Corn and Wine, and Milk, and every kind of Healthful Nourishment; . . . the Common Benefits of Air and Light; . . . useful Fire and delicious Water; . . . Knowledge, and Literature, and every useful Art; . . . my Friends and their Prosperity, and the

2. "A Remarkable and Curious Conversation between Sir Isaac Newton and Mr. Conduit," quoted by James Parton, *Life and Times of Benjamin Franklin* (Boston, 1892), I, 175.
3. Labaree (ed.), *Papers*, I, 104–109.

fewness of my Enemies; . . . all thy innumerable Benefits;
. . . Life, and Reason, and the Use of Speech; . . . Health
and Joy, and every Pleasant Hour."

The quest for virtue was an essential part of both the
"Articles of Belief" and the "Acts of Religion." In his liturgy, as we have already seen, Franklin devoted the section
entitled "Petition" to enumerating and defining the compo-
nents of virtue. And in his credo he asserted not only that
our God is pleased with the happiness of his creatures, but
also that "since without Virtue Man can have no Happiness
in this World," God "delights to see me Virtuous, because he
is pleas'd when he sees me Happy."

Franklin never entirely abandoned the combination of
ethics and polytheism in his "Articles of Belief" as he had
rejected his earlier necessitarianism. Indeed, he expanded his
notions throughout the years, and, as we shall see in a subsequent chapter, he associated his own polytheism with primitive beliefs he had observed among Indian tribes in Pennsylvania. It is true that in his autobiography and elsewhere,
Franklin states "that there is one God, who made all things,"
but we may also find in his later years many vestiges of
polytheism. Shortly after reaching the age of fifty, he referred
in a letter (April, 1757) to a military friend to a plurality of
gods and made a prayer to them *"That whatever I wish for
my Friends, shall come to pass."*[4] Remarking that "the Gods
will doubtless take Care of those they love," he recommended his friend to the *Dieux,* using the plural French
form. In commending Dupont de Nemours' benevolence to
mankind in 1768, he observed that this must be the govern-
ing philosophy "of superior beings in better worlds."[5] In
1773 he and the Welsh philosopher David Williams jointly
agreed on the possibility of the existence of plural deities.[6]
Nine years later he remarked to Joseph Priestley on the

4. *Ibid.,* VII (1963), 182.
5. Albert Henry Smyth (ed.), *Writings of Benjamin Franklin* (10 vols.,
New York, 1905–1907), V, 156.
6. See chap. xvi below.

"Light we are viewed by superior Beings."[7] And becoming more precise in a letter to the abbé Soulavie in the same year, he suggested that "superior beings smile at our theories, and at our presumption in making them."[8]

Most important of all, in a letter to Sir Joseph Banks, president of the Royal Society, reporting the first French experiments with flight by balloons (November 21, 1783), Franklin suggested that "Beings of a [rank] and nature far superior to ours have not disdained to amuse themselves with making and launching balloons, otherwise we should never have enjoyed the light of those glorious objects that rule our day and night, nor have had the pleasure of riding round the sun ourselves upon the balloon we now inhabit."[9] At this time Franklin had almost reached the age of eighty, and he was still speculating on the subject of "Beings of a [rank] and nature far superior to ours." To be sure, he may have been speaking in the sense of Greek gods or "whatever gods may be." It is significant, on the other hand, that of those friends to whom he spoke of plural deities, Priestley, Soulavie, and Banks were all scientists, a circumstance suggesting that his polytheistic references may have been based on the Newtonian concept of intelligent beings superintending the revolutions of the heavenly bodies.

Franklin's comparison of stars in the firmament to balloons flying over France also explains the phrase "Father of Lights" in his famous motion for prayers in the Constitutional Convention. "How has it happened, Sir," he asked, "that we have not hitherto once thought of humbly applying to the Father of Lights to illuminate our Understandings."[10] Previously the phrase "Father of Lights" has been understood merely as a poetic metaphor. It may just as well be based upon a scientific concept.

If any inconsistency between monotheism and polytheism exists in Franklin's thought, it can be resolved in the light of

7. Smyth (ed.), *Writings,* VIII, 452.   9. *Ibid.,* IX, 118.
8. *Ibid.,* p. 599.   10. *Ibid.,* 600.

his "Articles of Belief," which presuppose a *"Supremely Perfect"* or *"Infinite Father,"* who created "many Beings or Gods, vastly superior to Man." In other words, Franklin's perspective could embrace either a multiplicity of gods, each one controlling a system such as our own, or the single supreme god controlling all the subordinate gods and their systems. When engaged in scientific imagination, Franklin directed his thoughts toward several gods; when he devoted himself to worship, his perspective was limited to a single god, whom he considered as either "Father" or "Friend."

CHAPTER FOUR

SCIENTIFIC DEIST

A few months after Franklin drew up his polytheistic scheme of worship, he organized among his brightest acquaintances in Philadelphia a club for mutual improvement called the Junto. The rules which he drew up required that "every Member in his Turn should produce one or more Queries on any Point of Morals, Politics or Natural Philosophy, to be discuss'd by the Company, and once in three Months produce and read an Essay of his own Writing."[1] In 1730, a scant five years after publishing his pamphlet on liberty and necessity, he delivered to his "intimate pot-companions" a lecture, "On the Providence of God in the Government of the World," designed to prove the freedom of will and the divine control of human affairs.[2] Franklin chose the very existence of God as the essential point of his discourse, and he presented conventional demonstrations to prove it. The pendulum of his thought had moved to the opposite extreme from his necessitarian pamphlet. He now unequivocally asserted God's active participation in human affairs—a position from which he later more than once retreated when beset by doubt.

Perhaps the media of communication had something to do with the extreme divergences between his London pamphlet and his Philadelphia discourse. In an anonymous work published in the printing capital of the British Empire, Franklin had nothing to lose by maintaining radical paradoxes—and he could pose as an atheist and adopt sensational positions which he may not really have believed. But in a lecture delivered in person to his business associates and intimate friends in the provincial milieu of Philadelphia, he could not afford to run the risk of being labeled an atheist. Even to the

1. Leonard W. Labaree et al. (eds.), Autobiography of Benjamin Franklin (New Haven, 1964), pp. 116–117.
2. The lecture is printed in L. W. Labaree et al. (eds.), Papers of Benjamin Franklin, I (New Haven, 1959), 264–269, under the date 1732. Reasons for believing that it may have been 1730 appear in A. O. Aldridge's review of this volume of the Papers in American Literature, XXXII (1960), 208–210.

relatively sophisticated closed circle of the Junto, Franklin did not develop a complete deistical system but limited himself to arguments which would be accepted by both deists and orthodox Christians.

In his lecture, Franklin used as the initial proof of the existence of God the fact that the preponderance of mankind in all ages have believed it—the familiar argument of the *consensus gentium*. The second proof Franklin found in the admirable order and disposition of things in the universe. Physical perfection, he argued, could only be the product of infinite wisdom—and we will find it whether we consider the stellar system or the vegetable and animal kingdoms on this earth. Franklin marveled at the way each living creature is "adapted to its Nature, and the Way of Life it is to be placed in, whether on Earth, in the Air or in the Waters, and so exactly that the highest and most exquisite human Reason, cannot find a fault and say this would have been better so or in another Manner." Franklin had forgotten all his objections to Wollaston, who argued in this very same fashion. Indeed, as Franklin continued to give illustrations of the goodness of God in the creation, he could have served as a model for Voltaire's Dr. Pangloss. Franklin pointed out that God has made the most necessary elements for survival (water, air, and light) the most common and easy to attain. And his creatures acknowledge their gratitude for the life he has given them by their unwillingness to depart from it.

Although Franklin had abandoned the necessitarianism of his earlier pamphlet, he had not given up his notion of God as a super-mechanic. He tried to convey the infinite productive potentialities of God's infinite knowledge and wisdom by comparing them with mere human degrees of these qualities. "Weak and foolish Creatures as we are, by knowing the Nature of a few Things can produce . . . wonderful Effects"—such as mixing nitre and sea salt to form acid or mixing saltpeter, sulphur, and charcoal to form gunpowder. What power then "must he possess who not only knows the

Nature of every Thing in the Universe, but can make Things of new Natures with the greatest Ease and at his Pleasure!"

Having established the existence of his God-mechanic, Franklin next listed four possible relationships in which God could stand with regard to the universe which he had created.

First, he could unchangeably decree every action and leave nothing to the course of nature, admitting no free agency of any kind. This assumption, Franklin maintained, would be equivalent to atheism. Before making such an irrevocable decree covering every action in the universe, God would be a being of power almighty; but by determining everything, he would divest himself of all further power. It would be no exaggeration to say of such a God: "he has done and has no more to do, he has ty'd up his Hands, and has now no greater Power than an Idol of Wood or Stone; nor can there be any more Reason for praying to him or worshipping of him, than of such an Idol, for the Worshippers can never be better for such Worship." Even though Franklin avoided the term *necessity*, this comment represents a repudiation of the underlying presuppositions of his youthful *Dissertation*. The type of necessitarianism he had earlier propounded was indeed equivalent to making God unalterably determine every thing that comes to pass in the universe and hence effectively remove himself from consideration. In his recantation, Franklin pointed out that necessitarianism or the supposition of an unchangeable decree would be making God responsible for all the evil in the world as well as for all the blasphemy uttered against himself. It would also put him in the absurd light of causing the greatest part of mankind to address prayers and supplications which would be utterly unfounded and useless, for everything would be determined in advance. Surely, Franklin concluded, "it is not more difficult to believe the World was made by a God of Wood or

Stone, than that the God who made the World should be such a God as this."

The second supposition, that God would leave everything in the universe to the operation of general nature and free agency, Franklin found equally unsatisfactory, for it also removed God completely from his creation—putting him in the position of an indifferent spectator, or even worse, of a parent who has abandoned his creation. To the heroes in virtue who struggle to please a God, whom they think good, the divine being must answer, *"Take the Reward Chance may give you, I do not intermeddle in these Affairs."* To the evildoers and bringers of destruction, he must say, *"If Chance rewards you, I shall not punish you, I am not to be concerned."* And to the innocent and the beneficent in the hands of wicked oppressors, he is able to say nothing but, *"I cannot help you, 'tis none of my Business nor do I at all regard these things."* To make such assumptions about God would be to believe him "idle and unactive" and unconcerned with his attributes of "Power, Wisdom, and Goodness."

The third supposition, that some events are unalterably decreed and the rest left entirely to general nature and free agency, Franklin considered no less a form of un-Godding the creator. As in the two foregoing suppositions, "he is no more to be regarded than a lifeless Image, than Dagon, or Baall, or Bell and the Dragon."

We are driven, therefore, Franklin argued, to admit a fourth supposition, "that the Deity sometimes interferes by his particular Providence, and sets aside the Events which would otherwise have been produc'd in the Course of Nature, or by the Free Agency of Men."

This may appear to be a conclusion relatively clear and simple, hardly dependent upon the systematic rejection of the three foregoing suppositions. Yet such a conclusion was extremely rare in the eighteenth century, except in the works of a few orthodox Christian theologians who did not bother to prove it but merely assumed its truth on the authority of revelation. Very few of Franklin's contemporary deists made any such specific statement concerning the place of providence in the universe. Most never even faced the problem or, if they did, they successfully obscured it with ambiguous rhapsodies about the wisdom of God and the sublimity of law and order in the universe. Shaftesbury in his *Characteristics,* for example, suggested both that divine order has contrived the independent functioning of a perfect universe and, conversely, that a guiding providence intervenes to control particular events.

We see that Franklin, like Jonathan Edwards, did indeed take up the problem of free will and God's foreknowledge. But instead of vainly attempting to reconcile them, he concluded that both men and God are free. On the subject of God's powers, Franklin was not only more forthright than most of the deists but also more consistent than Edwards. The latter stoutly insisted on the law of cause and effect to prove his necessitarian argument but, on the other hand, argued with equal vehemence that God has the power to intervene directly in human affairs. The two notions are, of course, incompatible. One might say also that Franklin's notions of free will and divine control of human affairs are equally inconsistent. In a sense they are, but one could hypothecate God's interference in any situation in a manner which would not directly affect any involved human being's free will. Edwards' system will not admit even this kind of a loophole.

After claiming greater consistency for Franklin than for Edwards, we must still admit that Franklin's argument for occasional divine intervention rests on nothing more solid than a demonstration of the inadequacies of the other three suppositions (complete divine determinism, absolute freedom, partial divine determinism). Since Franklin himself probably recognized the weakness of his demonstration, he added a somewhat irrelevant and not very convincing exposition of free agency in human creatures. Since God has communicated to human beings a portion of his wisdom, power, and goodness, he argued, it is also possible for him to communicate a portion of his free agency. " 'Tis sufficient," Franklin declared, ". . . to shew 'tis not impossible, and no Man I think can shew 'tis improbable." In other words, men have free will because the contrary cannot be proved.

Franklin buttressed his argument for providence by means of a dilemma he posed to doubters: "If God does not sometimes interfere by his Providence 'tis either because he cannot, or because he will not." The first alternative denies his infinite power; the second, his infinite goodness. Franklin's case rests, therefore, on the proposition that it is reasonable to believe in providence since it is highly absurd to believe otherwise.

Faith in providence, Franklin concluded, represents the foundation of all true religion. "We should love and revere that Deity for his Goodness and thank him for his Benefits; we should adore him for his Wisdom, fear him for his Power, and pray to him for his Favour and Protection; and this Religion will be a Powerful Regulator of our Actions, give us Peace and Tranquility within our own Minds, and render us Benevolent, Useful and Beneficial to others."

Several years later when Franklin was in correspondence with the evangelist George Whitefield, he once more referred to the hypothesis that God controls only the physical universe and never interferes in human affairs—and he seemed, temporarily at least, to adopt it. "I *see* with you," he wrote, "that our affairs are not well managed by our rulers here below; I wish I could *believe* with you, that they are well attended to by those above: I rather suspect, from certain circumstances, that though the general government of the universe is well administered, our particular little affairs are perhaps below notice, and left to take the chance of human prudence or imprudence, as either may happen to be uppermost. It is, however, an uncomfortable thought, and I leave it."³ Whitefield was appalled at Franklin's "uncomfortable thought" and wrote at the foot of the letter: *"Uncomfortable indeed! and, blessed be God, unscriptural;* for we are fully assured that 'the Lord reigneth,' and are directed to cast *all* our own care on him, because he careth for us."⁴

At an even later period, almost fifty years after delivering his discourse on providence, Franklin remembered its doctrine and summarized it in a letter to Benjamin Vaughan, specifically labeling it a refutation of his dissertation on necessity. "I reasoned, that if all things are ordained, prayer must among the rest be ordained. But as prayer can produce no change in things that are ordained, praying must be useless and an absurdity. God would therefore not ordain praying if everything else was ordained. But praying exists, therefore all things are not ordained, etc."⁵

This letter provides a striking parallel to a passage in one of Jonathan Edwards' letters to his son Timothy. "Whatever your circumstances are," he wrote, "it is your duty not to despair, but to hope in infinite mercy, through a Redeemer. For God makes it your duty to pray to him for mercy; which would not be your duty, if it was allowable for you to despair."⁶ Both men use the argument that God exacts prayer as a duty, but Franklin concludes that the prayer may perhaps have a response united to it in a cause-and-effect relationship; Edwards concludes that the prayer and any subse-

3. Joseph Belcher, *George Whitefield* (New York, 1857), p. 415. This letter was written in 1769. In *Poor Richard* for 1757 (Labaree [ed.], *Papers,* VII [1963], 91) Franklin had affirmed his belief that the world would not be destroyed by fire or water. Ever since Newton, orthodox theologians had tried to demonstrate that it was within God's power to bring the world to an end. According to Poor Richard, "our Comfort is, the same great Power that made the Universe, governs it by his Providence. And such terrible Catastrophes will not happen till 'tis best they should." In his letter to Whitefield, Franklin makes a distinction between "particular little affairs" and "general government of the universe," which allows him to retain his faith that the world will not be destroyed.
4. Belcher, *George Whitefield*, p. 415.
5. Albert Henry Smyth (ed.), *Writings of Benjamin Franklin* (10 vols., New York, 1905–1907), VII, 412.
6. To Timothy Edwards, April, 1753, Edward Hickman (ed.), *Works of Jonathan Edwards* (London, 1840), I, cxcix.

quent event which seems to be related to it are merely ordained in a predetermined sequence. Franklin's view certainly provides the stronger justification for prayer.

One may perhaps raise the question whether the reasoning of Franklin's discourse should be called scientific deism or even deism at all. One could indeed argue that it is either a highly intellectualized kind of Christianity or watered-down Christianity, depending on one's point of view. Actually, it contains nothing inimical to either Christianity or deism. Few, if any, real deists argued for a completely mechanical universe, and Franklin's system of a guiding providence would be metaphysically compatible with the cosmologies of a rhapsodic deist such as Shaftesbury, with a Christian deist such as William Wollaston, and with an Arminian Christian such as John Taylor. The essence of scientific deism consists in reasoning from the harmony and order of the physical universe to the existence of God and his moral attributes. Franklin's brief demonstration has more in common with this method than with any other.

Although Franklin abandoned the necessitarianism of his early treatise, he never entirely discarded his mechanistic conception of the universe. A few years after his Junto address, a group of merchants in Philadelphia established a dancing club called the Assembly, at first proposing that "no mechanic or mechanic's wife or daughter should be admitted, on any terms." As we shall see in a later chapter, this was probably in 1740 during the revivals of George Whitefield. Franklin opposed the restrictive rules of the Assembly on the grounds that they would exclude even "God Almighty." He is, Franklin affirmed, *"notoriously the greatest mechanic in the universe;* having, as the Scripture testifies, made all things, and that by *weight* and *measure."*[7]

Throughout Franklin's life, his opinions wavered on the degree of divine control of human destiny. Many times he

7. William Temple Franklin (ed.), *Memoirs of the Life and Writings of Benjamin Franklin* (London, 1818), I, 448.

seemed to question the beneficence of providence, but more often he affirmed it. In a letter to his sister, Jane Mecom, in September, 1752, he remarked in the vein of Pangloss, "After all, having taken care to do what *appears to us to be for the best,* we must submit to God's Providence, which orders all things *really for the best."*[8] Somewhat later in reference to his own and Buffon's suffering from the stone, he reflected, "I do not understand these dispensations of Providence, though probably they are for the best. But it seems to me that if . . . I had the disposition of good and evil in this world, so excellent a man [Buffon] would not have an hour's pain during his existence."[9] Similarly he remarked on another occasion that "It is unlucky, I think in the Affairs of this World, that the Wise and Good should be as mortal as Common People and that they often die before others are found fit to supply their Places."[10]

In a famous passage in his autobiography, quoting the argument of an Indian orator that the Great Spirit had designed rum for Indians to get drunk with, Franklin added his own comment: "And indeed if it be the Design of Providence to extirpate these Savages in order to make room for Cultivators of the Earth, it seems not improbable that Rum may be the appointed Means."[11] This seems to be a serious judgment, but Franklin may have meant it partly in jest. He once quoted the proverb *"God sends meat, and the Devil cooks"* to illustrate the principle that "Heaven orders all things for the best" on ocean voyages—where notoriously bad ship cooks are providently intended to keep passengers from indulging extraordinary appetites created by the sea air.[12]

Also Franklin sometimes meant by providence nothing more than nature or a natural process. He once made a

8. Labaree (ed.), *Papers,* IV (1961), 357.
9. Smyth (ed.), *Writings,* IX, 572.
10. *Ibid.,* p. 331.
11. Labaree (ed.), *Autobiography,* p. 199.
12. Smyth (ed.), *Writings,* IX, 402.

connection between the flat-chestedness of French women and their practice of not nursing their children, observing "possibly, Nature, finding they made no use of Bubbies, has left off giving them any."[13]

These are all random comments, designed to fit particular events and circumstances, and it is hardly fair to consider them as statements of philosophical belief. The same may be said of an appealing passage in one of Franklin's letters to his old printing friend William Strahan on the conclusions to be drawn from the American victory in the Revolution. "I am," he wrote, "too well acquainted with all the Springs and Levers of our Machine [the mind?], not to see, that our human means were unequal to our undertaking, and that, if it had not been for the Justice of our Cause, and the consequent Interposition of Providence, in which we had Faith, we must have been ruined. If I had ever before been an Atheist, I should now have been convinced of the Being and Government of a Deity! It is he who abases the Proud and favours the Humble."[14] Franklin probably intended this passage for its political effect as much as for any philosophical meaning.

Later he applied essentially the same reasoning to the United States Constitution. Although he could not make a case for its being divinely inspired because of the opposition which it at first aroused, he nevertheless maintained that he had so much "Faith in the general Government of the world by *Providence,* that I can hardly conceive a Transaction of such momentous Importance to the Welfare of Millions now existing, and to exist in the Posterity of a great Nation, should be suffered to pass without being in some degree influenc'd, guided, and governed by that omnipotent, omnipresent, and beneficent Ruler, in whom all inferior Spirits live, and move, and have their Being."[15] This could be interpreted to mean that natural law working by itself creates

13. *Ibid.,* p. 334.
14. *Ibid.,* p. 262.

15. *Ibid.,* pp. 702–703.

proper and beneficent effects, but these good effects could be upset or prevented by irrational human agency. He stated this view more clearly in a much earlier letter to Peter Collinson, warning that "whenever we attempt to mend the scheme of Providence and to interfere in the Government of the World, we had need be very circumspect lest we do more harm than Good."[16] As an example, he cited the success of New England farmers in ridding themselves of blackbirds, but as a consequence being infected with a breed of worms which in the absence of the birds increased without check. Regretfully the farmers realized that the blackbirds were to be preferred to the worms.

Here, of course, Franklin can be accused of inconsistency, for his career as a scientist was certainly established on the policy of the deliberate control of natural forces, which is all that his parable of the blackbirds represented. In defense of his own invention of the lightning rod, moreover, he argued that it is legitimate for man to guard himself against thunder, which is "no more supernatural than the Rain, Hail or Sunshine of Heaven, against the Inconveniencies of which we guard by Roofs and Shades without Scruple."[17]

Many of the preceding quotations embody, in addition to the problem of divine control of human activities, the related problem of evil—how the demonstrable moral and physical evil in the world may be reconciled with the supposition of a benevolent and omnipotent deity. If Franklin can be considered as having given formal attention to the problem of evil, it was at the time of his youthful *Dissertation* on necessity. It carried as epigraph, we remember, the following lines from Dryden:

> Whatever is, is in its Causes just
> Since all Things are by Fate; but purblind Man
> Sees but a part o' th'Chain, the nearest Link,
> His Eyes not carrying to the equal Beam
> That poises all above.

16. Labaree (ed.), *Papers*, IV, 480.   17. *Ibid.*, p. 463.

In his pamphlet Franklin took the position that since each man's pain is balanced with an equal amount of pleasure, no real evil can be said to exist. Beyond this, he admitted the existence of sickness, want, and murder but excused these on the grounds that "whatever an infinitely good God hath wise Ends in suffering to *be,* must be good, is thereby made good, and cannot be otherwise." For the rest of his life, he never made a more specific declaration than this.

Parenthetically we might add that Franklin once expressed a doctrine resembling in its ramifications that of the Christian doctrine of original sin, which partially but only partially exempts God from being responsible for moral evil by ascribing it to the human race. After wondering toward the end of his life why "all good Men and Women are not by Providence kept free from Pain and Disease," Franklin added, "In the best of all possible Worlds, I should suppose it must be so; and I am piously inclin'd to believe that this World's not being better made was owing merely to the Badness of the Materials."[18] But this, of course, gives no explanation as to who is responsible for the materials.

If we extend the parallel between Franklin and Jonathan Edwards to cover the problem of evil, we discover once more that Franklin does not come out second best. Although Edwards wrote a bulky treatise on *Original Sin,* in it he treated merely the Calvinistic doctrine of each human being's bearing the taint of Adam's disobedience, and he neither there nor elsewhere in his works gave any treatment to the broader question of how any kind of evil (physical as well as moral) may consist with the perfections he attributes to God.

Edwards in all his works thought in terms of sin rather than evil, but his defense of God for allowing it to exist resembles Franklin's assurance that whatever "God hath wise Ends in suffering to *be,* must be good." Edwards admitted that God is "the Author of Sin" if this is taken to mean that he is a "permitter, or *not a hinderer* of Sin; and at the same

18. Smyth (ed.), *Writings,* IX, 506. See also IX, 579.

time, a disposer of the state of events, in such a manner, for wise, holy, and most excellent ends and purposes."[19] Neither Edwards nor Franklin ever went beyond this type of broad affirmation, and nobody can pretend that either man ever made a serious attempt to resolve the problem of evil.

19. *Freedom of the Will,* Pt. IV, sec. ix; *Original Sin,* Pt. IV, chap. ii.

CHAPTER FIVE

PRACTICAL MORALIST

As we have seen, Franklin satisfied his early urge for metaphysical speculation with his polytheistic supposi- tions and deistical syllogisms, but he also needed a system of practical morality for daily use. Since he always felt that doing good to man was serving God, his ethical system must be considered a fundamental part of his religion. Two years before he wrote his "Acts of Religion" Franklin drew up a plan for regulating his future conduct in life. At the age of twenty he began putting into practice the principles of this plan, and, according to his own testimony, he continued to adhere to it "pretty faithfully . . . quite thro' to old Age."[1]

His plan was inspired by classical critics on the art of poetry who had maintained that every literary composition should have a preconceived "regular plan and design." By applying this concept to everyday behavior, Franklin hoped to change his life from a "confused variety of different scenes" to an orderly progression—to form a scheme of ac- tion so that he could "live in all respects like a rational creature." The scheme which he drew up was brief and intensely practical, containing only four precepts.

1. It is necessary for me to be extremely frugal for some time, till I have paid what I owe.

2. To endeavour to speak truth in every instance; to give nobody expectations that are not likely to be answered, but aim at sincerity in every word and action—the most amiable excellence in a rational being.

3. To apply myself industriously to whatever business I take in hand, and not divert my mind from my business by any foolish project of growing suddenly rich; for industry and patience are the surest means of plenty.

4. I resolve to speak ill of no man whatever, not even in a matter of truth; but rather by some means excuse the faults I hear charged upon others, and upon proper occasions speak all the good I know of every body.[2]

1. Leonard W. Labaree *et al.* (eds.), *Autobiography of Benjamin Franklin* (New Haven, 1964), p. 106.
2. L. W. Labaree *et al.* (eds.), *Papers of Benjamin Franklin,* I (New Haven, 1959), 99–100.

This is the first recorded of a large number of plans and schemes devised by Franklin, all notable for their method and precision. Most significant in this earliest moral design is the complete absence of any religious sanction. His subsequent plans of conduct, however, either embodied elements of piety or took some notice of divine providence.

A few years after writing the "Acts of Religion," Franklin composed a parallel handbook for the attainment of moral perfection, also for his private use. This world-famous method of self-improvement is described at length in his autobiography. Reviewing the enumerations of moral virtue which he had encountered in his reading, Franklin determined what he considered to be the thirteen principal ones, comprising all necessary or desirable qualities. With each virtue he included a precept to help him attain it; for example: "MODERATION: Avoid Extreams. Forbear resenting Injuries so much as you think they deserve; TRANQUILITY: Be not disturbed at Trifles, or at Accidents common or unavoidable; HUMILITY: Imitate Jesus and Socrates."[3] The other ten virtues were temperance, silence, order, resolution, frugality, industry, sincerity, justice, cleanliness, and chastity.

Each virtue occupied a page of a small notebook with spaces for each day of the week where he could check infractions of his rules. He proposed "to give a Week's strict Attention to each of the Virtues successively" with the aim of gradual improvement until after a number of attempts he should succeed in keeping an unblemished book during thirteen weeks' daily examination.

His "Art of Virtue" and his "Articles of Belief" have an epigraph in common, a quotation from Addison's *Cato:*

> Here will I hold—If there is a Pow'r above us
> (And that there is, all Nature cries aloud
> Thro' all her Works), He must delight in Virtue
> And that which he delights in must be Happy.

3. Labaree (ed.), *Autobiography*, p. 150.

Franklin incorporated the essence of this unusual idea as one of his "Articles of Belief," merely changing the emphasis. According to Addison, God delights in virtue and therefore virtuous creatures must be happy. According to Franklin's paraphrase, God delights in the happiness of creatures and therefore happy creatures must be virtuous. Instead of "be good and you will be happy," Franklin taught "be happy and you will be good."

Franklin included also as mottos in his moral notebook a quotation from Cicero and another from the Book of Proverbs (3:16–17) : *"Length of Days is in her right hand, and in her Left Hand Riches and Honours; Her Ways are Ways of Pleasantness, and all her Paths are Peace."* The antecedent of the pronoun is virtue. Many years later in France Franklin repeated this proverb to a young protégé, Pierre Jean Georges Cabanis, and revealed that at the age of twenty he had determined to confirm its truth by his own life. Looking back at the age of eighty, he appealed to his friends, "Judge whether I have been deceived. My health was not more firm then than today. I enjoy, not opulence, but easy circumstances far above my needs; and it is well known in the world that King George has little reason to be content with his quarrels with the journeyman printer."[4] His little book also contained a brief prayer of his own in prose and another in verse by James Thomson.

To keep himself from the trouble of renewing his original book, which from the repeated scraping out of check marks became full of holes, Franklin transferred his tables and precepts to more durable form on ivory leaves. After several years he gave up checking lapses from virtue, but he always kept the little book with him. In France during his seventies he showed it to Cabanis, who was much impressed. "We have had in our hands this precious little book," Cabanis wrote.

4. A. O. Aldridge, *Franklin and His French Contemporaries* (New York, 1957) , p. 208.

49

"One perceives in it a sort of chronological history of Franklin's mind and character. One sees him develop, fortify and mold all the actions which constitute spiritual perfection, and the art of life and virtue taught in the same manner as that of playing an instrument or manufacturing weapons."[5]

Franklin remarked in his autobiography that although his scheme for attaining moral perfection "was not wholly without Religion there was in it no Mark of any of the distinguishing Tenets of any particular Sect."[6] Esteeming his method to be of universal utility, and therefore worthy of publication, he deliberately avoided references to religion which might alienate zealous sectarians.

Much had been written in the seventeenth and eighteenth centuries on the motives for virtue. At one time a vociferous group of Anglican clergymen held that concern for one's welfare in the next world represents the only common-sense reason for virtuous behavior.

This somewhat cynical opinion was not universally held among Anglican theologians but was denounced by a group of latitudinarians who recognized that establishing virtue solely upon expectation of reward and fear of punishment represented a surrender to the principles of Thomas Hobbes, the bête noire of seventeenth-century orthodoxy. Hobbes had propounded a materialistic "selfish system" of ethics, basing all social relations upon fear. Like the cynical theologians, he argued that "the Laws of Nature (as *Justice, Equity, Modesty, Mercy,* and (in summe) *doing to others, as wee would be done to,*) of themselves, without the terrour of some Power, to cause them to be observed, are contrary to our naturall Passions, that carry us to Partiality, Pride, Revenge, and the like."[7]

Liberal theologians such as Benjamin Whichcot, Richard Cumberland, and Benjamin Hoadly took a firm stand against the penetration of the selfish system into theology, but

5. *Ibid.,* p. 206. 7. *Leviathan,* chap. 17.
6. Labaree (ed.), *Autobiography,* p. 157.

the most famous and influential protest came from Shaftesbury, who denounced both Hobbes and the sin-obsessed
theologians. He opposed the Christian doctrine of rewards
and punishments not only because he considered it morally
repugnant as issuing bribes to virtue, but also because it was
antithetical to his own Platonically inspired conception of
the system of the universe: God is good, the universe is good,
and man's inherent affections are good. He concluded his
Inquiry concerning Virtue with a reconciliation of self-love
and altruism. To follow virtue for its own sake, or, more
properly, because it is the animating principle of the universe, he contended, is equivalent to seeking one's own highest welfare.

Although Franklin adopted as epigraph the sentiment
from Addison's *Cato* that virtue brings happiness, he had in
mind a more direct and material effect than spiritual welfare.
Franklin promised: "Nothing so likely to make a man's fortune as virtue." This terse statement appears as a note in Part
II of Franklin's autobiography.[8] In the text three paragraphs
later, he expanded and somewhat modified the notion: "no
Qualities were so likely to make a poor Man's Fortune as
those of Probity and Integrity."[9] Addison and Shaftesbury
both agreed with Franklin that it was "every one's Interest to
be virtuous, who wish'd to be happy even in this World."
But Franklin's view of interest was narrower than that of his
Augustan predecessors. Although not excluding the broader
possibilities of spiritual solace, Franklin meant that virtue
would pay rewards, not in the next world but in this. As he
interpreted Christian ethics in his autobiography, "vicious
Actions are not hurtful because they are forbidden, but
forbidden because they are hurtful, the Nature of Man
alone consider'd."[10] This principle was so important to

8. It is not printed in the Labaree edition of the *Autobiography* but is
included in the Max Farrand Parallel Text Edition, *Memoirs* (Berkeley,
1949) , p. 232.
9. Labaree (ed.) , *Autobiography*, p. 158.
10. *Ibid.*, p. 158.

Franklin that he included it in a slightly different version in another part of his autobiography in connection with his attitude toward Revelation: "tho' certain Actions might not be bad *because* they were forbidden by it, or good *because* it commanded them; yet probably those Actions might be forbidden *because* they were bad for us, or commanded *because* they were beneficial to us, in their own Natures, all the Circumstances of things considered."[11] We shall have occasion to refer again to this significant principle. For the moment, it is to be noted that it represents a relativist position, contrary to Shaftesbury's belief in the absolute nature of good and evil, practically the only ethical principle on which Franklin differed from the author of the *Characteristics*.

Throughout his life Franklin tried to convince young men that their probity and integrity would make them valuable agents for "rich Merchants, Nobility, States and Princes, who have need of honest Instruments for the Management of their Affairs."[12] His emphasis upon industry and frugality in *Poor Richard's Almanack* and his other works on prudence came primarily from his belief that there is a close connection between procuring wealth and securing virtue, "it being more difficult for a Man in Want to act always honestly, as . . . *it is hard for an empty Sack to stand upright.*"[13]

His belief in the importance of frugality Franklin derived in part from his father, who had instilled in him the verse of Proverbs, *"Seest thou a Man diligent in his Calling, he shall stand before Kings, he shall not stand before mean Men."*[14] When Franklin conceived the notion of publishing an expanded version of his system for self-improvement, he planned to write a little comment on each virtue showing "the Advantages of possessing it, and the Mischiefs attending its opposite Vice."[15]

Although this prudential system is akin to Puritanism, it

11. *Ibid.*, p. 115.
12. *Ibid.*, p. 158.
13. *Ibid.*, p. 164.

14. *Ibid.*, p. 144.
15. *Ibid.*, p. 157.

has very little in common with the *Characteristics* and even less with a sensational attack upon Shaftesbury in *The Fable of the Bees.* Mandeville accused Shaftesbury of asserting that men may be virtuous without self-denial—of assuming "Goodness in his Species, as we do a sweet Taste in Grapes and China Oranges."[16] If Shaftesbury was vulnerable to Mandeville's blast against easy virtue, Franklin was doubly so. Mandeville set forth a rigoristic definition of virtue which, if applied to Franklin's scheme, would have completely eliminated his thirteen forms of counting-house probity. According to Mandeville, mankind has recognized as virtuous only those acts "by which Man, contrary to the impulse of Nature, should endeavour the Benefit of others, or the Conquest of his own Passions out of a Rational Ambition of being good."[17] The trick in this definition is the phrase "contrary to the impulse of Nature." Automatically it removes from the running the acts dearest to Shaftesbury, those which he maintained are motivated by inherent benevolent affections. The obvious answer of the Shaftesburians was to deny that virtue was contrary to nature and to affirm that the highest virtue came from natural impulses.

In some later essays Franklin reviewed the abstract controversy between Shaftesbury and Mandeville and declared unequivocally for Shaftesbury. But even in his practical system he effectually scouted Mandeville by supplying his own definition for each of his thirteen virtues. Let us consider, for example, the first four:

1. TEMPERANCE. Eat not to Dulness. Drink not to Elevation.
2. SILENCE. Speak not but what may benefit others or yourself. Avoid trifling Conversation.
3. ORDER. Let all your Things have their Places. Let each Part of your Business have its Time.
4. RESOLUTION. Resolve to perform what you ought. Perform without fail what you resolve.[18]

16. F. B. Kaye (ed.), *The Fable of the Bees* (Oxford, 1924), I, 323.
17. *Ibid.*, pp. 48–49.
18. Labaree (ed.), *Autobiography*, p. 149.

Although these notions do not measure up to Mandeville's rigoristic prescription, few would deny that the first and last represent the rational ambition of being good.

Franklin's thirteen virtues are those which we might call prudential or personal because their effects are felt primarily by the individual who exercises them. They may be contrasted with the social or altruistic virtues, which have direct salutary effects upon others as well as upon the individual who possesses them. These would include such qualities as charity, friendship, patriotism, and kindness. In defending Franklin, one may point out that his prudential virtues do not interfere with the more sublime and altruistic sentiments. But one might still wonder why he did not include such qualities as truthfulness or honesty, which are not comprised in Franklin's notion of sincerity ("Use no hurtful Deceit. Think innocently and justly; and, if you speak, speak accordingly.") or in his notion of justice ("Wrong none, by doing injuries or omitting the Benefits that are your Duty."). It might also be objected that the practice of the thirteen virtues Franklin did include would not necessarily help a young man in making his fortune. To this, all that can be answered is that if they do not guarantee prosperity, they cannot hinder it.

Franklin gave more detailed instruction on the practical means of becoming rich in his *Advice to a Young Tradesman* (1740). The way to wealth, he insisted, "depends chiefly on two Words, INDUSTRY and FRUGALITY." Yet even the operation of these two qualities depends upon the orderly operation of the universe, and if something happens to upset the equilibrium of the economic or social system, then the individual is helpless. In a sense, this equilibrium is provided by providence. As Franklin put it, "He that gets all he can honestly, and saves all he gets (necessary Expenses excepted) will certainly become RICH; If that Being who governs the World, to whom all should look for a Blessing on their honest Endeavours, doth not in his wise Providence otherwise determine."[19] God is still more influential than individual character—and the tradesman who finds himself poor after following Franklin's prudential advice may conveniently have God to blame.

Franklin also believed, quite logically, that if the prudential virtues are good for the individual who practices them, they are good also for an entire religious sect. In one of his economic tracts, he made a calculating estimate of the salutary results of combining religion with thrift: "If there be a Sect therefore, in our Nation, that regard Frugality and Industry as religious Duties, and educate their Children therein, more than others commonly do; such Sect must consequently increase more by natural Generation, than any other Sect in Britain."[20]

Franklin is a made-to-order illustration of the thesis that Protestantism and capitalism developed hand in hand in the modern world. During the American Revolution, he actually recommended that the copper coins of the new nation carry prudential maxims from *Poor Richard* as well as Biblical injunctions such as *"The fear of the Lord is the beginning of Wisdom."*[21]

Franklin himself recognized, on the other hand, the sometimes unholy alliance between religion and commercialism, and he protested against it. In a satirical sketch "Concerning the Savages of North America," suggesting that the behavior of primitive American Indians is in many ways morally superior to that of civilized white men, Franklin condemned the role of the church in exploiting the natives. An Indian visiting Albany notices that once every seven days the white people shut up their shops and assemble in a large house. When he is told that they go there "to hear and learn *good Things*," the Indian is incredulous. On a previous trip he had gone to the meeting with a fur trader. "There stood up a

19. Labaree (ed.), *Papers*, III (1961), 308.
20. *Ibid.*, IV (1961), 232.
21. Albert Henry Smyth (ed.), *Writings of Benjamin Franklin* (10 vols., New York, 1905–1907), VII, 381.

Man in Black, and began to talk to the People very angrily."
After the meeting, the Indian discovered that all the fur
traders in Albany were paying the same low price for furs.
The Indian concludes, therefore, "that whatever they pretended of meeting to learn *good Things,* the real purpose was
to consult how to cheat Indians in the Price of Beaver."[22]
Without question, there existed an ambivalence in Franklin's attitude toward material success.

In the nineteenth century Renan became one of the harsh-
est critics of Franklin's prudential system, going so far as to
call it rank immorality. He deplored the attitude of a man
who could summarize the goal of life in the words "to make
one's fortune honestly," particularly when he seems to have
included honesty only because it is the best policy.[23] Renan
could not understand how a man with any moral or philosophic sense could write works with such titles as "Advice to a
Young Tradesman," "Necessary Hints to Those that would
be Rich," and "The Way to Make Money Plenty in Every
Man's Pocket." He found particularly reprehensible Franklin's promise of the rewards of money-catching: "The whole
hemisphere will shine brighter, and pleasure spring up in
every corner of thy heart. Now therefore embrace these rules
and be happy." Renan could not resist the ironical reflection: what a "charming means of ennobling human nature."

Wealth, instead of being enshrined as the goal of life,
Renan thought, should be "the last thing about which one
should think, a thing which has value only in serving an
ulterior idealistic end." From this perspective Franklin's
scheme is immoral, a narrow and limited conception of existence. It "could come only from a soul stripped of religion
and poetry."

Yet all Frenchmen did not agree with Renan's estimate. A
few years after Franklin's death, a society of French deists

22. *Ibid.,* X, 103–104.
23. Translated from Henriette Pschari (ed.), *Œuvres complètes* (Paris,
n.d.), III, 794–795.

made a précis of *The Way to Wealth,* gave it the title *The Moral Thoughts of Franklin,* and published it in a compilation of works of religious and moral contemplation, *The Religious Year of the Theophilanthropists, or Adorators of God and Friends of Men.*[24]

Despite the worst that Renan and others can say about Franklin's "mean" or "scoundrel" maxims, no one can seriously maintain that the practice of his thirteen virtues or even his rules for gaining wealth would be evil for either society or the individual.

Everyone must admit, moreover, that Franklin seriously included probity and virtue as personal ideals in life. He called upon divine aid in his "Acts of Religion" that he might "have a constant Regard to Honour and Probity, . . . possess a perfect Innocence and a good Conscience, and at length become truly Virtuous and Magnanimous."[25]

24. Aldridge, *Franklin and His French Contemporaries,* p. 52.
25. Labaree (ed.) , *Papers,* I, 109.

CHAPTER SIX

THEORETICAL MORALIST

M ANY critics besides Renan have been supercilious about
Franklin's materialistic morality, viewing his system as
a Horatio Alger formula for getting rich. But sneering does
not invalidate. Also, we must remember that Franklin's prudential schemes form only a small part of his complete moral
system. Franklin was actually a philosopher, not only in the
eighteenth-century sense of an experimenter with natural
science, but in the broader sense of one who reflects ma-
turely on all the problems of existence. He looked at fundamental ethical problems as they were related to the doctrines
of liberty and necessity, the chain of being, the ontological
basis of the universe, and the nature of God. And the system
he evolved was fundamentally altruistic. The contrary image
of Franklin as a self-seeking materialist has sprung up because not all of his works were known in the nineteenth
century and because his maxims of thrift and sobriety have
always had far greater circulation than his reflective works.

Even in his autobiography Franklin focused his discussion
of morality upon the prudential virtues and thus contributed to the impression that his ethical vision extended no
further than to commercial maxims. Actually he was acquainted with Shaftesbury and other idealistic moralists
from the time of his early youth and was fully aware of the
speculative ethical problems of the age. In his letters and
other personal documents Franklin showed himself acutely
concerned with altruistic virtues. His multitudinous private
benefactions and philanthropic projects are even more com-
pelling proof of his ethical consciousness. Yet the popular
mind has been unable to assimilate the two facets of Franklin's personality. Paradoxically, moral altruism is generally
considered to be a part of Franklin's life, but not his
thought.

Even though Franklin failed to make a precise list and
definition of the altruistic virtues, he praised them separately

in scattered letters and other works and exemplified them in his life. In his "Articles of Belief and Acts of Religion," for example, he begged God to help him to "have Tenderness for the Weak, and a reverent Respect for the Ancient; [and to] . . . be kind to my Neighbours, good-natured to my Companions, and hospitable to Strangers; . . . honest and Openhearted, gentle, merciful and Good, chearful in Spirit, rejoicing in the Good of Others."[1]

When Franklin spoke of virtue in general, it is sometimes difficult to know whether he understood only the prudential virtues or whether he included the social ones as well. In a statement such as, "Nothing so likely to make a man's fortune as virtue," he probably meant only the prudential ones.[2] But what did he imply by the statement, *"Virtue alone is sufficient to make a Man Great, Glorious and Happy"?*[3]

The great importance Franklin attached to virtue is revealed in one of his sayings which has come down to us through the recollections of Cabanis. Franklin "constantly repeated that [morality] was the single rational design of individual happiness as it was the sole guarantee of public happiness. One day when he had already spoken at length on this point, he finished by telling us . . . : 'If rascals knew all the advantages of virtue, they would become honest out of rascality.' "[4] This is typical of Franklin. Just as the moment when he was presumably supporting altruistic virtue, he seemed to nullify his idealism by adding that virtue pays material dividends. Yet it does not really diminish the nobility of a moral system to point out that it may at the same time be personally and socially advantageous.

Franklin's writings show that he fully understood the theoretical implications of ethical thought as well as the practical utility of rules of personal conduct. He may not have had

1. L. W. Labaree *et al.* (eds.), *Papers of Benjamin Franklin,* I (New Haven, 1959), 108–109.
2. See n. 8 of chap. v, above.   3. Labaree (ed.), *Papers,* I, 119.
4. A. O. Aldridge, *Franklin and His French Contemporaries* (New York, 1957), p. 205.

a high opinion of that kind of abstract morality which seems to have no relationship to practical behavior, but he realized that general principles have to be formulated in order that practice might be based upon them.

Evidence of the intellectual basis of Franklin's system of ethics may be found in the pages of the *Pennsylvania Gazette,* a newspaper which Franklin began to edit in 1728. Franklin remarked in his autobiography that he considered his newspaper a "Means of Communicating Instruction," and that for this reason he sometimes published moral pieces of his own which had been first composed for reading in the Junto.[5] Two of the pieces which he identified as his own writing belong in the realm of speculative rather than practical ethics and stem directly from the Platonic systems of Shaftesbury and Hutcheson. Franklin's pieces comprise a dialogue concerning the character of a man of sense and a discourse on the relation of self-denial to virtue.[6]

His dialogue, stylistically modeled on a paraphrase of Xenophon which Franklin had published some time earlier, concerns an eternal problem of human relations, whether great abilities or high morals are the more desirable attainments. In it, Franklin analyzed the mental equipment of a man of reason in order to demonstrate the pre-eminent importance of moral qualities. He showed himself in agreement with Bacon, who had declared in his essay "Of Great Place" that one should prefer an ignorant man with integrity to a dishonest man with ability.

A random comment of Franklin's interlocutor, Socrates, elicits the statement of his companion, Crito, that a certain gentleman of the city is "esteem'd a *Man of Sense,* but not very honest." In the remainder of the dialogue, Socrates by means of appropriate questions persuades Crito to declare

5. Leonard W. Labaree *et al.* (eds.), *Autobiography of Benjamin Franklin* (New Haven, 1964), p. 165.

6. Labaree (ed.), *Papers,* II (1959), 15–21. A fuller treatment appears in A. O. Aldridge, "Franklin's 'Shaftesburian' Dialogues Not Franklin's," *American Literature,* XXI (1949), 151–159.

that a man who is not honest cannot be a man of sense.

The next moral essay which Franklin wrote for the *Gazette* was designed to prove against Mandeville *"That* SELF-DENIAL *is not the* ESSENCE OF VIRTUE." The problem is an ancient one, to decide which man has the greater virtue, the temperate man with no inner temptations to evil who follows the path of virtue undisturbed, unopposed, and unruffled, or the continent man with strong urges to commit evil who resolutely persists in the path of virtue but must constantly overcome vicious inclinations. In the eighteenth century, the problem had been stated in Shaftesbury's *Characteristics* and resolved in favor of the temperate man. Previous philosophers had more generally held the contrary opinion.

At the outset Franklin condemned as obscure and erroneous the opinion that "without *Self-Denial* there is no Virtue, and that the greater the *Self-Denial* the greater the Virtue." He proposed as more intelligible the contrary of the proposition, that he who cannot deny his injurious inclinations lacks the virtue of resolution or fortitude. Franklin's conclusion, like that to his dialogue on a man of sense, is the most vigorous part of the piece.

> The Truth is, that Temperance, Justice, Charity, &c. are Virtues, whether practis'd with or against our Inclinations; and the Man who practises them, merits our Love and Esteem: And Self-denial is neither good nor bad, but as 'tis apply'd: He that denies a Vicious Inclination is Virtuous in proportion to his Resolution, but the most perfect Virtue is above all Temptation, such as the Virtue of the Saints in Heaven: And he who does a foolish, indecent or wicked Thing, meerly because 'tis contrary to his Inclination, (like some mad Enthusiasts I have read of, who ran about naked, under the Notion of taking up the Cross) is not practising the reasonable Science of Virtue, but is lunatick.

This conclusion is obviously a vindication of the philosophy of Shaftesbury against the aspersions of Bernard Mandeville. Shaftesbury, defining virtue as natural affection, had argued that love of virtue could enable a man completely to banish contrary impulses and that in so doing he would become more virtuous, not less. Mandeville, who maintained that man's basic impulses were brutish, cowardly, and selfish, insisted that self-denial was a necessary ingredient of virtue and ridiculed Shaftesbury for expecting a natural "goodness in his Species."

Franklin's exposition of the concept that virtue does not depend upon resistance to an innate contrary principle of evil offers a striking parallel with the thought of Jonathan Edwards, who devoted a large section of his *Freedom of the Will* to proving the same thing. Specifically, Edwards demonstrated first that the moral excellence of God and Christ exists in a pure form without any contrary force and is still praiseworthy, and second that the virtuous behavior of Christ was necessary but still worthy of reward.[7]

In his "Miscellanies," Edwards affirmed in a blunt style remarkably similar to Franklin's that it would be utterly preposterous to assume that "if a man be naturally a very ill-natured man, and from that ill nature does often treat his neighbors maliciously and with great indignity, his neighbors ought to excuse and not to be angry with him so far as what he does is from ill nature."[8]

The philosophic preoccupations of Franklin's mind are revealed not only in his newspaper essays, but also in a series of questions for discussion which he drew up for his intellectual club, the Junto. In morals, as well as in science, Franklin realized that the theoretical is the generating force which makes the practical possible even though it is the practical which creates the welfare and happiness of mankind.

The idea for the Junto—Franklin's association of tradesmen for mutual improvement—had come to him from the New England Puritan, Cotton Mather. In his *Essays to Do Good* (1710), Mather had proposed voluntary associations

7. A. O. Aldridge, *Jonathan Edwards* (New York, 1964), pp. 103–104.
8. Harvey G. Townsend, *The Philosophy of Jonathan Edwards From His Private Notebooks* (Eugene, Ore., 1955), p. 163.

for the promotion of religion and morality and prescribed for them a structure and order of business. Franklin drew up similar rules for his secular organization, requiring that every member in turn produce moral or philosophical queries for general discussion and once in three months deliver an original essay on any subject he pleased.

In one of the topics he proposed for general discussion Franklin touched on one of the most fundamental ethical problems of the century, "Whether Men ought to be denominated Good or ill Men from their Actions or their Inclinations?"[9] In other words, are acts to be judged by their results or their motives? Believers in absolutes of good and evil such as Shaftesbury argued that motives alone should be considered. Relativists such as Mandeville argued that results were more important. Franklin's opinions for the Junto are not on record, but we have seen that in the *Gazette* he decided unequivocally for Shaftesbury.

Franklin also proposed a number of queries concerning the respective value of riches and virtue. He was quite aware that wealth and goodness are not necessarily companion qualities even though his "prudential" writings do not show this comprehension. He asked:

> Which is best to make a Friend of, a wise and good Man that is poor; or a Rich Man that is neither wise nor good? Which of the two is the greatest Loss to a Country, if they both die?
> Which of the two is happiest in Life?
> Does it not in a general Way require great Study and intense Application for a Poor Man to become rich and Powerful, if he would do it, without the Forfeiture of his Honesty?
> Does it not require as much Pains, Study and Application to become truly Wise and strictly Good and Virtuous as to become rich?
> Can a Man of common Capacity pursue both Views with Success at the same Time?
> If not, which of the two is it best for him to make his whole Application to?[10]

9. Labaree (ed.), *Papers,* I, 263.   10. *Ibid.,* pp. 263–264.

Franklin also asked the question, which some of his critics have accused him of ignoring, whether there is any "Difference between Knowledge and Prudence? If there is any, which of the two is most Eligible?"[11]

And he took note of some of the ethical problems of political association long before he himself engaged in any form of government. He wondered:

> Is it justifiable to put private Men to Death for the Sake of publick Safety or Tranquility, who have committed no Crime?
> As in the Case of the Plague to stop Infection, or as in the Case of the Welshmen here Executed. . . .
> If the Sovereign Power attempts to deprive a Subject of his Right, (or which is the same Thing, of what he thinks his Right) is it justifiable in him to resist if he is able?[12]

In the commonplace book in which these queries are preserved, Franklin gave no answers. He attempted an answer, however, to a much more basic ethical question, one which every human being must consider: "Wherein consists the Happiness of a rational Creature?" His answer: "In having a Sound Mind and a healthy Body, a Sufficiency of the Necessaries and Conveniences of Life, together with the Favour of God, and the Love of Mankind."[13] Significantly, Franklin at this time considered man's relation to God equally important as his relation to his fellow men.

He gave an even more detailed answer to another purely ethical query based on fundamental religious and metaphysical concepts. "Can a Man arrive at Perfection in this Life as some Believe; or is it impossible as others believe?"[14] Franklin found his answer in the theory of the Great Chain of Being. "The Perfection of any Thing," he argued, is the highest point of development which "the Nature of that Thing is capable of." Although in the notion of the chain of being each species is ranked according to its closeness to or remoteness from God, individuals of every species are at the

11. *Ibid.*, p. 263.   13. *Ibid.*, p. 262.
12. *Ibid.*   14. *Ibid.*, p. 261.

same time capable of various degrees of perfection within that species. Thus, according to Franklin's scheme, "an Horse is more perfect than an Oyster yet the Oyster may be a perfect Oyster as well as the Horse a perfect Horse. And an Egg is not so perfect as a Chicken, nor a Chicken as a Hen; for the Hen has more Strength than the Chicken, and the C[hicken] more Life than the Egg: Yet it may be a perfect Egg, Chicken and Hen." Applying the notion to mankind, Franklin concluded that "a Man cannot in this Life be so perfect as an Angel, . . . for an Angel by being incorporeal is allow'd some Perfections we are at present incapable of, and less liable to some Imperfections that we are liable to." And it may also be true that "a Man is not capable of being so perfect here as he is capable of being in Heaven." But man is nevertheless capable of reaching the maximum degree of perfection which his rank in the scale of being permits. To assert the contrary would be nonsense. "It is as if I should say, a Chicken in the State of a Chicken is not capable of being so perfect as a Chicken is capable of being in that State. In the above Sense if there may be a perfect Oyster, a perfect Horse, a perfect Ship, why not a perfect Man? that is as perfect as his present Nature and Circumstances admit?" A few years later Alexander Pope expressed essentially the same idea in his *Essay on Man*.

> If to be perfect in a certain sphere,
> What matter, soon or late, or here or there.

This was Franklin's answer to the Calvinistic doctrine of "the total depravity and corruption of man's nature." Franklin's view of mankind was neither optimistic nor pessimistic but could be extended in either an optimistic or pessimistic direction. If one believes that the majority of mankind live up to their potentiality as a species in the chain of being, this is an optimistic view; if one believes that the majority of mankind fail to do so, this is pessimistic. During the remainder of his life Franklin shifted from one view to the other according to his prevailing mood. He frequently varied his opinion concerning moral progress or perfectibility, but he never wavered from his conception of man occupying a mid-way station in the Great Chain of Being.

Toward the end of his life Franklin graphically presented his conception of the chain of being in the guise of an oriental tale, a highly popular literary genre of the eighteenth century developed by such authors as Addison, Goldsmith, and Voltaire.[15] In keeping with the tradition, Franklin used an oriental philosopher, the good magician Albumazar, to convey his moral lesson. One night Albumazar was visited by one of the spirits of the first rank, Belubel the strong. "His height was seven leagues, and his wings when spread might overshadow a kingdom." Belubel laid himself gently down between the ridges of the mountain range, using the tops of the trees in the valley as his couch. Albumazar "spoke to him with rapturous piety of the wisdom and goodness of the Most High; but expressed his wonder at the existence of evil in the world, which he said he could not account for by all the efforts of his reason."

Belubel, in reply, advised the wise mortal not to value himself upon that quality called reason. "If thou knewest its origin and its weakness, it would rather be matter of humiliation."

Then Belubel called upon the magician to contemplate "the scale of beings, from an elephant down to an oyster. Thou seest a gradual diminution of faculties and powers, so small in each step that the difference is scarce perceptible. There is no gap, but the gradation is complete. Men in general do not know, but thou knowest, that in ascending from an elephant to the infinitely Great, Good, and Wise, there is also a long gradation of beings, who possess powers and faculties of which thou canst yet have no perception."

Although Franklin did not round out his tale with a moral

15. Albert Henry Smyth (ed.), *Writings of Benjamin Franklin* (10 vols., New York, 1905–1907), X, 123–124.

tag such as is usually found in the genre, his meaning is clear enough. Man exists in the scale of being just above the elephant, and his intellectual faculties are inadequate to enable him to understand the moral problems of the universe. This must certainly be taken as Franklin's final opinion concerning the problem of evil.

His moral tale illustrates not only the Great Chain of Being, but also the equally common eighteenth-century doctrine that "purblind Man" is in error if his pride causes him to overlook the limitations of his reason.

On still another occasion Franklin used his oyster and horse to illustrate the scale of being. In one issue of the *Pennsylvania Gazette* (August 1, 1734), he had published a dismal monologue by an English clergyman, Joshua Smith, "On the Vanity and Brevity of Human Life." Then he wrote twin repudiations which he printed in the next issue: a humorous and somewhat ribald parody and a parallel meditation reflecting a cheerful outlook.[16] In introducing his parody, he remarked that he not only disliked to view the dark side of things but considered gloomy philosophy unjust. "The World is a very good World, and if we behave our selves well, we shall doubtless do very well in it. I never thought even *Job* in the right, when he repin'd that the Days of a Man are *few* and *full of Trouble;* for certainly both these Things cannot be together just Causes of Complaint; if our Days are full of Trouble, the fewer of 'em the better." Smith's gloomy meditation Franklin compared to the perverse lamenting of a child that he cannot have his cake and eat it too. His irony is worthy of Swift.

[Smith:] *All the few days we live are full of Vanity; and our choicest Pleasures sprinkled with bitterness:*
[Franklin:] All the few Cakes we have are puffed up with Yeast; and the nicest Gingerbread is spotted with Flyshits!
[Smith:] *The time that's past is vanish'd like a dream; and that which is to come is not yet at all.*

16. A. O. Aldridge, "A Religious Hoax by Benjamin Franklin," *American Literature*, XXXVI (1964), 204–209.

[Franklin:] The Cakes that we have eaten are no more to be seen; and those which are to come are not yet baked. . . .

[Smith:] *But the longer we live, the shorter is our life; and in the end we become a little lump of clay.*

[Franklin:] And the more we eat, the less is the Piece remaining; and in the end the whole will become Sir-reverence! [a turd]

In his conclusion Franklin dismissed all such insignificant meditations. "I am for taking *Solomon's* Advice, *eating Bread with Joy, and drinking Wine with a merry Heart.* Let us rejoice and bless God, that we are neither Oysters, Hogs, nor Dray-Horses; and not stand repining that He has not made us Angels; lest we be found unworthy of that share of Happiness He has thought fit to allow us."

Franklin's companion address on the benevolence of the universe emphasizes smiles and pleasure. "Most happy are we, the sons of men, above all other creatures, who are born to behold the glorious rays of the sun, and to enjoy the pleasant fruits of the earth." After a life of using our reason in doing good, we are rewarded with "the sweet sleep of death, pleasant as a bed to a weary traveller after a long journey."

During the same period that Franklin was drawing up his queries for the Junto, he also wrote for his private use a series of "Observations on Reading History." Here he expressed an opinion of human nature which seems at variance with the Shaftesburian direction of his thought in other writings. Starting with the principle that all the great affairs of the world are carried on by parties, he observed "That while a Party is carrying on a general Design, each Man has his particular private Interest in View. . . . That few in Public Affairs act from a meer View of the Good of their Country, whatever they may pretend; and tho' their Actings bring real Good to their Country, yet Men primarily consider'd that their own and their Country's Interest was united, and did not act from a Principle of Benevolence. That fewer still in public Affairs act with a View to the Good of Mankind."[17]

In one sense there does not seem to be much benevolent altruism in these views, and the statement that men act according to their own particular interest seems to reflect the "selfish" system of Hobbes and Mandeville. Indeed, in 1737 Franklin was inclined to consider Hobbes's notion somewhat "nearer the Truth than that which makes the State of Nature a State of Love."[18] There is a paradox here which can be understood only by considering a "great and extensive Project" which Franklin envisaged in the final paragraphs of his observations on history.

> There seems to me at present to be great Occasion for raising an united Party for Virtue, by forming the Virtuous and good Men of all Nations into a regular Body, to be govern'd by suitable good and wise Rules, which good and wise Men may probably be more unanimous in their Obedience to, than common People are to common Laws.
>
> I at present think, that whoever attempts this aright, and is well qualified, cannot fail of pleasing God, and of meeting with Success.

In his autobiography Franklin revealed that he hoped to organize this party of virtue under the name of The Society of the Free and Easy, in a sense a Junto for the whole world, but the project was never carried out.

The paradox may be resolved in this way: Franklin agreed with Mandeville that observation of society indicates that the majority of men indeed act upon primarily selfish motives. But this is true only for society as it is now constituted —not necessarily as it must remain for all time. Franklin also agreed with Shaftesbury that man possesses benevolent instincts which can be nurtured and developed. There *can* be a perfect man just as there *can* be a perfect oyster. Franklin's Party for Virtue was designed to organize the existing altruists, to increase their number, and to bring the commonal-

17. Labaree (ed.), *Autobiography*, p. 161.
18. Labaree (ed.), *Papers*, II, 185.

ity of men closer to the Shaftesburian ideal. Franklin consequently emphasized the existing division between common men and good and wise men, a consequence of Shaftesbury's theories rather than Mandeville's.

Franklin's opinion of human nature is obviously an important part of his religion. Although in theory he shared the benevolent philosophy of Shaftesbury and the English latitudinarian divines, he veered during his moments of disillusion toward the views of Mandeville and exponents of Calvinistic depravity. "Whatever may be the Musick of the Spheres," he wrote in *Poor Richard* for 1735, "how great soever the Harmony of the Stars, 'tis certain there is no Harmony among the Stargazers; but they are perpetually growling and snarling at one another like strange Curs."

Most famous of Franklin's gloomy observations are those in which he similarly contrasts the inanimate "Works of Nature" with the animate or moral part. The more he discovered of the former, he affirmed, the more he admired them; the more he learned of the latter, the more he became disgusted with them.[19] In one of his most extreme passages, he expressed the rhetorical hope "that moral Science were in as fair a way of Improvement" as physical science, "that Men would cease to be Wolves to one another, and that human Beings would at length learn what they now improperly call Humanity."[20]

In the midst of the Revolution, Franklin expressed revulsion at man's perverse attitude toward procreating and killing his own species:

> Men I find to be a Sort of Beings very badly constructed, as they are generally more easily provok'd than reconcil'd, more disposed to do Mischief to each other than to make Reparation, much more easily deceiv'd than undeceiv'd, and having more Pride and even Pleasure in killing than in begetting one another; for without a Blush they assemble in great armies at NoonDay to destroy, and when they have kill'd as many as they can, they exaggerate the Number to augment

19. Smyth (ed.), *Writings*, VIII, 451.   20. *Ibid.*, p. 10.

the fancied Glory; but they creep into Corners, or cover themselves with the Darkness of night, when they mean to beget, as being asham'd of a virtuous Action. A virtuous Action it would be, and a vicious one the killing of them, if the Species were really worth producing or preserving; but of this I begin to doubt.[21]

This is indeed a very gloomy view—but not as deep-seated as it appears. Franklin was not actually presenting sentiments which had originated in his own despondent heart—instead he was paraphrasing a passage from the French essayist Montaigne, who had written: "Every one avoids seeing a Man born, every one runs to see him die. To destroy a Man, a spacious Field is sought out, and in the Face of the Sun; but to make him, we creep into as dark and private a Corner as we can. 'Tis a Man's Duty to withdraw himself from the Light to do it; but 'tis Glory, and the Fountain of many Vertues to know how to destroy what we have done: The one is Injury, the other Favour." This passage comes from a long essay "On Some Verses of Virgil," dealing principally with sex.[22] Franklin's temporary pessimism may have been as much affected by his reading as by any of the events of the war or the diplomatic crisis.

Franklin once wrote to his sister that "Mankind were Devils to one another," but he meant by this merely that man's greatest sufferings come from other men rather than from other animals.[23] He had been led into this reflection by recalling a printer's widow he had known during his first visit to London when he was nineteen. This lady, Elizabeth Ilive, had held the doctrine of pre-existence and by the terms of her will obliged her son to deliver a public discourse "the purport of which was to prove, that this world is the true Hell, or place of punishment for the spirits, who had transgressed in a better state, and were sent here to suffer for their

21. *Ibid.*, pp. 451–452.
22. Robert Newcomb, "Benjamin Franklin and Montaigne," *Modern Language Notes*, LXXII (1957), 489–491.
23. Carl Van Doren (ed.), *Letters of Benjamin Franklin and Jane Mecom* (Princeton, 1950), p. 125.

sins in animals of all sorts."[24] This theory was supported by the assumption that "though we now remembered nothing of such a preëxistent state, yet after death we might recollect it, and remember the punishments we had suffered, so as to be the better for them; and others, who had not yet offended, might now behold and be warned by our sufferings."

In a letter to his sister, December 30, 1770, Franklin seemed partly convinced by this reasoning. "We see here, that every lower animal has its enemy, with proper inclinations, faculties, and weapons, to terrify, wound, and destroy it; and that men, who are uppermost, are devils to one another; so that, on the established doctrine of the goodness and justice of the great Creator, this apparent state of general and systematical mischief seemed to demand some such supposition as Mrs. Ilive's, to account for it consistently with the honor of the Deity."[25] But Franklin held back from any positive affirmation because our reasoning powers lack the materials necessary to inform us about our existence either before or after this life. "Revelation only can give us the necessary information, and that, in the first of these points especially, has been very sparingly afforded us."

Since Franklin's sister seems to have been completely unreceptive to the doctrine of pre-existence, Franklin tried to show in a subsequent letter that it was not entirely nonsensical. He explained that "it had been invented with a good Intention, to save the Honour of the Deity, which was thought to be injured by the Supposition of his bringing Creatures into the World to be miserable, without any previous misbehaviour of theirs to deserve it."[26] But Franklin himself did not accept this reasoning. In Biblical symbols, he denominated the doctrine "an officious Supporting of the Ark." When God has "thought fit to draw a Veil, our Attempting to remove it may be deem'd at least an offensive Impertinence. And we shall probably succeed little better in

24. *Ibid.*, p. 124.
25. *Ibid.*

26. *Ibid.*, p. 125.

such an Adventure to gain forbidden Knowledge, than our first Parents did when they ate the Apple."

Seeking to remove some of the sting from his comparison of men to devils, he added: "Upon the whole, I am much disposed to like the World as I find it, & to doubt my own Judgment as to what would mend it. I see so much Wisdom in what I understand of its Creation and Government, that I suspect equal Wisdom may be in what I do not understand: And thence have perhaps as much Trust in God as the most pious Christian." In his final sentence, Franklin virtually separated himself from the body of Christianity, perhaps without realizing it, almost wistfully portraying himself as on the outside, looking in.

His propensity to like the world as it is explains the view of mankind which he held most of the time—whenever his natural cheerful disposition was not overcome by temporary clouds of gloom. In France during a conversation with English friends at the close of the American war, he reprobated the maxim that all men are equally corrupt. "A man," he affirmed, "who has seen nothing but hospitals, must naturally have a poor opinion of the health of mankind."[27]

Although Franklin is usually considered as one of the outstanding rationalists of the eighteenth century, his faith in pure reason diminished as he grew in years. He made his most positive assertion of the supreme importance of reason in his Junto lecture on providence in the course of which he repudiated "Art and Ornament," "Flourishes of Rhetorick," "the false Glosses of Oratory," and "a musical Accent in delivery." "I know," he affirmed, "that no Authority is more convincing to Men of Reason than the Authority of Reason itself."[28]

In contrast to this confident rationalism, the spirit Belubel in Franklin's oriental tale warns us against placing a high value on human reason, which because of its origin and

27. Journal of John Baynes, *Life of Sir Samuel Romilly Written by Himself* (London, 1841), I, 447–448.
28. Labaree (ed.), *Papers*, I, 265.

weakness is rather a matter of humiliation.[29] Franklin once complained to his sister that reason sometimes not only fails to help us prevent evil but even actually misleads us. Occasionally he was "almost tempted to wish we had been furnished with a good sensible Instinct instead of it."[30]

To one of his friends he suggested that reason may be best fitted for some people, instinct for others. "As those Beings, . . . who have Reason to regulate their Actions, have no Occasion for Enthusiasm. However, there are certain Circumstances in Life, sometimes, wherein 'tis perhaps best not to hearken to Reason."[31] One of Franklin's best examples of the deficiencies of reason is the man who knows the theory of swimming but loses his head in deep water.[32]

To a close friend in France, he once wrote that reason must be a thing quite uncertain "since two people like you and me can draw from the same principles conclusions diametrically opposite. This reason seems to me a guide quite blind. A good and certain instinct would be worth much more to us. All the inferior animals together do not go so far astray in a year as a single man in a month—although this man pretends to act according to reason."[33] This paradoxical view of the irrationality of human reason, Franklin supported in a witty anecdote which he related to John Adams in 1775:

> "Man, a rational Creature"! said Franklin. "Come, Let Us suppose a rational Man. Strip him of all his Appetites, especially of his hunger and thirst. He is in his Chamber, engaged in making Experiments, or in pursuing some Problem. He is highly entertained. At this moment a Servant Knocks, "Sir dinner is on Table." "Dinner! Pox! Pough! But what have you for dinner?" "Ham and Chickens." "Ham"! "And must I break the chain of my thoughts, to go down and knaw a morsel of damn'd Hogs Arse"? "Put aside your Ham." "I will dine tomorrow."[34]

29. Smyth (ed.), *Writings*, X, 124.
30. Van Doren (ed.), *Letters of Benjamin Franklin and Jane Mecom*, p. 112.
31. Smyth (ed.), *Writings*, V, 225.
32. *Ibid.*, p. 547.
33. Papers of the abbé de la Roche in Institut de France.
34. Lester J. Cappon (ed.), *The Adams-Jefferson Letters* (Chapel Hill, 1959), II, 399.

CHAPTER SEVEN

RELUCTANT METAPHYSICIAN

WE have seen that Franklin used a priori reasoning in his necessitarian pamphlet and a priori reason to refute it. We have also seen that on occasion he even called in question reason itself. In 1745, a group of his scientific friends forced him to return once more to the area of metaphysics, which he had abandoned almost concomitantly with his repudiation of necessitarianism. In that year a friend in New York, Cadwallader Colden, published a treatise on physics which reminded Franklin forcibly of his own *Dissertation on Liberty and Necessity*. Even for Franklin, Colden's work, *An Explication of the First Causes of Action in Matter, and, of the Cause of Gravitation*, was difficult to comprehend. And Franklin's scientifically inclined companions in Philadelphia found it necessary to do background reading in order to prepare themselves for the understanding of Colden's doctrine. They found particularly helpful a book written by a Scotsman, Andrew Baxter, *An Inquiry into the Nature of the Human Soul, wherein its Immateriality is evinced* (2d ed.; London, 1737). When they insisted that Franklin read it, he turned out to have quite the contrary opinion of its merits. In company one night he dissented from Baxter's view of the foundation "on which all Philosophy and even Religion are to be built."[1] He was asked to present his reasons in writing—and did so the next morning. Apparently he also sent his reflections on Baxter to a number of scientific friends in other cities.

In one of these letters Franklin included a paragraph in which he confessed to feeling great reluctance about returning to the method of metaphysical reasoning. "The great Uncertainty I have found in that Science, the wide Contradictions and endless Disputes it affords; and the horrible Errors I led my self into when a young Man, by drawing a Chain of plain Consequences as I thought them, from true

---

1. L. W. Labaree *et al.* (eds.), *Papers of Benjamin Franklin*, III (New Haven, 1961), 91.

Principles, have given me a Disgust to what I was once extreamly fond of."[2] In a marginal note, Franklin made clear that he was referring to his *Dissertation on Liberty and Necessity.*

Colden's treatise had forced Franklin against his will to cross once more the line between physics and metaphysics. Although the titles of Colden's and Baxter's books lead one to believe that one is on a purely scientific subject, and the other on a subject purely theological, both books attempted to solve the apparently unsolvable problem of how spirit can react upon matter.

Baxter's proof of the existence of God was one of many adaptations of the Newtonian system current in the eighteenth century. His particular emphasis was upon the inertness of matter—a quality to which he applied the paradoxical term *vis inertiae,* or force of inertness. He argued that since matter has no active powers, it is necessary to suppose the existence of an immaterial being or God to explain the various effects of matter observable in the universe. According to Baxter, "If the immateriality of the soul, the existence of God, and the necessity of a most particular incessant providence in the world, are demonstrable from such plain and easy *principles* [as the force of inertness of matter]; the atheist has a desperate cause in hand."[3]

Franklin did not question the existence of God but objected to Baxter's paradox of asserting a power in inert matter. Franklin, to use his own words, stumbled "at the threshold of the building." He argued that the supposed power of matter is illusory since "the greatest assignable mass of matter will give way to, or be moved by the *least* assignable force." To prove his point Franklin asked his correspondent to imagine "two Globes each equal to the Sun and to one another, exactly equipoised in Jove's Ballance" and to "suppose no Friction in the Center of Motion, in the Beam or

2. *Ibid.,* pp. 88–89.
3. Quoted by Franklin in another version of his letter in the archives of the Yale Franklin Papers.

elsewhere." Then if a mosquito were to alight on one of these globes, would not one descend and the other rise? It would be no valid objection to argue that the force of gravity helps one globe to ascend, for the same force would oppose the other globe from rising. "Here is an Equality, that leaves the whole Motion to be produc'd by the Musketo, without whom those Globes would not be moved at all." Where in all this, Franklin scoffed, is the alleged *vis inertiae*? And what other effect could we expect if there were no such inert force in matter? Surely if it were anything but a phantom, "there might be enough of it in such vast Bodies to annihilate, by its Opposition to Motion, so trifling a Force."[4]

Baxter had grounded his hypothesis of *vis inertiae* upon a fundamental law of motion, that a body moving with a certain velocity requires a certain degree of force or resistance to stop its motion. Franklin accepted the principle of motion but denied that it had anything to do with Baxter's mystical property. Franklin insisted "that there is no Body how large soever, moving with any Velocity how great soever, but may be stopped by any opposing Force how small soever, continually apply'd. . . . [Let] me turn the Thing in what Light I please, I cannot [discover] the Vis Inertiae, nor any Effect of it." After subjecting Baxter's hypothesis to a number of similar objections, Franklin concluded his observations almost in the author's own words: "That if the Doctrines of the Immateriality of the Soul, and the Existence of God, and of Divine Providence are demonstrable from *no plainer* Principles, the *Deist* has a desperate Cause in Hand."[5]

James Bowdoin, one of Franklin's friends to whom he sent a version of these comments, replied January 27, 1755, discussing them in detail. Bowdoin also quoted a significant paragraph which Franklin had placed at the end of his letter.

4. Labaree (ed.), *Papers*, III, 86.
5. *Ibid.*, p. 88. In Benjamin Vaughan's edition, the words *"i. e. theist"* were interpolated in parentheses after *"Deist"* in this sentence, presumably to indicate that Franklin was not abdicating the principles of deism, but that he considered deism and theism as equivalent.

If God was before all things, and filled all space; then when he formed what we call matter, he must have done it out of his own thinking immaterial substance. The same, though he had not filled all space; if it be true that *ex nihilo nihil fit*. From hence may we not draw this conclusion, that if any part of matter does not at present act and think, 'tis not from an incapacity in its nature, but from a positive restraint. I know not yet what other consequences may follow the admitting of this position, and therefore I will not be obliged to defend it.[6]

This part of Franklin's thought and writings is related to the section labeled "Of Being" in Jonathan Edwards' "Notes on Natural Science"—the section of his works in which he attempts to answer the fundamental problems of ontology. The basic problem is existence per se. Since both Edwards and Franklin assumed the existence of a divine power, both needed to explain the relation between God and the universe of human experience.

Edwards began with the assumption of the existence of necessary, eternal, infinite, and omnipresent being. This eternal being, he reasoned, cannot be solid since solidity is nothing but resistance to other solids. It is possible to imagine the non-existence of any solid, but we cannot conceive of the non-existence of space. Existence in itself implies consciousness, or in Edwards' own words, "consciousness and being are the same thing exactly," and space is God.[7]

Edwards' conception of the atomic theory leads to the same conclusion. An atom, he defined, as a *minimum physicum*, a body which cannot be made smaller. Everything in the universe is composed of atoms, which are held together by an infinite force or power, and this power is God. These atoms are not composed of a substance called matter but represent individual powers of resistance.

The problem of creation—the single problem which

6. *Ibid.*, V (1962), 486.
7. "Of Being," Harvey G. Townsend, *The Philosophy of Jonathan Edwards From His Private Notebooks* (Eugene, Ore., 1955), pp. 1–20.

Franklin chose to deal with—Edwards resolved by considering the created universe as part of God himself, space and God being the same. "Since . . . body is nothing but an infinite resistance in some part of space caused by the immediate exercise of divine power, it follows that as great and as wonderful power is every moment exerted to the upholding of the world as at first was to the creating of it."[8]

Neither Franklin nor Edwards adequately explained creation, but there is no reason for claiming greater profundity for the hypothesis of Edwards. Franklin, assuming matter as distinct from God, could at least suppose the creating of matter by God. Edwards, by assuming that body is merely an extension of God's power, could not make a distinction between the universe as it now exists and before it came into being. His idealism removes the problem of explaining the interaction of spirit upon matter, but in so doing it nullifies the distinction between the world and a superior intelligence guiding it. God is merged into the whole universe and every atom into God.

Bowdoin wrote five lengthy pages of comment on Franklin's single-paragraph speculation on creation—an illustration of the endless perplexities and ramifications which made Franklin deplore metaphysical abstraction. As far as he was concerned, Franklin's hypothesis created more difficulties than the one which assumes that matter was created out of nothing.

> If God formed matter out of his own thinking immaterial substance, then the substance of God must be diminished, and therefore he cannot be infinite: or if not diminished, the matter formed out of it must be God, or a part of God: in which case he must greatly debase and degrade himself, if matter be less excellent than thinking immaterial substance, and therefore he cannot be unchangeable: in which case he must be a compound of matter and spirit, and therefore not a pure and simple being: he must be both cause and effect, creator and creature, and therefore holy and unholy,

8. *Ibid.*, pp. 16–17.

wise and foolish, just and unjust, good and mischievous, eternal and temporal, unchangeable and mutable, almighty and frail, true and a liar, happy and miserable.[9]

Bowdoin had other objections to Franklin's hypothesis, but we may well stop here. Before asking Franklin's pardon for the freedom he had taken, Bowdoin admitted to being "very little versed in metaphysics." But so far as he was able to judge, he was quite of Franklin's opinion " 'that there is great uncertainty in that science, and that the contradictions and disputes it affords are endless'; and it is no wonder that this should be the case, for its object is beyond our ken."

Franklin's own aversion to metaphysical speculation had been strong when he wrote his letter against Baxter. He was probably none the more attracted to it when he saw the criticisms which could be leveled against his own reasoning —criticisms which he could not subject to an objective standard. Here all was opinion and conjecture.

After this chastening experience, Franklin never again wrote on primarily metaphysical subjects although his interest in religion remained as vital as ever. He had discovered that science did not really demonstrate the existence of God —nor did it satisfy any other of man's religious needs. Franklin's disillusionment with metaphysics is reflected in one of his surreptitious pieces, "To The Royal Academy of Brussels," written many years later during his diplomatic mission to Paris. Here he asked a series of questions disparaging scientific and metaphysical speculation: "Are there twenty Men in Europe at this Day, the happier, or even the easier, for any Knowledge they have pick'd out of Aristotle? What Comfort can the Vortices of Descartes give to a Man who has Whirlwinds in his Bowels? The Knowledge of Newton's mutual *Attraction* of the Particles of Matter, can it afford Ease to him who is rack'd by their mutual *Repulsion,* and the cruel Distensions it occasions?"[10] To be sure, this passage is

9. Labaree (ed.) , *Papers*, V, 489.
10. Richard E. Amacher, *Franklin's Wit and Folly* (New Brunswick, 1953) , pp. 68–69.

highly ironical, and Franklin certainly did not intend it as a repudiation of science. But it reveals the same basic distrust of metaphysics which he had expressed to Bowdoin.

Franklin, nevertheless, saw no need to abandon either science or religion. After Bowdoin's strictures, he merely affirmed his religious principles without attempting to prove them by natural law. He became a humanitarian deist rather than a scientific deist, establishing his belief in God upon moral rather than scientific principles. A humanitarian deist instead of looking for the existence of God in the wonders of the physical universe, as Franklin had done in his Junto lecture, looks instead into his own heart for the evidence of moral order and assumes that it has been implanted by God. Franklin henceforth built his religious system upon the Shaftesburian assumption of moral integrity pervading the universe. Satisfied with this faith, he confined himself either to admittedly fanciful speculation with no pretensions of ascertaining objective truth or to practical manifestations of the religious spirit in worship and in good behavior.

CHAPTER EIGHT

"WE ZEALOUS PRESBYTERIANS"

THE first religious sect with which Franklin had any connection was the Presbyterian, regarded in his day as identical with the Congregational. On the very day of his birth he was baptized in the Old South Church in Boston (January 17, N.S. 1706), and he was reared by his pious parents in the faith of Calvin.

He never forgot the disdain for his coreligionists which as a boy he once heard expressed by a High Church Episcopalian trader, who had bought a large cargo of Connecticut onions which began to sprout on his hands. "Here they are," he exploded, "and they are *growing* too! I damn 'em every day; but I think they are like the Presbyterians; the more I curse 'em, the more they *grow*."[1]

As a man, Franklin quoted with approval an anecdote concerning a member of Parliament who "began one of his Speeches with saying, he thank'd God he was born & bred a Presbyterian; on which another took leave to observe, that a Gentleman must needs be of a most grateful Disposition, since he was thankful for such very small Matters."[2]

For the benefit of his own pious sister, Franklin once reflected against the dogmatic nature of "our Sect." "We zealous Presbyterians," he observed, are "too apt to think ourselves alone in the right, and that besides all the Heathens, Mahometans and Papists, whom we give to Satan in a Lump, other Sects of Christian Protestants that do not agree with us, will hardly escape Perdition."[3]

As we have already noticed from the pages of Franklin's autobiography, he was imbued during childhood with such dogmas as the eternal decrees of God, election, and reprobation. He not only found these concepts unintelligible and

1. Albert Henry Smyth (ed.), *Writings of Benjamin Franklin* (10 vols., New York, 1905–1907), IX, 329.
2. L. W. Labaree *et al.* (eds.), *Papers of Benjamin Franklin*, VI (New Haven, 1963), 463.
3. Carl Van Doren (ed.), *Letters of Benjamin Franklin and Jane Mecom* (Princeton, 1950), p. 71.

later untenable but through them acquired a distaste for the doctrinal side of religion. Conversely he dedicated himself to morality—to an investigation of its elements and practice of its highest forms. As he developed his attachment to ethics, he increased his aversion for dogma. Particularly throughout his youth and middle age he carried on an unrelenting campaign to exalt morality over doctrine wherever he could make his influence felt.

As editor and publisher of the *Pennsylvania Gazette* for a period of thirty years, Franklin maintained a policy of silently promoting rational religion and openly defending diversity of religious belief. For the first ten years he published a number of essays promoting deism and liberal theology, and until the advent of Whitefield in 1739 he published nothing on the other side.

His most specific affirmation of religious toleration came as a consequence of his having printed a handbill or poster announcing that a certain ship destined for Barbados would take freight and passengers. At the bottom of this advertisement, he later explained, "this odd Thing was added, N.B. *No Sea Hens nor Black Gowns will be admitted on any Terms.*"[4] Sea Hens were probably old women; Black Gowns were clergymen. Since many people were offended by this disrespectful reference to the cloth, Franklin wrote an editorial vindicating himself for printing it (June 10, 1731). As Milton had written *Areopagitica* to defend the freedom of the press against censorship, Franklin wrote to expose the unhappy lot of the printer, who, dealing with the multifarious opinions of men, is hardly able to get a living without giving offense to somebody. In excusing himself for the anticlerical phrase, Franklin explained that he had printed it without malice, he had not intended to traduce the clergy, he had been paid five shillings for the advertisement, and this was the first out of more than a thousand he had printed to carry anything objectionable.

4. Labaree (ed.), *Papers*, I (1959), 197.

Soon after taking up management of his newspaper, Franklin reprinted from the pages of the *Maryland Gazette* a series of nine latitudinarian essays entitled "The Plain Dealer" (April 2—June 25, 1730), designed to substitute reasoned belief for blind belief in religion as well as in every other subject. Like the works of Bayle, Shaftesbury, and Anthony Collins, these essays proposed that religion be subjected to every light of reason and evidence.[5]

At the time that Franklin announced the series as a forthcoming feature, he suggested to his own subscribers that they might be able to produce essays of equal interest, but none of the local residents responded to his appeal. Three months later Franklin tried to stir up his readers with a new series "On Original Primitive Christianity" taken from the *London Journal*. Some of his readers disliked the essays, he reported, because of their "false, heretical and pernicious Positions and Opinions," but although he offered to print any refutations, none ever appeared.

Two years later Franklin printed a letter in the *Gazette* under the pseudonym Marcus (March 30, 1732) answering charges of a correspondent in the other Philadelphia newspaper, Franklin's rival, the *American Weekly Mercury*, that irreligion and profaneness were rife among the leaders of the Pennsylvania government. After a number of replies and counter-replies branching out into questions of plagiarism, coxcombery, and provincialism, the wrangle got quite out of hand, and Franklin was forced to halt it with the comment, "I do not love to have the Gazette filled with these controversies about Religion."

Franklin's first known exposition of the Bible in any form was an essay on visiting and caring for the sick which he wrote and published in the *Gazette* (March 25, 1731) during an epidemic of smallpox.[6] He subconsciously indicated

---

5. "Benjamin Franklin and the *Maryland Gazette*," *Maryland Historical Magazine*, XLIV (1949), 177–189.
6. This essay is identified by A. O. Aldridge in "Benjamin Franklin and the *Pennsylvania Gazette*," *Proceedings of the American Philosophical Society*, CVI (1962), 77–81.

his aversion to the dogmatic parts of religion by observing that the famous good Samaritan was "esteemed no better than an Heretick or an Infidel by the Orthodox of those Times." Franklin crammed his essay with scriptural allusions and quotations, not because he accepted the authority of the Bible, but because most of his readers did. Also, he revised a number of verses to fit the local situation but presented them as direct quotations, not paraphrases. Few writers besides Franklin at this time would have been bold enough to take these liberties. In commenting on the parable of the good Samaritan, for example, he remarked: *"I was* SICK *and ye* VISITED *me,* is one of the Terms of Admission into Bliss, and the contrary a Cause of Exclusion: That is, as our Saviour himself explains it, *Ye have visited, or ye have not visited, assisted and comforted those who stood in need of it, even tho' they were the least or meanest of Mankind."*

In this essay Franklin pretended to be appalled by heresy, like most of his readers, but in a private letter to an intimate friend late in life, he revealed that he considered that all of the heretics he had ever known had been virtuous men. "They have the virtue of fortitude, or they would not venture to own their heresy; and they cannot afford to be deficient in any of the other virtues, as that would give advantage to their many enemies; and they have not, like orthodox sinners, such a number of friends to excuse or justify them."[7]

In addition to printing deistical essays in the *Pennsylvania Gazette,* Franklin used his printing press to support his own views concerning the local Presbyterian congregation of which he was himself a prominent member. Franklin regularly paid his annual subscription to the church. But he had little regard for the pastor, the Rev. Jedediah Andrews, a man of intense missionary zeal and organizing ability who persistently urged Franklin to attend his services in addition to according financial support. Franklin put in an appearance from time to time, once for five successive Sundays, and

7. Smyth (ed.), *Writings,* IX, 677.

would have continued regularly, he tells us in his autobiography, had Andrews been a good preacher. "But his Discourses were chiefly either polemic Arguments, or Explications of the peculiar Doctrines of our Sect, and were all to me very dry, uninteresting and unedifying, since not a single moral Principle was inculcated or enforc'd, their Aim seeming to be rather to make us Presbyterians than good Citizens."[8] Franklin, who sought moral discourses, was disgusted and henceforth stayed away from public worship. He was by no means the only member of the congregation to be dissatisfied with Andrews. According to the Rev. Ashbel Green, a Presbyterian historian of the latter part of the eighteenth century, Andrews' "unyielding attachment to certain measures, which he judged to be important in organizing the congregation and settling its government and worship, dismembered it of several persons who had been most active in its formation, and who from that time joined the episcopal church."[9]

Franklin's attitude toward the Presbyterian clergy changed in September, 1734, when an assistant to Andrews arrived in the person of the Rev. Samuel Hemphill, formerly of the Presbytery of Straban in Ireland. The new arrival, according to Franklin, "delivered with a good Voice, and apparently extempore, most excellent Discourses, which drew together considerable Numbers of different Persuasions, who join'd in admiring them. Among the rest I became one of his constant Hearers, his Sermons pleasing me, as they had little of the dogmatical kind, but inculcated strongly the Practice of Virtue, or what in the religious Stile are called Good Works."[10] It turned out later that Hemphill, who had a photographic memory, did not write his own sermons but

8. Leonard W. Labaree *et al.* (eds.), *Autobiography of Benjamin Franklin* (New Haven, 1964), p. 147.
9. *General Assembly's Missionary Magazine,* II (1806), 45.
10. Labaree (ed.), *Autobiography,* p. 167. Background is given by Merton A. Christensen, "Franklin on the Hemphill Trial: Deism Versus Presbyterian Orthodoxy," *William and Mary Quarterly,* 3rd ser., X (1953), 422–440.

instead preached printed sermons of well-known English divines. This in itself would not have counted much against him had he chosen doctrinal discourses similar to those favored by Andrews. Instead of this, however, he preached moral sermons by liberal clergymen. This naturally delighted Franklin but infuriated Andrews. Franklin once more began to spend his Sundays in church, and Andrews reported to a brother minister that "freethinkers, Deists, nothings," getting a scent of Hemphill, "flocked to him." Andrews' sectarian zeal, coupled no doubt with professional jealousy, led him to prefer charges of heterodoxy in the synod. Before the trial he went around from door to door calling Hemphill a "Deist and Socinian" and requesting the congregation not to attend his sermons. As Franklin put it,

> Those . . . of our Congregation, who considered themselves as orthodox Presbyterians, disapprov'd his Doctrine, and were join'd by most of the old Clergy, who arraign'd him of Heterodoxy . . . in order to have him silenc'd. I became his zealous Partisan, and contributed all I could to raise a Party in his Favour; and we combated for him a while with some Hopes of Success. There was much Scribbling pro and con upon the Occasion; and finding that tho' an elegant Preacher, he was but a poor Writer, I lent him my Pen and wrote for him two or three Pamphlets, and one Piece in the Gazette of April 1735. Those Pamphlets, as is generally the Case with controversial Writings, tho' eagerly read at the time, were soon out of Vogue, and I question whether a single Copy of them now exists.[11]

Franklin's piece in the *Gazette* (April 10) appeared exactly one week before Hemphill's trial, which, incidentally, occurred only eight months after Hemphill's arrival in Philadelphia. At the trial it was brought out that Hemphill had earlier been accused of heterodoxy in Ireland but had been exonerated. One of his Irish enemies had written to a brother-in-law in Philadelphia, describing Hemphill as "a vile heretic, a preacher of morality rather than dogma." He had also run afoul of the Presbytery of New Castle because

11. Labaree (ed.), *Autobiography,* p. 167.

of two sermons preached at New London, but apparently no formal charges were there pressed against him.

Franklin in the *Gazette* and in his pamphlets did not attempt to deny the accusations leveled against Hemphill. Instead, he defended Hemphill for preaching morality and argued that he was in this way performing his legitimate duties as a minister of the gospel. Apparently Hemphill realized from the first that the synod could never be persuaded to accept this liberal view. He seems to have stayed in the fight largely because of Franklin's urging.

Franklin's piece in the *Gazette* was a dialogue, in which he presented two primary ideas: morality over faith and relativism over dogmatism.[12] The first theme was already familiar to readers of the *Gazette;* the second was a new concept, directly inspired by the accusations against Hemphill. Franklin argued broadly that ecclesiastical synods have only relative authority and that no such group is infallible. Doctrines, therefore, should not be irrevocably fixed but should remain fluid, constantly subject to reinterpretation. The piece was not a Socratic dialogue, for Franklin did not even pretend to give both sides of the question or to show an adversary being persuaded. He merely presented a series of brief questions inimical to Hemphill and gave lengthy answers vindicating him.

Franklin cast his two speakers as members of the Presbyterian meeting, and described Hemphill's offense as talking of nothing but the duties of morality. The unfriendly member complained, *"I do not love to hear so much of Morality: I am sure it will carry no Man to Heaven, and I do not think it fit to be preached in a Christian Congregation."* Franklin's spokesman replied that morality constituted an important part of the preaching of Christ and his disciples, not only of Hemphill. Indeed the Sermon on the Mount is a moral discourse "towards the End of which, (as foreseeing that People might in time come to depend more upon their *Faith* in him,

12. Labaree (ed.), *Papers,* II (1959), 28–33.

than upon *Good Works*, for their Salvation) he tells the Hearers plainly, that their saying to him, *Lord, Lord* (that is, professing themselves his Disciples or *Christians*) should give them no Title to Salvation, but their *Doing* the Will of his Father; and that tho' they have prophesied in his Name, yet he will declare to them, as Neglecters of Morality, that he never knew them." In this sense, doing the will of God means living "virtuous, upright, and good-doing Lives."

In answer to the question whether faith is not recommended in the New Testament as well as morality (a question which Andrews and his colleagues would undoubtedly never have phrased except in reverse), Franklin shrewdly interjected his private definition of a Christian faith—that it means belief in the efficacy of Christ as a teacher of morality or virtue. "Thus Faith would be a Means of producing Morality, and Morality of Salvation. But that from such Faith alone Salvation may be expected, appears to me to be neither a Christian Doctrine nor a reasonable one. And I should as soon expect, that my bare Believing Mr. *Grew* to be an excellent Teacher of the Mathematicks, would make me a Mathematician, as that Believing in Christ would of it self make a Man a Christian." Since Hemphill's advocate did not believe that faith alone can produce a man's salvation, he was next asked whether morality alone may. He answered that "Morality or Virtue is the End, Faith only a Means to obtain that End: And if the End be obtained, it is no matter by what Means." Once more, therefore, as well as in his *Dissertation on Liberty and Necessity* Franklin argued that the end justifies the means.

His next point is less sensational—although perhaps no less controversial. Faith in Christ helps not at all toward salvation if it is not accompanied by virtuous conduct. This argument Franklin supported with "the Instance of the Devils, who are far from being Infidels, *they believe,* says the Scripture, *and tremble.*" This illustration comes straight from Pierre Bayle, who in his *Pensées diverses sur la comète* makes a good deal of the point that devils and mortals in league with them all believe in God. Further to support the pre-eminence of good works, Franklin cited a number of passages from Scripture, including a description of the last judgment. From these he concluded that "Our Saviour . . . says nothing of *Faith* but what he says against it, that is, that those who cry *Lord, Lord,* and profess to have *believed* in his Name, have no Favour to expect on that Account; but declares that 'tis the Practice, or the omitting the Practice of the Duties of Morality, *Feeding the Hungry, cloathing the Naked, visiting the Sick,* &c. in short, 'tis the Doing or not Doing all the Good that lies in our Power, that will render us the Heirs of Happiness or Misery."

Having apparently admitted that faith has some—although limited—efficacy, Franklin next justified Hemphill for not occasionally preaching faith as well as morality. As the good physician suits his medicine to the disease of the patient, Hemphill had given his present congregation instruction in morality. Were his audience composed of heathen, he might need to preach faith, but the citizens of Philadelphia, already abounding in doctrine and having been baptized in the name of Christ, had a much greater need of morality in which they were deficient. "For our late Want of Charity to each other, our Heart-burnings and Bickerings are notorious."

In shifting attention to the commission of the synod which would bring Hemphill to trial, Franklin suggested that Hemphill had actually committed no offense. "Is Virtue Heresy; and Universal Benevolence False Doctrine, that any of us should keep away from Meeting because it is preached there." He could not believe that an official board of Presbyterians could "persecute, silence and condemn a good Preacher, for exhorting them to be honest and charitable to one another and the rest of Mankind." The issue which Franklin presented is whether ministers and congregations must conform to ecclesiastical fiat or whether they have freedom of individual interpretation. Hemphill's opponents had argued that Hemphill as a Presbyterian teacher was bound to conform to the Westminster Confession of Faith and preach no doctrines but those it authorized. Franklin argued that the church had developed in gradual stages. According to his view, it had changed from the primitive simplicity of the Gospel to the hierarchical government of the Middle Ages and then returned once more in the direction of simplicity. The Protestant Reformation, he argued, had taken place slowly and gradually. Luther had at first preached only against the selling of pardons and then later retreated further from Rome. Calvin widened the breach even more, and the Church of England attempted to stop the process by means of the Thirty-nine Articles.

> The Presbyterians not satisfied, went yet farther; but being too self-confident to think, that as their Fathers were mistaken in some Things, they also might be in others; and fancying themselves infallible in *their* Interpretations, they also ty'd themselves down by the Westminster Confession. But has not a Synod that meets in King George the Second's Reign, as much Right to interpret Scripture, as one that met in Oliver's Time? And if any Doctrine then maintain'd is, or shall hereafter be found not altogether orthodox, why must we be for ever confin'd to that, or to any, Confession?

Franklin argued not only that subsequent official synods have the right to depart from the Westminster Confession but that individual preachers, disagreeing with subsequent synods, have the right to preach their own views. Franklin had no faith in infallibility and opposed giving the rights of infallibility to any church authority. "That is as much as to say, if the Majority of the Preachers be in the wrong, they may justly hinder any Man from setting the People right; for a *Majority* may be in the wrong as well as the *Minority*, and frequently are."

After expressing the tolerant view that the Turks had the same right to send a Mahometan missionary to Pennsylvania as the Philadelphians had to send a Christian to Turkey and that the citizens of Pennsylvania could not reasonably prohibit his preaching—since he would come to them out of a charitable disposition—Franklin concluded that the synod could not reasonably silence Hemphill even though it failed to approve his doctrine in all respects.

> We have justly deny'd the Infallibility of the Pope and his Councils and Synods in their Interpretations of Scripture, and can we modestly claim *Infallibility* for our selves or our Synods in our way of Interpreting? Peace, Unity, and Virtue in any Church are more to be regarded than Orthodoxy. In the present weak State of humane Nature, surrounded as we are on all sides with Ignorance and Error, it little becomes poor fallible Man to be positive and dogmatical in his Opinions. No Point of Faith is so plain, as that *Morality* is our Duty, for all Sides agree in that. A virtuous Heretick shall be saved before a wicked Christian: for there is no such Thing as voluntary Error. Therefore, since 'tis an Uncertainty till we get to Heaven what true Orthodoxy in all points is, and since our Congregation is rather too small to be divided, I hope this Misunderstanding will soon be got over.

This reasoning had no effect whatsoever upon the commission of the synod which tried Hemphill, April 17, 1735. "Never was there such a trial known in the American World."[13] Although eight articles were alleged against Hemphill during the nine days of the trial, he was convicted primarily on one—that he preached that "the gospel is a revival, or new edition, of the law of nature." He was thereupon suspended from the ministry provisionally until the regular meeting of the synod in September, which made the suspension permanent. Hemphill, not at all surprised, sent the synod a message with the postscript, "I shall think you do me a deal of honor, if you entirely excommunicate me."

Franklin took an even firmer stand, publishing pamphlets denouncing the synod's decision in July, September, and October. The first of these, *Some Observations on the Proceedings against The Rev. Mr. Hemphill,* consists of a point-

13. Richard Webster, *A History of the Presbyterian Church in America* (Philadelphia, 1841), p. 115.

by-point examination of the charges brought by Andrews.[14]
Since Franklin correctly labeled most of these accusations as
"trifling," his rebuttal was inevitably confined to the same
level of pedestrian aspersion. Occasionally he rose to a vigorous phrase as he detected "the crafty Malice . . . and the hot
distemper'd Zeal" of Hemphill's detractors. Franklin approached his own personal theology only in a passage defending Hemphill's deistical contention that Christianity is
an illustration and improvement of the law of nature. Franklin argued that this notion is not at all contrary to the Gospel,
for "our Saviour's Design in coming into the World, was to
restore Mankind to the State of Perfection in which Adam
was at first created." Franklin also affected amazement that
the synod should argue that Christianity required other
sanctions or observances. By and large, the rest of the pamphlet illustrates the kind of polemical divinity which Franklin
deplored when he found it in other writers: that is, examining a controverted passage, comparing it with a text of
Scripture, and concluding that the passage is indeed scriptural, logical, and sound.

In the only vigorous thrusts in the pamphlet, Franklin
compared the synod to "that hellish Tribunal the *Inquisition,* who rake up all the vile Evidences, and extort all the
Confessions they can from the wretched Object of their
Rage, and without allowing him any Means of invalidating
the Evidence, or convincing 'em of their own Mistakes, they
assemble together in secret, and proceed to Judgment." The
commission, in publishing an extract of its proceedings, had
observed in conclusion that all its consultations had "been
carried on with an undisturbed Unanimity." Franklin satiri-
cally conjectured that they mentioned this as an argument
for the justice of their censure. "But this will likewise prove
that the Spanish Inquisition is in the right, which is as unanimous in all its Transactions as the Commission. The Reverend Inquisitors go to Prayer, they call upon God to direct

14. Labaree (ed.), *Papers,* II, 37–65.

them in every [one] of their Censures (altho' they have unanimously determined to condemn all who are so unfortunate as to be call'd before them) and, I am sorry to say it, all this is too applicable to the present Case."

Franklin's next pamphlet consisted of the reconstruction of a sermon against the synod preached during the summer by one of Hemphill's defenders. Franklin contributed only the preface, calling upon his brother laymen to resist clerical domination. He warned that their happiness would be at an end if they allowed "the Clergy to get upon our Backs, and ride us, as they do their Horses, where they please."[15] In the meantime, a spokesman for the synod, probably Jonathan Dickinson, had answered Franklin's *Observations* with a moderately phrased *Vindication of the Reverend Commission of the Synod*. Franklin thereupon wrote and published another pamphlet, *A Defence of the Rev. Mr. Hemphill's Observations: or, an Answer to the Vindication of the Reverend Commission,* his most witty and urbane contribution to the controversy.[16] He probably wrote it for the sake of the principle alone without any thought of gaining victory for Hemphill. The latter's enemies were making the most of the evidence of his plagiarism, and Hemphill himself had declined making any further defense before the synod, which on September 22 made his suspension complete.[17]

Among the quotations on his title page, Franklin included one attributed to Tillotson, which may be spurious, "I never knew any Good to come from the Meetings of Priests." This sets the tone of burlesque and abuse for the entire pamphlet. At the outset Franklin labeled the persecution of Hemphill as an outcome of the autocratic spirit of the Commission.

Perhaps the more Pains they have taken, by invented Surmises, wrested Constructions of Hemphill's Words and Actions, and sinister and palpable Prostitutions of Scripture-

15. *Ibid.*, p. 67.   16. *Ibid.*, pp. 91–126.
17. Wm. M. Engles (ed.) , *Records of the Presbyterian Church in the United States of America* (Philadelphia, 1841) , p. 115.

Phrase, to hang him up, as a Scare-crow to the People, and represent him as a dangerous Innovator; the more Occasion they have given to many to call in question their slavish and arbitrary Principles; and the more they have convinc'd them, even in these remote Parts of the Earth, (where they thought themselves secure) of their Inconsistency to every Thing that is real Virtue, Religion and Christian Liberty.

The Commission had argued that it had the privilege, common to all societies, of judging the qualifications of its members and expelling those whom it judged to be heretical. Franklin denied this right by repeating his analogy to the Inquisition.

According to this way of Reasoning, the Spanish Inquisitors may say to a Person they imagine heretical, You, 'tis true, have a Right to judge for your self, to quit our Communion, and declare yourself Protestant; but we have likewise the common and natural Right of Societies, to expel you our civil and ecclesiastical Society, destroy your Reputation, deprive you of your Estate, nay your Life, or in other Words do you all the Mischief we please, notwithstanding your Right of declaring Non-Communion with us. How so? Because we have the Power, and Inclination to do it. Are not these Reasons by which they vindicate themselves every whit as good to justify the Practice of the Inquisition?

In accusing the Commission of pride and arrogance, Franklin quoted "the Advice of a great Author," whom he did not identify—possibly because this author was the notorious deist, Lord Shaftesbury. In the passage quoted by Franklin, Shaftesbury had derided ecclesiastical pompousness and had admonished the clergy against adopting "those high Characters, Appelations, and Titles, which may be Tokens perhaps of what they expect hereafter, but which as yet don't answer the real Power and Authority bestowed on them."[18]

But this was only warming up. Franklin directly accused the Commission of dishonesty and manipulation in the presentation of evidence and then ironically observed that they

18. *Characteristicks,* "Miscellaneous Reflections," Misc. 5, Ch. 3.

considered it lawful to swear to anything to promote "the glorious Cause of Christ and his Church."

Franklin's strongest blow against the Commission came in a mock syllogism portraying its members as dull witted.

> *Asses are grave and dull Animals,*
> *Our Authors are grave and dull Animals; therefore*
> *Our Authors are grave, dull,* or if you will, *Rev. Asses.*
> This Reasoning is every Whit as conclusive, and as infallibly just as theirs.

While attacking the literary integrity of the Commission, Franklin felt obliged to defend that of Hemphill, particularly against the charge of plagiarism. He argued that all ministers compose their sermons by drawing upon books. They receive a good salary because "they are at great Expence in Learning, and in purchasing books. If they preach from their own natural Fund or by immediate Inspiration, what need have they either of Learning or Books?" According to Franklin, the generality of ministers chose the dullest authors to read and study and pass on to the public; whereas "when Hemphill had Occasion to borrow, he gave us the best Parts of the best Writers of the Age. Thus the Difference between him and most of his Brethren, in this part of the World, is the same with that between the Bee and the Fly in a Garden. The one wanders from Flower to Flower, and for the use of others collects from the whole the most delightful Honey; while the other (of a quite different Taste) places her Happiness entirely in Filth, Corruption, and Ordure." This is, of course, a paraphrase of Jonathan Swift's apologue of the spider and the bee, in which the two insects represent modern and ancient learning respectively. It is also a complete reversal in attitude from the *Dogood Letters,* in which Franklin had derided Harvard divinity students for alleged plagiarism.

Although the main principle which Franklin defended in his pamphlet is that of religious toleration or the freedom of individual interpretation without duress from authority, he never clearly formulated the principle. There is one subsidiary principle, however, on which he clearly declared himself and which is of fundamental significance in an interpretation of his religion—the question of the authority of the Scriptures. Franklin spoke out boldly in the first person against the fundamentalist position—the obligation of literal interpretation. He made it quite clear that in a conflict between Scripture and reason or the nature of things, he would unequivocally accept the authority of the latter. He had no hesitation in calling one of the doctrines of the Commission, that of *"our lost and undone State by Nature,"* an absurd notion "to fright and scare an unthinking Populace out of their Senses, and inspire them with Terror, to answer the little selfish Ends of the Inventors and Propagators." If it were ever alleged that certain passages in Scripture insinuate this doctrine, Franklin replied, he would answer that such passages are intricate and obscure. "And I would ingeniously confess I did not understand them, sooner than admit of a Sense contrary to Reason and to the Nature and Perfections of the Almighty God." Although in a sense taking refuge in protestations of intellectual modesty, Franklin nevertheless affirmed the supremacy of reason over Scripture.

In November, weeks after the synod had taken final action and Hemphill had departed from Pennsylvania, another printer in Philadelphia, Andrew Bradford, published a sharp pamphlet devoted exclusively to invective against Franklin's *Remarks*.[19] According to its author, Obadiah Jenkins (possibly a pseudonym), only "a Pagan, a Jew, or a Mahometan" could have produced the "impertinent Scrawl" of the *Remarks* or its "prophane Rant against the most important Articles of Christianity."

Jenkins made no attempt to meet Franklin's arguments beyond contrasting his chief doctrines with opposing passages in Scripture. He charged Franklin with treating the

19. *Remarks upon the Defence of the Reverend Mr. Hemphill's Observations* (Philadelphia, 1735).

fundamentals of Christianity "in the most ludicrous Manner with Scorn, Banter & Grimace"; with proposing a new method of salvation by moral law alone to which "both the Gospel and the Protestant Churches have ever been strangers to" and with "renouncing as an Idol the Confession of Faith, received by the Presbyterian Churches in *England, Scotland, and Ireland*" as well as by his own synod.

This abusive pamphlet was the only concrete return which Franklin received from all his writings on Hemphill. Yet he probably learned many lessons—particularly that unrelieved satire may gratify personal feelings but do little to change public opinion. His temperate dialogue in the *Gazette* was far more persuasive than his vitriolic pamphlets denouncing the smugness and tyranny of the clergy.

The legalistic Andrews, although winning a temporary victory, later felt the hand of the ecclesiastical court raised against his own reputation. Toward the close of his life "a rumour was spread" that he had "suddenly fallen by a disgraceful act." At his trial he denied "drunkenness, criminal intent or act" but confessed to "imprudence and foolish tampering with evil" and deplored "the shame brought on the ministry, by a levity so unbecoming his advanced life." He was suspended, but in a few months restored.

In the meanwhile rumors of Franklin's warfare against the synod had reached the ears of his parents in Boston. Alarmed at his deviation from orthodoxy, they wrote from Boston expressing anxiety over his spiritual welfare. Franklin replied (April 13, 1738) with a serious and respectful vindication of individual conviction in matters of religion. He admitted to his share of erroneous opinions but in extenuation pointed to "the natural Weakness and Imperfection of Human Understanding" and "the unavoidable Influences of Education, Custom, Books and Company, upon our Ways of thinking." He concluded that "a Man must have a good deal of Vanity who believes, and a good deal of Boldness who affirms, that all the Doctrines he holds, are true; and all he rejects, are false." And applying his remarks to religious zealots, he suggested that "the same may be justly said of every Sect, Church and Society of men when they assume to themselves that Infallibility which they deny to the Popes and Councils."

Taking a pragmatic position which he retained throughout most of his life, Franklin argued that "Opinions should be judg'd of by their Influences and Effects; and if a Man holds none that tend to make him less Virtuous or more vicious, it may be concluded he holds none that are dangerous."

Franklin expressed sorrow that his religious opinions had given uneasiness to his parents but appealed to their understanding and charity. "Since it is no more in a Man's Power *to think* than *to look* like another, methinks all that should be expected from me is to keep my Mind open to Conviction, to hear patiently and examine attentively whatever is offered me for that end." And if he persists in error, he should be pitied rather than blamed.

> My Mother grieves, that one of her Sons is an Arian, another an Arminian. What an Arminian or an Arian is, I cannot say that I very well know; the Truth is, I make such Distinctions very little my Study; I think vital Religion has always suffer'd, when Orthodoxy is more regarded than Virtue. And the Scripture assures me, that at the last Day, we shall not be examin'd what we *thought,* but what we *did;* and our Recommendation will not be that we said *Lord, Lord,* but that we did GOOD to our Fellow Creatures.[20]

No doubt Franklin exaggerated in professing ignorance of the meaning of Arian and Arminian, but by so doing he was able unobtrusively to diminish doctrinaire absolutes. Franklin's Christianity was not fundamental enough to make him either an Arian or an Arminian—although he agreed with the Arians that Christ was not the son of God and with the Arminians that each man's eternal fate had not been inevitably pre-ordained. Some years later Franklin repeated the

20. Labaree (ed.), *Papers,* II, 203.

humorous saying of a Scottish divine that an *ism* worse than *Arianism* and *Socinianism* was rheumatism.[21]

Even though not a believer in inspiration, Franklin cited Scripture to good effect, referring his parents to the same passage which he had paraphrased in his Hemphill dialogue. The expression *"Lord, Lord"* comes from the parable of the foolish virgins, who were repudiated for their failure to provide oil for their lamps. In the same chapter appears a description of the last judgment in which the King rewards those who had fed the hungry and cared for the sick.

Five years later, Franklin's sister Jane also expressed uneasiness concerning his doctrinal divagations. She had come to believe that he opposed worshiping of God and that he believed good works alone to be a passport to heaven. Franklin gently chided her for these fancies. "I am so far from thinking that God is not to be worshipped, that I have compos'd and wrote a whole Book of Devotions for my own Use. And I imagine there are few, if any, in the World so weake as to imagine, that the little Good we can do here, can *merit* so vast a Reward hereafter."[22]

There were some things in his sister's "New England Doctrines and Worship" which he admitted he did not agree with, but he did not condemn them or try to shake his sister's faith in them. "We may dislike things that are nevertheless right in themselves." He asked only that she show him the same tolerance. To that end he urged her to read a passage in Jonathan Edwards' *Some Thoughts concerning the present Revival of Religion in New-England,* published in 1742. Here Edwards had affirmed that "The internal Acts & Principles of the Worship of God . . . are the most essential and important of all Duties of Religion." He added, however, that there are two external manifestations or expressions of this inward religion: one consists of outward acts of worship such as attending religious ceremonies, taking sacraments,

21. Smyth (ed.), *Writings*, V, 376.   22. Labaree (ed.), *Papers*, II, 385.

and honoring God with such gestures as bowing and kneeling and such words as prayer and praise. "And the other Sort, are the Expressions of our Love to GOD, by obeying his moral commands, of Self-denial, Righteousness, Meekness, and Christian Love, in our Behaviour among Men." The latter, Edwards insisted, "are of vastly the greatest Importance in the Christian Life. God makes little Account of the former, in Comparison of them." Edwards stated just as unequivocally as Franklin that showing our religion by deeds is vastly more important than showing it by words. "We can't express our LOVE to GOD, by doing any Thing that is profitable to GOD: GOD would therefore have us do it in those Things that are profitable to our Neighbours, whom he has constituted his Receivers."

After citing Edwards, Franklin closed his letter by appealing to the authority of the New Testament: "If you can perceive the Fruit to be good, don't terrify your self that the Tree may be evil, but be assur'd it is not so; for you know who has said, *Men do not gather Grapes of Thorns or Figs of Thistles.*" This exposition of the principle of judging by results is a paraphrase from a parable in Matthew 7, which is preceded by the even more pertinent admonition, "Ye shall know them by their fruits."

Franklin's quoting Edwards in defense of his moral doctrines reveals a resemblance between the two men perhaps more important than the metaphysical parallels previously indicated. The passage reveals also that Franklin soon lost the anticlerical animus of his Hemphill pamphlets. We should not forget that Hemphill, although discredited by the Philadelphia synod, was still a Presbyterian minister, and Franklin accorded him friendship and support. In condemning the synod, Franklin was attacking a group of narrow sectarians, not the Presbyterian denomination at large.

When Franklin later served in London as agent for several of the American colonies, he frequently defended the Presbyterians of New England on political grounds. In at least one regard, he argued, they were more tolerant than Anglicans, for the Massachusetts legislature regularly turned over to the Church of England all sums levied for the support of religion, whereas in England all of the tax levied for religion went to the established church. He also stressed the theme that during the seventeenth century, Presbyterians had saved the English people "from the Tyranny of the Stuarts." Joining political liberty with religious freedom, he invented one of his most forceful sayings, "Rebellion to Tyrants is Obedience to God."[23]

An episode toward the close of Franklin's life shows, moreover, that he harbored no resentment whatsoever against the Presbyterians. The leaders of a new town which had sprung up in Massachusetts named it Franklin in his honor and proposed to build a steeple to their meeting house if he would donate a bell. Franklin advised them to spare the expense of a steeple for the present but offered a collection of books as a nucleus for a parochial library. The books he gave, worth twenty-five pounds, were designed "to inculcate Principles of sound Religion and just Government." The clergyman of the parish subsequently preached a sermon to commemorate Franklin's bounty, which he printed under the title of *The Dignity of Man.*[24] On his title page he referred to Franklin as "the Ornament of Genius, the Patron of Science, and the Boast of Man" and in his message enforced the necessity of intellectual and moral culture. This was a theme dear to Franklin's heart, from which he probably received as much satisfaction as from the compliments of his beneficiaries. He could very well have interpreted it as a tardy vindication of Hemphill and the social gospel.

---

23. A. O. Aldridge, *Benjamin Franklin: Philosopher and Man* (New York, 1965), p. 257.
24. Smyth (ed.), *Writings,* IX, 301.

CHAPTER NINE

WHITEFIELD AND METHODISM

WHILE Franklin was backing up Hemphill in asserting the right of individual conscience, the religious atmosphere of Philadelphia was heavy and unyielding, although not oppressive. The received orthodoxy was enforced by acquiescent indifference rather than by militant zeal, and it was possible for Franklin to promote liberal notions without endangering his respected position in the community. In the 1740's with the advent of the evangelist George Whitefield, however, the entire religious climate of Pennsylvania changed. As personal convictions became intense and enthusiastic, Franklin abandoned the attempt to foster his own religious ideas in his newspaper. He published several pieces supporting Whitefield and his revivals partly out of personal inclination and partly as a concession to the spirit of the times.

In his autobiography, Franklin revealed respectful amazement at Whitefield's powers.

> The Multitudes of all Sects and Denominations that attended his Sermons were enormous, and it was matter of Speculation to me who was one of the Number, to observe the extraordinary Influence of his Oratory on his Hearers, and how much they admir'd and respected him, notwithstanding his common Abuse of them, by assuring them they were naturally *half Beasts and half Devils*. It was wonderful to see the Change soon made in the Manners of our Inhabitants; from being thoughtless or indifferent about Religion, it seem'd as if all the World were growing Religious; so that one could not walk thro' the Town in an Evening without Hearing Psalms sung in different Families of every Street.[1]

Whitefield stirred up so much religious feeling during one of his visits that for a year afterward public worship was held regularly twice a day and three or four times on Sunday. The enthusiasm to hear him preach was so great that many fol-

---

1. Leonard W. Labaree *et al.* (eds.), *Autobiography of Benjamin Franklin* (New Haven, 1964), p. 175. In the edition of Whitefield's *Sermons* which Franklin printed in 1740 appears the remark, "I know that by Nature I am but half a Devil, and half a Beast" (II, 40).

lowed him on foot from Philadelphia to other cities, sometimes as far as sixty miles.[2]

During Whitefield's first visit, in the autumn of 1739, Franklin reported in the *Gazette* (November 15) that he preached nightly from the Court-House Gallery to nearly 6,000 people, "who stood in an awful Silence to hear him." Franklin continued to fill the *Gazette* with reports of Whitefield's campaign, letters from Whitefield himself on doctrine and social evils, letters and poems in praise of Whitefield, and essays from Whitefield's disciples. He also printed some material against Whitefield, by and large inspired by the regular clergy, who resented his superior success, both in declamation and finance.

In his autobiography, Franklin pointed out the histrionic advantage which Whitefield as an itinerant preacher enjoyed over his brothers who were stationary. "The latter can not well improve their Delivery of a Sermon by . . . many Rehearsals," but Whitefield's speech "was so improv'd by frequent Repetitions, that every Accent, every Emphasis, every Modulation of Voice, was so perfectly well turn'd and well plac'd, that without being interested in the Subject, one could not help being pleas'd with the Discourse, a Pleasure of much the same kind with that receiv'd from an excellent Piece of Musick."[3]

The local divines were upset, however, by dangers to their intellectual prestige through conflicting opinions. Whitefield may have had no conscious intention of disputing the authority of the regular parish minister, but it proved to be practically impossible for two expounders to think alike on all aspects of the Scriptures. The itinerant preacher inevitably aroused questioning, bewilderment, and confusion; and the parishioners, after they had been confronted with new interpretations, were deprived of their spiritual complacency

2. Ashbel Green, "Memoir of Hannah Hodge," *General Assembly's Missionary Magazine*, II (1806), 45.
3. Labaree (ed.), *Autobiography*, p. 180.

and rendered acutely aware of their own minister's fallibility.

An even more disturbing element in the relations between Whitefield and the local clergy was his practice of taking up collections for the support of an orphanage which he had established in Bethesda, near Savannah, Georgia. Whitefield frequently affirmed that his main reason for touring the northern colonies was to gather money for his orphans, and he used every rhetorical device at his command in appealing to the generosity of his audiences. In Philadelphia and elsewhere, attacks against Whitefield were commonly focused upon his fund-gathering.[4] Local ministers who at first welcomed him to their pulpits as an exalted servant of the Lord cooled off as they began to realize the amount of his collections. They charged him with divesting their congregations of more money in a few days of impassioned preaching than they themselves garnered during a whole year of devoted service. Resentful of both the admiration and the monetary contributions bestowed upon Whitefield, they ultimately closed their doors to him and forced him to preach in the fields.

The paradox underlying the close and friendly relations between Franklin and Whitefield is that Whitefield's theology of faith over good works was the antithesis of Franklin's. The deist and the Methodist developed mutual respect and admiration despite the fact that the doctrine which Whitefield preached was of a piece with that of the ultra-orthodox Presbyterians, which Franklin deplored, condemned, and vigorously attacked.

One of Whitefield's constant themes was the insufficiency of good deeds as an instrument of salvation. To take one example, he categorically asserted in his sermon "The Wise and Foolish Virgins," "None but such as have a living faith in Jesus Christ, and are truly born again, can possibly enter into the kingdom of heaven. You may perhaps live honest

---

4. *Ibid.*, p. 177.

and outwardly moral lives, but if you depend on that morality, or join your works with your faith, in order to justify you before God, you have no lot or share in Christ's redemption."

The explanation of why Franklin could in spite of this doctrine admire and respect Whitefield lies in the ambivalence of Whitefield's character. Although preaching consistently against reliance upon good works, Whitefield in practice labored tirelessly and selflessly to promote a number of fundamental social reforms. By establishing his orphanage, fostering education for Negroes, denouncing cruelty to slaves, and initiating a number of private charities, Whitefield became one of America's pioneer humanitarians. It was this side of Whitefield's personality which appealed to Franklin. In his autobiography he praised "the benevolent Heart of Mr. Whitefield." Franklin was undoubtedly enough of a diplomat in his contacts with the evangelist to evade discussion of doctrinal topics, and Whitefield probably exercised the same tact. The inherent fund of humanitarianism which both possessed served to cement their friendship. Yet neither concealed his religious opinions from the other. Franklin particularly affirmed in his autobiography that Whitefield "us'd indeed sometimes to pray for my Conversion, but never had the Satisfaction of believing that his Prayers were heard. Ours was a mere civil Friendship, sincere on both Sides, and lasted to his Death."[5]

During his first visit to Philadelphia, Whitefield at the age of twenty-four was already somewhat of a celebrity. Franklin, nine years older, was still merely a local printer. In the ordinary course of events, Whitefield would probably have had little to do with Franklin, but there was something in their personalities which drew them together. Perhaps subconsciously Whitefield recognized and admired Franklin's sexual vigor and ease with ladies of all kinds. Whitefield had undertaken his travels in part for the purpose of finding a

5. *Ibid.,* p. 178.

suitable wife, but he consistently failed in his romantic enterprises. His theatrical appeals were effective for a mass audience, but apparently failed to warm individual hearts. Because of his obsession with marriage, he openly complimented Jonathan Edwards for the possession of his wife, Sarah, but he had little complimentary to say about Edwards himself.

Even though Whitefield and Edwards shared the same clerical profession, espoused the same doctrine, and practiced the same form of "experimental" (emotional) preaching, they were never personally drawn to each other. Their coolness makes the cordial relations between Franklin and Whitefield all the more remarkable. They seem to have been mutually attracted at the first meeting, and a warm friendship and correspondence lasted until Whitefield's death.

During Whitefield's first sojourn in Philadelphia, Franklin as a business venture undertook the publication of his sermons and journals but did not in any sense identify himself with Whitefield's religious views. Indeed, he strongly disapproved of some of the expressions which Whitefield had used in his journals. Although Whitefield was not a narrow sectarian in his attitude toward dissenters from the Church of England, he was extremely intolerant of anyone who rejected fundamentalist doctrine. Franklin opposed this confined outlook in Whitefield as he opposed bigotry and fanaticism wherever he found them. In writing to a friend some years later on the distinction between an atheist and a deist, Franklin remarked that "they are diametrically opposite; and not near of kin, as Mr. Whitefield seems to suppose, where (in his Journal) he tells us, '*Mr. B. was a Deist, I had almost said an Atheist*'; That is, *Chalk*, I had almost said *Charcoal*."[6]

Franklin did not by any means consider his press as pro-Whitefield. On polemic divinity, which he despised, he

6. L. W. Labaree *et al.* (eds.), *Papers of Benjamin Franklin*, III (New Haven, 1961), 88.

printed almost anything in the way of pamphlets which was brought to him and in which he could see a profit. Some of the most rancorous colonial vilifications of Whitefield emanated from Franklin's press.

Franklin also was the sole American printer to publish a letter by Whitefield which brought greater abuse upon him than anything else he ever wrote. This was an attack on Archbishop Tillotson, a much-beloved latitudinarian, affirming that he knew no more about true Christianity than did Mahomet, an attack engendered by Tillotson's broad interpretation of doctrine. Franklin published Whitefield's letter in both the *Gazette* and in a separate pamphlet, despite the fact that his personal religious views were much closer to Tillotson's than to Whitefield's.[7]

On Whitefield's second trip to Pennsylvania, his traveling companion was William Seward, a well-to-do English widower thirteen years Whitefield's senior, who had recently adopted Methodist notions under the influence of Charles Wesley. He embarked with Whitefield for America in August, 1739, and in 1740 published a *Journal of a Voyage from Savannah to Philadelphia, and from Philadelphia to England,* a full record of his activities.

Seward was a pious, dedicated, and generous servant of the Lord and a loyal henchman of Whitefield, but like his young mentor he sometimes allowed his zeal to triumph over his tact. In Philadelphia he involved Whitefield in an altercation with the worldly segment of society in which Franklin, as editor of the *Pennsylvania Gazette,* played a principal role.

The social center of the community was a room used for select balls and concerts as well as for a dancing school. Two days after Whitefield and Seward arrived in Pennsylvania, April 14, Seward persuaded the proprietor of the dancing

7. "A Letter from the Rev. Mr. Whitefield, at Georgia, to a Friend in London, wherein he vindicates his Asserting, that Archbishop Tillotson knows no more of Christianity than Mahomet," *Pennsylvania Gazette,* April 10, 1740.

school, Robert Bolton, who rented out his premises for concerts and assemblies, to lock the doors and turn over the keys to him. Seward was especially indignant that "the *Assembly-Room, Dancing-School,* and *Musick-Meeting,*" should be "supported in Part . . . by the Proprietor [Thomas Penn], whose Father bore a noble Testimony against those Devilish Diversions." It appears that Bolton's wife came under Whitefield's influence and that she persuaded her husband to turn over his keys to Seward. But before doing so, Bolton warned Seward that he had already leased the room for regular meetings of the Assembly and the Concert Society, and Seward promised to pay for any damage Bolton should sustain thereby.

On the day after Seward locked up the dancing room, the adherents of the Assembly publicly threatened to cane him, and that night they broke open the door even though there were no scheduled activities. Five days later (April 22) the Assembly danced as usual on its assigned day. Despite the resumption of social festivities, Seward considered his original interference as a personal triumph as well as a victory for Whitefield and God. On April 27 he wrote a news release for publication in the New York papers affirming that as a direct result of Whitefield's preaching the Philadelphia dancing school and concert room had been closed down.

Had Seward contented himself with publishing this comment in New York alone, he might have been able to enjoy an unruffled triumph. But he made the mistake of asking Franklin to publish in the *Pennsylvania Gazette* on May 1 a second and slightly more current bulletin: "Since Mr. Whitefield's Preaching here, the Dancing School, Assembly and Concert Room have been shut up, as inconsistent with the Doctrine of the Gospel: And though the Gentlemen concern'd caus'd the Door to be broke open again, we are inform'd that no Company came to the last Assembly Night." Seward also made a self-congratulatory remark in his journal, "Neither the Gentlemen of the *Assembly* or *Concert* have met this Week, so that I hope we have taken *Satan's strongest Hold in this City.*"

On the same day that he delivered his news release to Franklin (April 30), Seward heard that there was talk of legal action being taken against him for his high-handed behavior. He thereupon visited a number of the leaders of the Concert Society to ask pardon for his indiscretion, and, according to their version, he repeatedly assured them "that he knew nothing of any Gentlemen's having hired the Rooms, and that if he had had the least Intimation of it, he would not have caused them to be shut up." This was, of course, a falsehood if, as the Assembly leaders maintained, he had previously been informed by Bolton of the terms on which the premises were leased.

On the day after the appearance of the item in the *Gazette*, Seward, according to his journal, "call'd at Mr. *Franklin's* the Printer's." Just at that moment some of the irate patrons of the Assembly were there demanding to know who had written the libelous paragraph, and Franklin revealed that it was Seward. Franklin apparently acted as arbiter while the adherents of the Assembly confronted Seward and accused him of publishing falsehoods in the *Gazette*. Apart from Bolton, the only known members of the Assembly were Tench Francis, who played "a very indifferent finger upon an excellent violin"; Thomas Penn, the proprietor of the colony; and Richard Peters, a former bigamous Episcopalian clergyman, then serving as secretary to Penn. Since Peters had been one of the most vindictive opponents of White-field's activities in Philadelphia, he acted as "the chief Speaker" in Franklin's office. Seward, according to his own account, behaved with "great Sweetness and Calmness of Temper." He told Peters that "if he could prove that JESUS CHRIST, or his *Apostle,* or the *Primitive Christians,* approved of these Diversions," he would yield the point.

Peters and his supporters insisted that the paragraph in the *Gazette* falsely implied that the members of the Assembly had been convinced of the error of their ways by Whitefield's preaching. They maintained that, to the contrary, the Assembly actually abhorred Whitefield's methods and his doctrine. Logic was certainly on their side, but impervious sweetness on Seward's. He replied that the paragraph would not be construed in their sense, and even if it were, such a construction would be an honor to them. He himself had once been as fond of balls and assemblies as any of them but was now convinced that such amusements were pernicious. "Poor Men, tho' they boil'd with Rage when I came to talk to them of the *Truth as 'tis in* JESUS, they retired One by One, and left me alone."

Not content with venting their wrath upon Seward in person, the Assembly members then insisted that Franklin print a caustic letter contradicting his news release and accusing Whitefield's supporters of circulating dishonest reports. Franklin deplored these aspersions but decided nevertheless to print the letter as a means of proving that his press was not under the control of the Whitefield faction. "I have often said," he asserted, "that if any Person thinks himself injured in a Publick News-Paper, he has a Right to have his Vindication made as publick as the Aspersion."[8]

In the letter the Assembly members insisted that their dancing activities had been discontinued merely because the winter season had come to an end. Also they charged that the implication of Whitefield's having had anything to do with the closing was an imposition upon the public and a crafty device to spread Whitefield's fame in England. They even alleged that news reports of the great crowds composing Whitefield's audience were frauds and exaggerations, the numbers being often doubled or trebled.

In the next issue Franklin printed a letter signed Obadiah Plainman analyzing the original news story in the light of these objections.[9] It is possible that Obadiah Plainman was

8. Labaree (ed.), *Papers,* II (1959), 258.
9. *Pennsylvania Gazette,* May 8, 1740.

Franklin's pseudonym. Obadiah was at any rate pro-White-field. He defended the accuracy and objectivity of the original news story and satirized the proprietors of the Assembly for their arrogant assumption that the best people in Philadelphia were the patrons of the Assembly. In subsequent issues of the *Gazette* other writers joined the controversy.

On this same visit to Philadelphia, Whitefield had vigorously appealed for funds for his orphanage. On one Sunday, he raised 150 pounds sterling, preaching at morning and afternoon services to an estimated fifteen thousand auditors, a somewhat remarkable congregation for a city of ten thousand total population.[10] It was probably about this time, when Franklin's relations with Whitefield were still somewhat distant and uncertain in the direction they would take, that Franklin allowed a firm resolve not to contribute to the orphanage to melt under the influence of Whitefield's oratory. The passage in his autobiography is well known:

> I silently resolved he should get nothing from me. I had in my Pocket a Handful of Copper Money, three or four silver Dollars, and five Pistoles in Gold. As he proceeded I began to soften, and concluded to give the Coppers. Another Stroke of his Oratory made me asham'd of that, and determin'd me to give the Silver; and he finish'd so admirably, that I empty'd my Pocket wholly into the Collector's Dish, Gold and all.[11]

Franklin was from the first sympathetic to the idea of an orphanage but opposed to the undeveloped colony of Georgia as a site. He considered that it would be far more efficient to transport the orphans from Georgia to Philadelphia than to transport materials and workmen from Philadelphia for the construction in Georgia.

The gathering of funds for the Bethesda orphanage turned out to be one of Whitefield's most vulnerable spots. Clergymen who opposed his doctrine or his fervent preaching had difficulty in turning their congregations against him for these

10. *Ibid.*, April 24, 1740.
11. Labaree (ed.), *Autobiography*, p. 177.

reasons, but they successfully stirred up doubts and suspicions by circulating rumors concerning large sums of money carried by Whitefield out of the community. As a writer in the *Georgia Gazette* put it, "He was . . . maligned, traduced, and persecuted with unrelenting virulence, as a cheat, an impostor, and a public robber, who, under the specious pretence of promoting a charitable design, was amassing great wealth to himself."[12]

In his autobiography, Franklin reported his decided opinion that Whitefield "was in all his Conduct, a perfectly *honest Man.*" And even in the *Pennsylvania Gazette* he supported Whitefield's integrity. Although printing the letter of a sea captain who had visited Bethesda and had allegedly not found a single orphan installed,[13] he at the same time printed other communications justifying Whitefield, including a letter from the evangelist himself, setting forth the receipts and expenditures of the orphanage and declaring that he had not converted any part of the receipts to his private use.[14] Franklin also gave Whitefield advice on fund-raising and offered to compose a preamble for a subscription appeal for the orphanage. During the summer of 1747, Franklin wrote to his brother John expressing pleasure at Whitefield's presence in America: "He is a good Man and I love him."[15]

In his autobiography Franklin offered the following incident as an example of the intimate terms on which he and Whitefield stood.

Upon one of his Arrivals from England at Boston, he wrote to me that he should come soon to Philadelphia, but knew not where he could lodge when there, as he understood his old kind Host Mr. Benezet was remov'd to Germantown. My Answer was; You know my House, if you can make shift with its scanty Accommodations you will be most heartily welcome. He reply'd, that if I made that kind Offer for Christ's sake, I should not miss of a Reward. And I return'd,

12. John Gillies, *Memoirs of the Life of the Reverend George Whitefield* (New Haven, 1812), p. 275.
13. June 2, 1745.   14. May 22, 1746.
15. Labaree (ed.), *Papers*, III, 169.

*Don't let me be mistaken; it was not for Christ's sake, but for
your sake.* One of our common Acquaintance jocosely remark'd, that knowing it to be the Custom of the Saints,
when they receiv'd any favour, to shift the Burthen of the
Obligation from off their own Shoulders, and place it in
Heaven, I had contriv'd to fix it on Earth.[16]

For free-thinkers this passage is the *locus classicus* in Franklin's works to prove that he held anti-Christian sentiments. It
was, for example, the best that Robert Dale Owen, the famous New Harmony reformer, could offer to support his
charge that Franklin should be classed among the world's
unbelievers.[17] But as a Unitarian observer argued, the passage reveals merely that "Franklin wished to have a joke with
the *canting* Whitefield, and let him know that he had a
sufficient respect for himself to give him his board, without
doing it as a deed to the absent Christ."[18]

Franklin's retort is a remarkable example of a parallel
between life and literature, for a century earlier Molière had
incorporated an almost identical comment in a key scene of
his comedy *Dom Juan ou le festin de pierre.* In the play, Dom
Juan and his servant are approached in a forest by a poor
hermit who asks charity, in return for which he promises to
pray heaven for his benefactor's reward. Dom Juan, after
cynically observing that the hermit's ten years of prayer had
been remarkably inefficacious in providing for his own personal material welfare, remarks, "I want to give you a Louis
d'or, but I give it to you for the love of humanity." Despite
Franklin's echo of Dom Juan, it is highly doubtful that he
knew of the scene in Molière, for it was banned from the
stage after the second representation and not restored until
the nineteenth century.

Another striking literary parallel in Franklin's works is the
result, not of chance, but of conscious influence. Unlikely as
it may seem, Franklin based one of his own moral allegories

16. Labaree (ed.), *Autobiography*, p. 178.
17. *Record of Unitarian Worthies* (London, 1874), p. 173.
18. *Ibid.,* p. 174.

on a parable introduced by Whitefield in a sermon which Franklin heard him preach in Philadelphia. According to one of Whitefield's early biographers, he delivered the following apostrophe while preaching from the balcony of the courthouse on Market Street.

> "Father Abraham, who have you in heaven? any Episcopalians?" "No." "Any Presbyterians?" "No." "Any Baptists?" "No." "Have you any Methodists, Seceders, or Independents there?" "No, no!" "Why, who have you there?" "We don't know those names here. All who are here are Christians, believers in Christ—men who have overcome by the blood of the Lamb, and the word of his testimony." "Oh, is that the case? then God help me, God help us all, to forget party names, and to become Christians, in deed and in truth."[19]

We cannot state for certain during which one of his visits to Philadelphia Whitefield delivered his denunciation of sectarianism, but the principle was very much on his mind in November, 1739. Writing to a well-wisher he declared, "I long for professors to leave off placing religion in saying 'I am a Churchman,' 'I am a Dissenter.' My language to such is, 'Are you of CHRIST? If so, I love you with all my heart.'" John Adams in a letter to Jefferson, December 3, 1813, repeated Whitefield's parable and affirmed that if Whitefield really delivered it, there was "no Philosopher, or Theologian, or Moralist, ancient or modern, more profound, more infallible" than he.[20]

Whitefield's parable stayed in Franklin's memory forty years. During his sojourn in France in the midst of the American Revolution, he composed and set up on his private printing press a variant in French of Whitefield's plea for tolerance in which he used Catholic instead of Protestant symbols. The following is a translation.

> There was an officer, a man of virtue, named Montresor, who was seriously ill. His curate, believing that he was going to die, advised him to make his peace with God in order to

19. Joseph Belcher, *George Whitefield* (New York, 1857), pp. 206–207.
20. Lester J. Cappon (ed.), *The Adams-Jefferson Letters* (Chapel Hill, 1959), II, 406.

be received in Paradise. "I have not much anxiety on this subject," said Montresor, "for last night I had a vision which has given me complete tranquillity." "What vision did you have?" asked the good priest. "I was at the gate of Heaven," replied Montresor, "with a crowd of people who wanted to enter. And St. Peter asked each one what his religious profession was. One replied, 'I am Roman Catholic.' 'Very well,' said St. Peter, 'enter and take your place among the Catholics.' Another said that he was of the Anglican church. 'Very well,' said St. Peter, 'enter and take your place among the Anglicans.' Another said that he was a Quaker. 'Enter,' said St. Peter, 'and take your place among the Quakers.' Finally my turn coming, he asked me what my religion was. 'Alas!' I replied, 'unfortunately the poor James Montresor has none.' 'That is too bad,' said the Saint, 'I do not know where to put you; but enter anyway; and find a place where you can.' " [21]

Of course, only the form of this parable and the general theme of tolerance derive from Whitefield. Whereas Whitefield criticized sectarianism only within the limits of Protestantism and extended his tolerance no further, Franklin deplored all attention to religious distinctions as such and expounded his favorite notion of deeds over doctrine.

The French text of Franklin's parable was reprinted in a book by Cerutti and in two French periodicals during the eighteenth century. [22] It was also adapted by Mme Brillon d'Hardancourt, a charming married lady in her thirties with whom Franklin carried on a literary flirtation during his sojourn in Paris. Franklin and Mme Brillon exchanged a series of witty and sentimental notes in the process of which Franklin played the role of a gallant and Mme Brillon evaded an outright surrender with grace and dexterity. In one of her epistles, she retold his story after her own fashion. "When I go to paradise, if St. Peter asks me of what religion I am, I will reply—of that in which one believes the Eternal Being perfectly good and indulgent—of that in which one loves those who resemble the Eternal Being. And I loved

21. A. O. Aldridge, *Franklin and His French Contemporaries* (New York, 1957), pp. 172–173.
22. *Ibid.*, p. 173.

with idolatry Dr. Franklin. St. Peter will say, I am sure. Enter and take a place near Mister Franklin. You will find him seated near the eternal."[23]

Franklin's version of the parable on tolerance may have been partly suggested by an episode connected with a large building erected in Philadelphia for Whitefield's preaching. Trustees of the structure had been chosen from the principal sects, "one Church of England-man, one Presbyterian, one Baptist, one Moravian, &c."[24] The Moravian had been a very unpopular member, and when he died the remaining trustees determined not to have another Moravian and so were faced with the problem of keeping from having two of some other sect. Franklin explained in his autobiography, "At length one mention'd me, with the Observation that I was merely an honest Man, and of no Sect at all; which prevail'd with them to chuse me."[25]

Franklin further indicated in his autobiography that the meeting house was expressly intended "for the Use of any Preacher of any religious Persuasion who might desire to say something to the People of Philadelphia," but he was probably the only trustee liberal enough to take this formula literally. He added that the design in building was not "to accommodate any particular Sect, but the Inhabitants in general, so that even if the Mufti of Constantinople were to send a Missionary to preach Mahometanism to us, he would find a Pulpit at his Service." Whitefield in 1740 set forth his own understanding—quite different from Franklin's—in no uncertain terms. "The house is intended for public worship and a charity school. None but orthodox experimental ministers are to preach in it, and such are to have free liberty, of whatever denomination."[26] One wonders whether Franklin and Whitefield would have remained friends if a Mohamme-

---

23. Franklin Papers, American Philosophical Society.
24. Labaree (ed.), *Autobiography*, p. 176.
25. *Ibid.*, p. 194.
26. Walter Herbert Stowe, *Life and Letters of Bishop William White* (New York, 1937), p. 11.

dan missionary had actually turned up with a desire to use the building.

During Whitefield's absences from Philadelphia attendance at the preaching house fell off—but not the debt which had been incurred in constructing it. In 1749 Franklin published *Proposals relating to the Education of Youth in Pennsylvania* suggesting the founding of an academy, and in two years instruction began. As the enterprise flourished larger quarters became necessary, and Franklin negotiated with the trustees of the meeting house for use of the building. It was agreed that the debt should be paid, that the main hall be kept available for Whitefield and other preachers, and that a free school be established for needy children. As is well known, the academy eventually became the University of Pennsylvania—and Franklin and Whitefield can be considered joint founders. When Whitefield visited the academy on one of his last trips to Philadelphia, he heard "several Youths speak in it so oratorically, as would have delighted even a Cicero or Demosthenes."

As soon as Franklin published his *Proposals* for the academy he sent a copy of his work to Whitefield. As was to be expected, Whitefield thoroughly approved of the principle of fostering education but felt that the project needed more of formal Christianity.[27]

Franklin had said in his *Proposals* that "the youth are to be taught some public religion, and the excellency of the Christian religion in particular," but Whitefield felt that the mention of Christianity was too late and too perfunctory.

> As we are all creatures of a day; as our whole life is but one small point between two eternities, it is reasonable to suppose, that the grand end of every Christian institution for forming tender minds, should be to convince them of their natural depravity, of the means of recovering out of it, and of the necessity of preparing for the enjoyment of the Supreme Being in a future state. These are the grand points in which Christianity centers. Arts and sciences may be built

27. Whitefield to Franklin, February 26, 1750. Luke Tyerman, *Life of the Rev. George Whitefield* (London, 1890), II, 251–252.

on this, and serve to embellish and set off this superstructure, but without this, I think there cannot be any good foundation.

Actually Franklin's *Proposals,* which he sent to Whitefield, give greater consideration to religion than the printed statement of principles which Franklin and Tench Francis drew up to define the scope of the institution. In the formal *Constitutions of the Publick Academy in the City of Philadelphia,* there is no mention of either religion or God, let alone Christianity.[28]

Whitefield had spoken to the German chaplain of George III about Franklin's educational project, and the chaplain had given Whitefield for transmission to Franklin a book in German which he thought might be of some service. Whitefield expressed his own willingness to give advice but modestly demeaned the value of anything he could offer, deferring to the other gentlemen concerned as "every way superior . . . both in respect to knowledge of books and men." He particularly recommended, however, that "in such an institution, there should be a well-approved christian Orator, who should not be content with giving a public lecture in general upon oratory, but who should visit and take pains with every class, and teach them early how to speak, and read, and pronounce well." He also advocated that the students board in the academy in order to be constantly under the master's eye and that a fund be raised for the free education of the most promising poor. The one indisputable quality for the success of the institution, Whitefield concluded to be "the integrity, disinterestedness, and piety" of its promoters.

Since Whitefield included something of Christ in nearly all of his letters (*"aliquid Christi"* was one of his favorite expressions), it was only natural that he should frequently refer to Franklin's spiritual condition. In his very first letter to Franklin (November 26, 1740), giving the young trades-

28. Labaree (ed.), *Papers,* III, 422–428.

man permission to print his sermons and journals, he had remarked, "I do not despair of your seeing the reasonableness of christianity. Apply to GOD; be willing to do the divine will, and you shall know it."[29] This indicates that the two men had had some discussion of theology—that Franklin had admitted his inability to accept the literal beliefs of the prevailing Protestant sects but had, nevertheless, placed more emphasis upon his faith in a superintending providence than upon his opposition to orthodoxy. Whitefield seems to have considered him as a backsliding Christian momentarily disturbed by a doctrinal scruple, rather than as a confirmed deist.

Once more in England, Whitefield wrote to Franklin (July 6, 1749) an account of his success in spreading evangelical doctrines amid titled and wealthy society, where he had been introduced by the Countess of Huntingdon. Franklin congratulated Whitefield on his opportunities of preaching among the great and predicted that if he could "gain them to a good and exemplary life, wonderful changes will follow in the manners of the lower ranks; for, *Ad Exemplum Regis* &c."[30] Franklin buttressed this principle of reform from the top down by appealing to the life and teachings of Confucius. In praising the Chinese philosopher, Franklin was following a common practice of the deists, who traditionally eulogized the Chinese and excoriated the Jews. Not that the deists had any personal feelings about Jews or Chinese—the two nations merely represented contrary symbols which could be used to disparage the prevailing Christian religion. The deists looked with disapproval upon every form of particular revelation, arguing that God makes his existence known to all men through the wonders of the creation and that his justice would not permit him to prefer one group over the rest of mankind by any special communication. By relentlessly mocking the pretensions of the Jews to be a

29. Tyerman, *Life of the Rev. George Whitefield,* I, 439.
30. Labaree (ed.), *Papers,* III, 383.

chosen race, the deists supported their own theory of natural revelation and weakened the Christian system because of its dependence upon the Jewish. The Chinese, on the other hand, represented a civilization older and more highly developed than the Jewish. Not only were they completely independent of the Hebrew-Christian tradition, but they made no claims whatsoever to divine revelation or special guidance.

Franklin had long been acquainted with the works of Confucius, having printed in the *Pennsylvania Gazette* lengthy extracts from his *Morals.* In one passage, the philosopher observed that if "the Understanding of a Prince is well enlighten'd, ... his Family being arriv'd at this Perfection, 'twill serve as an Example to all Subjects of the particular Kingdoms, and the Members of the particular Kingdoms to all those that compose the Body of the Empire. Thus the whole Empire will be well govern'd."[31] In writing to Whitefield, Franklin referred to this principle: when Confucius

> saw his country sunk in vice, and wickedness of all kinds triumphant, he applied himself first to the grandees; and having by his doctrine won them to the cause of virtue, the commons followed in multitudes. The mode has a wonderful influence on mankind; and there are numbers that perhaps fear less the being in Hell, than out of the fashion. Our more western reformations began with the ignorant mob; and when numbers of them were gained, interest and party-views drew in the wise and great. Where both methods can be used, reformations are like to be more speedy. O that some method could be found to make them lasting! He that shall discover that, will, in my opinion, deserve more, ten thousand times, than the inventor of the longitude.

This is one of the most revealing comments Franklin ever made concerning his values in life. It shows that he unequivocally elevated morality over scientific progress.

In 1751 Franklin published his *Experiments and Observations on Electricity,* and he became almost instantaneously famous in England, France, and Belgium. Whitefield be-

31. May 7, 1738.

came concerned lest the plaudits of the learned world turn his friend's head. Referring to Franklin's "pretty considerable progress in the mysteries of electricity," he wrote to him (August 17, 1752) recommending the "diligent unprejudiced pursuit and study [of] the mystery of the new birth. It is a most important, interesting study, and when mastered, will richly repay you for all your pains. One, at whose bar we are shortly to appear, hath solemnly declared, that, without it, 'we cannot enter into the kingdom of heaven.' You will excuse this freedom. I must have *aliquid Christi* in all my letters."[32]

There is no evidence concerning the effect of this well-meaning but not exactly tactful advice, but when Whitefield repeated it several years later, Franklin replied somewhat tartly—but within the limits of politeness—that he had as much likelihood as Whitefield himself of attaining continued divine favor.

> Your frequently repeated Wishes and Prayers for my Eternal, as well as temporal Happiness are very obliging. I can only thank you for them and offer you mine in return. I have myself no Doubts that I shall enjoy as much of both as is proper for me. That Being who gave me Existence, and thro' almost threescore Years has been continually showering his Favours upon me, whose very Chastisements have been Blessings to me; can I doubt that he loves me. And, if he loves me, can I doubt that he will go on to take care of me, not only here but hereafter? This to some may seem Presumption; to me it appears the best grounded Hope; Hope of the Future, built on Experience of the Past.[33]

Franklin did not write this merely to put Whitefield in his place. It was a sentiment he honestly believed. Less than a week later he expressed it in very similar terms to his printer friend William Strahan, adding that if Strahan had greater Christian faith, this cheerful admonition would not be necessary. Franklin pointed out that his friend could be sure of

32. Tyerman, *Life of the Rev. George Whitefield*, II, 283.
33. Albert Henry Smyth (ed.), *Writings of Benjamin Franklin* (10 vols., New York, 1905–1907), IV, 248.

God's love "and that he will take at least as good Care of your future Happiness as he has done of your present. What Assurance of the *Future* can be better founded than that which is built on Experience of the *Past?*"[34]

Whitefield, always more preoccupied than Franklin with the approach of death, once wrote regretting the short span of life and predicting that he and Franklin would "soon go out of it." Although Franklin was nine years Whitefield's senior, he actually survived the evangelist for twenty years. After Whitefield's death in 1770, Franklin expressed his sorrow both publicly and privately. "I knew him intimately," he wrote, "upwards of thirty years. His Integrity, Disinterestedness and indefatigable Zeal in prosecuting every good Work, I have never seen equalled, I shall never see exceeded."[35]

---

34. *Ibid.*, p. 250.   35. *Ibid.*, V, 308.

CHAPTER TEN

MORE FAITH AND WORKS

DESPITE Franklin's disagreement with evangelical Christians on the subject of the relative value of faith and works, he never systematically took up all the issues of the complex question of how vital religion is to ethics. In his youth he affirmed that religious profession requires a corresponding high moral behavior, and there is no reason to believe that he ever wavered from that position. But apart from various essays in his *Pennsylvania Gazette* reflecting the opinion of Bayle that a society of atheists could attain to as high a degree of morality as a society of religionists—the doctrine suggested by his Hemphill pamphlets—we may look in vain for an unequivocal statement on the subject of morals completely independent of religion.

In his autobiography, written toward the close of his life, he adopted the ambiguous position, which we have already noted, "that vicious Actions are not hurtful because they are forbidden, but forbidden because they are hurtful, the Nature of Man alone consider'd: That it was therefore every one's Interest to be virtuous, who wish'd to be happy even in this World."[1] On the surface this seems to be nothing but humanistic ethics, but the phrases "the Nature of Man alone consider'd" and "even in this World" indicate that Franklin was not entirely neglectful of divine sanctions. In an earlier passage of the autobiography he confirmed the opinion that revelation is the agency which forbids hurtful actions, but he was not exactly sure of the nature of the forces which had kept him in his youth from wilful immorality or injustice, whether it was "the kind hand of Providence, or some guardian Angel, or accidental favourable Circumstances and Situations, or all together."[2]

Franklin made his most specific declaration on the subject

1. Leonard W. Labaree *et al.* (eds.), *Autobiography of Benjamin Franklin* (New Haven, 1964), p. 158. See also p. 115 of the *Autobiography* for an almost identical statement.
2. *Ibid.*, p. 115.

of faith and works in the decade after the Hemphill controversy when his attention had turned from business and civic affairs to his electrical experiments. During this period he wrote two almost contradictory letters on the subject, and toward the end of his life he sent copies to Ezra Stiles as evidence of his concern for religion. The first of these letters, on his adherence to the gospel of good works (June 6, 1753), he addressed to a zealous religionist whose paralysis he had relieved through electricity.[3] The recovered saint had thanked Franklin for the service but gratuitously added a "serious though rather impertinent Caution" that his benefactor should not expect to reach heaven on the strength of his social service. This ungracious correspondent was once thought to be George Whitefield but is now known to be a certain Joseph Huey, who has no other claim to fame except receiving this letter. Franklin ingeniously used Huey's expressions of gratitude to support one of his fundamental principles—one which Huey would presumably either have rejected or condemned as being of secondary order—that serving man is equivalent to serving God. Since it was impossible for Franklin to make a return in kind either for the mercies of God or for the kindnesses from other men which he had received when away from home, his only means of expressing gratitude, he explained, was through a constant readiness to help God's other children, his own brothers. But he founded no expectation of heaven upon his good works.

> By Heaven we understand, a State of Happiness, infinite in Degree, and eternal in Duration: I can do nothing to deserve such Reward: He that for giving a Draught of Water to a thirsty Person should expect to be paid with a good Plantation, would be modest in his Demands, compar'd with those who think they deserve Heaven for the little Good they do on Earth. Even the mix'd imperfect Pleasures we enjoy in this World are rather from God's Goodness than our Merit; how much more such Happiness of Heaven. For my own part, I have not the Vanity to think I deserve it, the Folly to expect

3. L. W. Labaree *et al.* (eds.), *Papers of Benjamin Franklin*, IV (New Haven, 1961), 504–506.

it, nor the Ambition to desire it; but content myself in submitting to the Will and Disposal of that God who made me, who has hitherto preserv'd and bless'd me, and in whose fatherly Goodness I may well confide, that he will never make me miserable, and that even the Afflictions I may at any time suffer shall tend to my Benefit.

Franklin had no desire to disparage the opposing concept of faith which Huey had extolled. He merely wished it were productive of good works: "real good Works, Works of Kindness, Charity, Mercy, and Publick Spirit; not Holiday-keeping, Sermon-Reading or Hearing, performing Church Ceremonies, or making long Prayers, fill'd with Flatteries and Compliments, despis'd even by wise Men, and much less capable of pleasing the Deity." These observances, he admitted, are useful in fulfilling man's duty to worship God, "but if Men rest in Hearing and Praying, as too many do, it is as if a Tree should value itself on being water'd and putting forth Leaves, tho' it never produc'd any Fruit."

In pointing out that Huey's "great Master tho't much less of these outward Appearances and Professions than many of his modern Disciples," Franklin repeated some of the arguments of his Hemphill dialogue and added some fresh ones. Christ himself "prefer'd the Doers of the Word, to the meer Hearers," for example, the heretical but charitable Samaritan to the sanctified Levite; Christ also declared that those who have ministered to the suffering shall be preferred on the last day to those "who cry Lord! Lord!" and value themselves on their faith. Finally, Christ professed "that he came not to call the Righteous but Sinners to Repentance; which imply'd his modest Opinion that there were some in his Time so good that they need not hear even him for Improvement; but now a days we have scarce a little Parson, that does not think it the Duty of every Man within his Reach to sit under his petty Ministrations, and that whoever omits them offends God."

Franklin was here attacking narrow spirits, not the clergy as a body, and certainly not religious ceremonies or church organizations. He later sent the letter to Stiles as a commentary on his doctrine that the most acceptable service we render to God is "doing good to his other Children."

In a similar letter to his sister Jane, Franklin used his sense of humor as well as his blunt and vigorous style to affirm the pre-eminence of charity over faith and hope in the Christian edifice. Instead of quoting Scripture, he used a simple children's verse to show that the world is too full of compliments and pious talk:

> A Man of Words and not of Deeds,
> Is like a Garden full of Weeds.

> 'Tis pity that *Good Works* among some sorts of People are so little Valued, and *Good Words* admired in their Stead; I mean seemingly *pious Discourses,* instead of *Humane Benevolent Actions.* These they almost put out of countenance, by calling Morality *rotten Morality,* Righteousness, *ragged Righteousness* and even *filthy Rags;* and when you mention *Virtue,* they pucker up their Noses as if they smelt a Stink; at the same time that they eagerly snuff up an empty canting Harangue, as if it was a Posie of the Choicest Flowers. So they have inverted the good old Verse, and say now

> A Man of Deeds and not of Words
> Is like a Garden full of ———

> I have forgot the Rhime, but remember 'tis something the very Reverse of a Perfume. So much by Way of Commentary.[4]

The second of the letters on religious faith which Franklin sent to Stiles presents the contrary emphasis. It is a determined defense of religion which he had written to persuade an acquaintance to destroy a deistical manuscript lest he seduce weak minds away from their faith by publishing it.

At the present time there exist three manuscript drafts of Franklin's sharply worded rebuke to his deistical acquaintance, but all are without date or addressee. Some editors have assumed that Franklin wrote his letter to urge Thomas

---

4. *Ibid.,* VIII (1965) , 155.

Paine not to publish *The Age of Reason,* despite the obvious fact that Franklin died before Paine even began writing his deistical work. The copy which Franklin sent to Stiles is in the hand of his grandson, William Temple Franklin, and is inscribed—probably by Franklin just before his death— "London, May 7, 1758"—"To Mr. J. H."[5]

Franklin's correspondent, the unknown Mr. J. H., had admitted a general providence but rejected a particular providence "that takes Cognizance of, guards and guides and may favour particular Persons." Franklin felt that this doctrine was striking at the foundation of all religion, for it took away all "Motive to Worship a Deity, to fear its Displeasure, or to pray for its Protection."

Also, Franklin felt strongly at this time (much more than on other occasions) that religion was a bulwark to morality —that it helped check the vicious inclinations of illiterate or irrational men. He wrote:

> You yourself may find it easy to live a virtuous Life without the Assistance afforded by Religion; you having a clear Perception of the Advantages of Virtue and the Disadvantages of Vice, and possessing a Strength of Resolution sufficient to enable you to resist common Temptations. But think how great a Proportion of Mankind consists of weak and ignorant Men and Women, and of inexperienc'd, and inconsiderate Youth of both Sexes, who have need of the Motives of Religion to restrain them from Vice, to support their Virtue, and retain them in the Practice of it till it becomes *habitual,* which is the great Point for its Security; And perhaps you are indebted to her originally that is to your Religious Education, for the Habits of Virtue upon which you now justly value yourself. You might easily display your excellent Talents of reasoning on a less hazardous Subject, and thereby obtain a Rank with our most distinguish'd Authors.

Franklin stressed the purely practical point of view. "Tho' your Reasonings are subtle, and may prevail with

5. *Ibid.,* VII (1963), 293–295.

some Readers, you will not succeed so as to change the general Sentiments of Mankind on that Subject, and the Consequence of printing this Piece will be a great deal of Odium drawn upon your self, Mischief to you and no Benefit to others. He that spits against the Wind, spits in his own Face." Adapting another proverb—one which he had published many years previously in *Poor Richard*—Franklin advised his friend "not to attempt unchaining the Tyger, but to burn this Piece before it is seen by any other Person. . . . If Men are so wicked as we now see them *with Religion,* what would they be if *without it.*"

Nowhere else does Franklin affirm a more intimate relationship between religion and morality, and, as we have already seen, he elsewhere subscribes to the contrary doctrine that morality may be independent of religious faith. Moreover, even in the letter to J. H. he does not really address himself to the theological question underlying both letters of whether there is a divine providence which intervenes to control the destinies of individual men. We have already noticed his "uncomfortable thought" communicated to Whitefield that providence does not so intervene.

In the absence of any simple declaration on the subject, the best one can do to reconcile Franklin's apparently divergent attitudes is to assume that he believed with Shaftesbury that "the Perfection and Height of VIRTUE must be owing to *the Belief of a* GOD."[6] But this could be either a Christian or a deistical god. Shortly after Franklin's death, Thomas Paine used him as the best example of the high morality which may be attained by a disbeliever in Christianity. Quoting Franklin's reference in his autobiography to the polemical books against deism which succeeded only in turning him into a perfect deist, Paine added: "All America, and more than all America, knows Franklin. His life was

---

6. *Characteristicks, Inquiry concerning Virtue,* Bk. I, Pt. III, sec. iii, Conclusion.

devoted to the good and improvement of man. Let, then, those who profess a different creed, imitate his virtues, and excel him if they can."[7]

We have already presented a considerable amount of evidence to show that Franklin believed that religious doctrines should be considered good or bad, not because of their inherent truth or falsehood but because of their results. This is the underlying meaning of the opinion concerning revelation in his autobiography cited at the beginning of this chapter. Very late in his life, he confided to James Madison "that he should be glad to see an experiment made of a religion that admitted of no pardon for transgressions; the hope of impunity being the great encouragement to them."[8] As an illustration of the pernicious consequences of forgiving evil, Franklin gave a recollection from his own youth. He had frequently suffered attacks of indigestion because of overeating until one of his friends prescribed a few drops of oil of wormwood as a remedy, which he found to be efficacious. "And then said he, having my absolution in my pocket, I went on sinning more freely than ever." Here is a concrete episode confirming Franklin's empirical attitude toward religion. He would have liked "to see an experiment made."

Another anecdote of his old age gives further evidence that he considered social utility to be the ultimate test of every religion, including Christianity. In France, he participated in a discussion of the question, "What is the strongest evi-

---

7. Philip S. Foner (ed.), *Complete Writings of Thomas Paine* (New York, 1945), II, 897.

8. James Madison, "Detached Memoranda," *William and Mary Quarterly*, 3rd ser., III (1946), 538. This anecdote confirms the view that Franklin might have become the leader in establishing a new religious sect had it not been for the channeling of his energies in other directions. William Tudor, for example, remarked with great insight, "His early bias [toward scepticism] seems still to have left his mind in an unsettled state, and it was a strange vagary, that appears from some passages in his writings to have occasionally passed through it, of establishing a new sect." *Life of James Otis* (Boston, 1823), p. 390.

dence of the divine origin of the Christian religion?"[9] One
learned man suggested the institution of the church, "a per-
petual monument and unfailing tradition, indissolubly con-
necting us with the past." A second named the miracles of
Christ, revealing supernatural power. A third adduced prophecy, a link between heaven and human destiny. A fourth
"enlarged upon the intrinsic reasonableness and beneficence
of the Gospel, as compared with all mythology." The debate
continued with cleverness and vigor until at last the company
asked Franklin for his opinion. His short and neat answer
not only closed the discussion but epitomized his personal
belief. "I think that the man has the strongest evidence of
the divine origin of the Christian religion, who most sincerely practises its precepts."

In a personal letter of the same period, Franklin applied
exactly the same standard to nations—their Christianity
must be judged according to their practice. No nation, he
felt, could consider itself either rational or Christian if it
persisted in the "repeated follies" of "repeated wars." In
reference to France and England he remarked, "You are all
Christians. One is *The Most Christian King,* and the other
Defender of the Faith." But these titles, he insisted, had to
be made valid in future conduct. " 'By this,' says Christ,
'shall all men know that ye are my Disciples, if ye love one
another.' 'Seek peace, and ensue it.' "[10]

The concept of making Christianity concrete in practice
was so important in Franklin's career that Sainte-Beuve considered him one of the strongest intellectual forces of the age
in secularizing Christianity. He based his contention largely
on the testimony of Mallet du Pan, a leading journalistic
acquaintance of Franklin in Paris, that Franklin "repeated

9. *The Year-Book of the Unitarian Congregational Churches for 1856*
(Boston, 1856), p. 63. This anecdote was communicated to the *Year-Book* by
Benjamin Vaughan.
10. Albert Henry Smyth (ed.), *Writings of Benjamin Franklin* (10 vols.,
New York, 1905–1907), IX, 108.

more than once to his pupils of Paris that the one who would transfer to the political state the principles of primitive Christianity would change the face of society."[11] According to Sainte-Beuve, Franklin was one of those spirits who had most successfully exalted the doctrine of secularizing Christianity, "of obtaining, if possible, good and useful results on earth."[12]

11. Translated from *Causeries du lundi* (Paris, n.d.), VII, 174–175.

12. By now it has become apparent that a persistent theme in Franklin's writing is the preference of works over faith at the Day of Judgment. The pertinent passages use almost identical language: "Dialogue" in defense of Hemphill (Labaree [ed.], *Papers*, II [1959], 29); letter to Josiah and Abiah Franklin, April 10, 1735 (*ibid.*, p. 204); letter to Joseph Huey, June 6, 1753 (*ibid.*, IV, 505).

On the basis of these passages it is possible to identify as Franklin's the following paragraph from *Poor Richard* for 1757 contrasting learning and godliness. It is printed in the Franklin *Papers* (VII, 89) with the comment: "Neither this paragraph nor the verses which follow has been identified." The paragraph is clearly Franklin's, but in my opinion the verses do not have the ring of his style.

"*Learning* is a valuable Thing in the Affairs of this Life, but of infinitely more Importance is *Godliness*, as it tends not only to make us happy here but hereafter. At the Day of Judgment, we shall not be asked, what Proficiency we have made in Languages or Philosophy; but whether we have liv'd virtuously and piously as Men endued with Reason, guided by the Dictates of Religion. In that Hour it will more avail us, that we have thrown a Handful of Flour or Chaff in Charity to a Nest of contemptible Pismires, than that we could muster all the Hosts of Heaven, and call every Star by its proper Name. For then the Constellations themselves shall disappear, the Sun and Moon shall give no more Light, and all the Frame of Nature shall vanish. But our good or bad Works shall remain forever, recorded in the Archives of Eternity."

To be sure, in the above passage Franklin contrasts learning and works rather than faith and works. The reason for the substitution of learning is almost certainly the place of publication, *Poor Richard*. Franklin's almanac was one of his most dependable sources of income, and he could not afford to offend his customers, most of whom accepted the orthodox doctrine of the pre-eminence of faith and at the same time, theologically at least, had no great regard for learning. By his apparent anti-intellectualism Franklin was able to drive home his lesson concerning the importance of good works, perhaps hoping that some of his readers would make the association between learning and religious faith.

It need hardly be added that Franklin did not share the opinion of a number of his orthodox contemporaries that the end of the world was imminent. See chap. iv, n. 3, above.

CHAPTER ELEVEN

RELIGION BY HOAX

O BVIOUSLY if religion is to be judged by a pragmatic standard, it must be subjected to rigid investigation and criticism. Franklin believed with Shaftesbury that religion should not be exempt from ridicule, and he shared with Swift a proclivity for exposing the amusing side of Christian doctrine and ceremonies. His mockery of religious manifestation, however, never touched the fundamentals of Christianity. We have already commented on one of his literary pranks with religious overtones: the burlesque of lugubrious religious meditations in the *Pennsylvania Gazette*.

Franklin's most celebrated hoax, *The Speech of Polly Baker,* which he wrote probably in 1746, also touches upon the theme of religion, striking at pharisaical morality and ministerial dogmatism. Anyone who knows Franklin at all knows the story of the mythical Polly Baker, who was prosecuted in New England for bearing five bastard children.[1] As Franklin allows Polly to defend herself against the charge that she has violated the precepts of religion by her transgressions, he combines two of his favorite themes, rational religion and philoprogenitiveness—the vindication of maximum procreation.

"If mine, then," Polly pleads, "is a religious Offence, leave it to religious Punishments. You have already excluded me from the Comforts of your Church-Communion. Is not that sufficient? You believe I have offended Heaven, and must suffer eternal Fire: Will not that be sufficient? What Need is there, then, of your additional Fines and Whipping? I own, I do not think as you do; for, if I thought what you call a Sin, was really such, I could not presumptuously commit it. But, how can it be believed, that Heaven is angry at my having Children, when to the little done by me towards it, God has

---

1. Max Hall treats Polly Baker exhaustively in *Benjamin Franklin and Polly Baker* (Chapel Hill, 1960). It is printed there and in L. W. Labaree *et al.* (eds.) , *Papers of Benjamin Franklin,* III (New Haven, 1961) , 120–125.

been pleased to add his Divine Skill and admirable Workmanship in the Formation of their Bodies, and crown'd it, by furnishing them with rational and immortal Souls." Polly's strongest argument is that she has merely been performing her religious duty—"the Duty of the first and great Command of Nature, and of Nature's God, *Encrease and Multiply.*"

Notwithstanding Polly's deistical talk, it can hardly be argued that Franklin hoped to use his *jeu d'esprit* as deistical propaganda—although writers such as Peter Annet and the abbé Raynal utilized it for just that purpose by playing down its comical elements. For Franklin the comic appeal was supreme. One may even believe with Polly's biographer, Max Hall, "that Franklin, by letting Polly talk in this manner and then go on to demand a statue to her memory, was having a little fun at the expense of the dedicated deists. It is conceivable that the satire of the speech was directed both at the orthodox religionists who wished to impose their own moral ideas on others and the unorthodox who were forever appealing to Nature."[2] It is likely, however, that Franklin also intended the speech as a rebuke to clerical domination. The protest against ecclesiastical authority is far more explicit and emphatic than the implied satire of the deists. Franklin wrote it not long after his struggle with the Presbyterian synod of Philadelphia in which he had damned "the Impositions of Priests, whether Popish, Presbyterian or Episcopal." With Polly Baker he was still letting loose his anticlerical animus.

So far as we know, *The Speech of Polly Baker* appeared for the first time in a London newspaper, the *General Advertiser,* in 1747. Franklin perpetrated another hoax with religious overtones, a purported account by a fictitious prisoner of American Indians, William Henry, in another London newspaper, the *London Chronicle,* in June, 1768.[3] Like *Polly*

2. Hall, *Benjamin Franklin and Polly Baker,* p. 111.
3. A. O. Aldridge, "Franklin's Deistical Indians," *Proceedings of the American Philosophical Society,* XCIV (1950), 398–410.

Baker, the account of William Henry portrays deism in a vein partly serious, partly mocking. Even more amazing, Franklin combines his early polytheism with deism—and associates both notions with the religious beliefs of North American Indians.

Many English deists of the period who had never seen an Indian assumed that the American natives would have a religion akin to deism—one based on the commonly observed phenomena of nature and dedicated to worship of nature's God. Franklin held these primitivistic suppositions along with the English deists and also apparently saw them confirmed in his personal relations with actual Indians.

In *Poor Richard* for 1751 he wrote:

> To Christians bad, rude Indians we prefer,
> 'Tis better not to know, than knowing err.

Franklin's hoax in which he combines his own religious notions with observations of the rude natives grew out of a series of treaties which the colony of Pennsylvania made with the local tribes from 1736 to 1762, the texts of which Franklin published at his Philadelphia press. His second primary source was an anonymous deistical essay published several times in the colonies during the same period. This essay, concerning the rational superiority of Indian natural religion to Christianity as it was preached by a Swedish missionary, was in turn based upon a Latin dissertation published by the missionary's son at Upsala, Sweden, in 1731. Franklin extracted the droll elements from this situation and used them in a famous pamphlet which he published in France, *Remarks concerning the Savages of North America* (1784). With refined deistical irony, Franklin gave his own version of the Swedish minister's unsuccessful efforts to convert the Indians.

Having assembled the chiefs of the Susquehannas, Franklin's minister "made a Sermon to them, acquainting them with the principal historical Facts on which our Religion is founded; such as the Fall of our first Parents by eating an

Apple, the coming of Christ to repair the Mischief, his Miracles and Suffering, &c. When he had finished, an Indian orator stood up to thank him. 'What you have told us,' says he, 'is all very good. It is indeed bad to eat Apples. It is better to make them all into Cyder.' " After offering this primitive wisdom, the Indian chief thanked the missionary for his kindness " 'in coming so far, to tell us these Things which you have heard from your Mothers.' " In return he delivered an oration setting forth the religious beliefs which the Indians had accepted from their ancestors.

Franklin's pamphlet relating this droll episode has been known and associated with Franklin ever since the year of its publication. The much longer hoax on which it is based, however, has been discussed and attributed to Franklin only within the last decade. In 1768 Franklin published in two issues of the *London Chronicle* a pretended "Extract from an Account of the Captivity of William Henry in 1755, and of his Residence among the Senneka Indians six Years and seven Months till he made his Escape from them. Printed at Boston, 1766. 4to, Pages 160."

After three years of captivity, Henry succeeded in learning the Indian language and in so doing gained the respect of his captors. He frequently engaged in conversation with "Old Canassatego," a "Warrior, Counsellor, and the chief man of our village." This Canassatego (elsewhere in the work spelled Canasseteego) was in actual life the Onondago chief of one of the Indian treaties which Franklin had published.

One day while William Henry contemplated the task of making the Indians perceive the wisdom and goodness of the European economic system, a young warrior began a discourse on the creation of the vegetable kingdom.

Nine *Oneida* Warriors passing near a certain hill, not far from the head of Sasquehanah, saw a most beautiful young Woman descend naked from the clouds, and seat herself on the ground upon that hill. Then they said, this is the great Manitta's Daughter, let us go to her, welcome her into our country, and present her some of our venison. They gave her a fawn's tongue broiled, which she eat, and thanking them, said, come to this place again after twelve moons, and you will find, where I now sit, some thing that you have never yet seen, and that will do you good. So saying she put her hands on the ground, arose, went up into the cloud, and left them. They came accordingly after twelve moons, and found growing where she had pressed the ground with her right hand, corn, where her left hand, beans; and where her back parts had pressed it, there grew tobacco.

This cosmogony immediately aroused the laughter of all the young Indians, and Old Canassatego rebuked the narrator for telling this foolish Oneida tale to their white captive. "If you tell him such tales, what can you expect but to make him laugh at our Indian stories as much as you sometimes do at his." To atone for the foolishness of the young warrior, Old Canassatego told the true story of the beginning of the country. Before doing so, however, he corrected William Henry's notion that there is but one "great good Manitta," usually called the "Great Manitou" in other Indian literature.

If there were but one, how unhappy must he be without friends, without companions, and without that equality in conversation, by which pleasure is mutually given and received! I tell you there are more than a hundred ([Franklin's note:] They commonly use a hundred to express any great unknown or indeterminate number.) of them; they live in the sun and in the moon; they love one another as brethren; they visit and converse with each other; and they sometimes visit, though they do not often converse with us. Every country has its great good Manitta, who first peopled that country.

This notion of the plurality of gods stems from Franklin's early "Articles of Belief" in which he hypothecated the existence of "many Beings or Gods, vastly superior to Man." In his youth Franklin conceived merely of one god for each sun and its system of planets instead of one god for each country, but the notion of plural deities is the same. The "Captivity of William Henry," aside from its intrinsic literary merits, has the biographical significance of showing that at the age of sixty-two Franklin had retained his interest in the doctrine of a plurality of worlds and of gods. To be sure, he may have been merely reporting the facts of Indian religion, but he did so with interest and apparent sympathy.

After establishing a "good Manitta" to people every land, Old Canassatego continued with an account of the peopling of Akanishionegy, the land of the five Indian nations. The good Manitta simply sows the fertile fields of Onondaga with five handfuls of red seeds, which produce little worms. After nine moons they become perfect boys and girls. For the next nine summers, the great Manitta nurses them and then for nine more summers he instructs them how to live. Eventually he explains to them the cycle of life, death, and reincarnation. "The bodies I have given you will in time grow old and wear out, so that you will be weary of them; or from various accidents they may become unfit for your habitation, and you will leave them. . . . I have enabled you therefore, among your selves, to produce new bodies, to supply the place of old ones, that every one of you when he parts with his old habitation may in due time find a new one, and never wander longer than he chuses under the earth, deprived of the light of the sun." In a note to this passage, Franklin wrote:

> They believe spirits ramble about under the earth, in a country where there is only a kind of twilight. That in that country are also the spirits of birds, beasts and fishes, and even of trees and plants. That all these spirits, a spirit can see and handle, without eyes or hands; but if he comes again above ground, he finds he cannot see the sun, or move even a grain of sand without eyes and hands; and therefore, he seizes the first opportunity of getting a new body, by entering and possessing an embrio just forming in its mother's womb; from which moment he forgets every thing but love to his country. The returning spirits of birds, beasts and fishes, they say do not forget every thing: The birds retain the memory of the manner of walking, flying, copulating, and building of nests; the beasts of walking, coupling, swimming, &c. and the fish of swimming, and other actions which the great spirit first taught them, and therefore now need no fresh teaching in those particulars.

Since these notions of metempsychosis and pre-existence are not seriously reflected elsewhere in Franklin's writings in the way that the concept of polytheism appears in his early "Articles of Belief," we have no reason to believe that they represent anything more than Franklin's reporting of Indian lore. But his motives are not entirely those of an anthropologist. His sympathetic attitude toward Indian religion enables him to expose the authoritarianism of orthodox Christianity. William Henry, for example, refuses to let pass Old Canassatego's account of creation without remarking that it is subject to great uncertainty, being trusted to memory only, from woman to woman through many directions; whereas the Christian account "was written down by direction of the great spirit himself, and preserved carefully in a book, which was never altered, but had ever remained the same, and was undoubtedly the truth." There seems to be more of irony than sincerity in this panegyric. Old Canassatego's answer is a humorous tribute to Indian politeness. He laments that William Henry has failed to learn the civil behavior of men, for despite his long residence among the polite Indians, he is almost as rude as when he first arrived. "You see, I always believed your stories, why do you not believe mine?" Some of the younger Indians make excuses for William Henry, observing that his stories "indeed might be best for white people, but Indian stories were undoubtedly best for Indians."

Franklin's narrative of William Henry reflects the unsatisfactory nature of the compromise between deism and orthodox Christianity which he was forced to make throughout most of his life. Intellectually he was closer to deism than to Christianity, but he also realized that primitive religions, highly prized in deistical theory, may obscure rather than enlighten truth. The good-natured ridicule in his narrative exposes both the dogmatic insularity of orthodox Christianity and the rather sterile primitivism of deism.

Another of Franklin's hoaxes in the genre of the imaginary

traveler is a spurious "Letter from China," which he wrote in 1785 and published in a London magazine three years later. Nobody then or since has understood Franklin's purpose in writing it. Biographers have given it practically no attention, and literary critics have given it none whatsoever.

For our needs, it is necessary merely to say that it purports to be a letter concerning one of two sailors who left the expedition of Captain Cook in Macao and engaged in a series of picaresque adventures in China. One paragraph concerns the adventurer's observations of Chinese religious customs:

> That they have a sort of religion, with priests and churches, but do not keep Sunday, nor go to church, being very heathenish. That in every house there is a little idol, to which they give thanks, make presents, and show respect in harvest time, but very little at other times; and, inquiring of his master why they did not go to church to pray, as we do in Europe, he was answered, they paid the priests to pray for them, that they might stay at home and mind their business; and that it would be a folly to pay others for praying, and then go and do the praying themselves; and that the more work they did while the priests prayed, the better able they were to pay them well for praying.[4]

Like "William Henry," this letter is an ironical allegory in the vein of *Gulliver's Travels* and, like Swift's masterpiece, it offers difficulties in interpretation. We might ask, for example, whether Franklin is offering the Chinese customs for our approbation or for our derision. As in his other narrative hoaxes, he is probably combining the two perspectives. His target is the paid clergy, and he makes the Chinese ridiculous in paying for prayers as for services performed. At the same time he seems to be saying that each man is better off in worshiping at home by himself. This unusual combination probably represents a compliment to the Quakers, who in Franklin's time did not maintain paid ministers. Shortly before writing his Chinese letter, Franklin confided to an Englishman in Paris, John Baynes, that he rather inclined "to

4. Albert Henry Smyth (ed.), *Writings of Benjamin Franklin* (10 vols., New York, 1905–1907), IX, 204.

doubt of the necessity of having teachers, or ministers, for the express purpose of instructing the people in their religious duties."[5] Several times he explicitly praised the Quakers for dispensing with both ministers and lawyers.

This subject was much on his mind during the period of the Constitutional Convention. Although Franklin accepted the salaries attached to all the diplomatic posts he ever held, he believed that the honor in public service should be the prime inducement in seeking office and argued during the convention that executive positions should not be remunerated. In a speech, he praised the Quakers for abstaining from law and settling all their controversies in their own meeting.[6] More important, as a warning against allowing government to become tainted with profit, he drew a parallel with religion "and related very pleasantly the progression in ecclesiastical benefices from the first departure from the gratuitous provision for the Apostles, to the establishment of the papal system."[7] In a subsequent chapter we shall see further examples of Franklin's opposition to the involvement of finances in religion.

Franklin's final hoax with religious overtones was written just three months before his death—an amusing defense of the Quakers against a congressman from Georgia, James Jackson, who had denounced the sect for advocating the abolition of slavery.[8] Failing to understand why they had set themselves up against slavery, the indignant lawmaker demanded: "Do they understand the rights of mankind, and the disposition of Providence, better than others? If they were to consult that book, which claims our regard, they will find that slavery is not only allowed but commended. Their Saviour, who possessed more benevolence and commiseration than they pretend to, has allowed of it."

5. *Memoirs of the Life of Sir Samuel Romilly Written by Himself* (London, 1842), I, 449.
6. Smyth (ed.), *Writings*, IX, 594; see also pp. 259–260.
7. Max Farrand, *Records of the Federal Convention* (New Haven, 1934–1937), I, 216.
8. Smyth (ed.), *Writings*, X, 86–91.

Franklin, who in the past had used the authority of the Bible to support political principles which he himself favored, refused to take Jackson seriously. In a letter to the *Federal Gazette,* March 23, 1790, he pretended to quote from a speech in which a mythical Arab politician of the seventeenth century used identical reasoning with Jackson's to condemn an Algerian sect called Erika, or the Purists (Quakers), for agitating for the abolition of piracy and the keeping of Christian slaves.

In one of the parallels to Jackson's speech, Franklin's Arab pointed to what he considered to be the Purists' gross misinterpretation of the Alcoran in suggesting that it opposed slavery. "Are not the two Precepts, to quote no more, *'Masters, treat your Slaves with kindness; Slaves, serve your Masters with Cheerfulness and Fidelity,'* clear Proofs to the contrary? Nor can the Plundering of Infidels be in that sacred Book forbidden, since it is well known from it, that God has given the World, and all that it contains, to his faithful Musselmen, who are to enjoy it of Right as fast as they conquer it."

This is exactly the method of Jonathan Swift in *Gulliver's Travels* as he discussed the Lilliputians and their scriptures, the Brundecral. Swift had shown that either Protestants (Little Endians) or Catholics (Big Endians) could be supported by the text: *That all true believers shall break their eggs at the convenient end.* In Franklin's parody, his target was a political abuse, but his satire touched interpretation of the Scriptures as well. Franklin's contemporaries, however, interpreted the squib exclusively as a defense of the Quakers and an indictment of slavery.

Parenthetically it should be observed that although Franklin frequently co-operated with Quakers and other sects in opposing slavery, he ordinarily did not use religious arguments to combat the evil. He based his opposition on moral and humanitarian grounds, condemning slavery as "such an atrocious debasement of human nature, that its very extirpation, if not performed with solicitous care, may sometimes open a source of serious evils."[9]

It is not at all surprising that Franklin should have used the hoax as a method of portraying his religious ideas since throughout his life he found this literary form an effective and efficient means of conveying his political notions and swaying public opinion. Franklin had his serious side and his comic side, and he felt that both were appropriate for the expression of religious concepts.

9. *Ibid.,* p. 67.

CHAPTER TWELVE

SECTARIAN CONTACTS

So far in our study of Franklin's religion we have been concerned with the development of his ideas. We have seen him journey intellectually the entire distance from atheism to polytheism. All the evidence indicates that he made a vigorous and sincere effort to resolve metaphysical problems common to all religions, but that he abandoned the quest as hopeless. Eventually he settled down to a common-sense deism from which he henceforth never varied.

Franklin's religious experience had a historical as well as a purely intellectual side. In other words, significant encounters which he had with sectarian leaders or groups profoundly affected his life without materially changing his ideas. In subsequent pages we shall be mainly concerned with these primarily biographical relations—just as much a part of the story of his religion as are his intellectual processes. Particularly during his early years in Philadelphia, when he was highly uncertain about his own convictions, he investigated the variety of religious beliefs around him as one means of discovering truth for himself.

Most eighteenth-century Europeans thought of Philadelphia as a Quaker city, and even today one is likely to assume that the Quakers were the predominant religious group. Statistics which Franklin printed in his *Pennsylvania Gazette*, however, show that there were more Anglicans buried in a year than members of all the other denominations combined.

Church	81	Strangers	
Quakers	39	Whites	41
Presbyterians	18	Blacks	39
Baptists	18	In all 227 (29 December 1730)	

The category "strangers" may also have included unbelievers who preferred not to join any congregation.

Apparently the unaffiliated continued to represent a respectable number. A visitor from Germany reported in 1743, "There is no lack of Atheists, Deists, Materialists, and

Free Masons. In short, there is no sect in the world that is not cherished here."[1] This diversity of belief became even more widespread with the influx of immigrants, particularly Germans. Another traveler remarked in 1750: "Greater freedom exists here than in other English colonies, and sects of every belief are tolerated. You meet here Lutherans, Reformed, Catholics, Quakers, Mennonites, Herrenhuter or Moravian Brethren, Seventh Day Baptists, Dunkers, Presbyterians, the New Born, Free Masons, Separatists, Free Thinkers, Negroes and Indians. Still the Evangelical and Reformed compose the greater number."[2]

Although the Quakers may not have been numerically the largest sect in Pennsylvania, they occupied a favored position in its government and succeeded in controlling public policy during most of the colonial period.

Franklin, as a printer and community leader, had various matter-of-fact relations with the Quaker hierarchy. He also considered himself a close friend of such eminent Quakers as Anthony Benezet, Isaac Pemberton, and James Logan. But he had no particular interest in their theology. Unlike Thomas Paine, who considered the Quakers close to deists and therefore the only Christian sect of any merit, Franklin never expressed any prepossession whatsoever for the Friends.[3] He commended them for their opposition to slavery and just as vigorously condemned them when they refused to pull their weight in colonial defense.

From the time of his first encounter with Quaker worship, Franklin admired its simplicity, the custom by which individual members addressed the meeting in clear, intelligible language and thus dispensed with the need of supporting a

1. C. W. Schaeffer (trans.), *Hallische nachrichten, Reports of the United German Evangelical Lutheran Congregations in North America* (Reading, Pa., 1882), I, 26.
2. Gottlieb Mittleberger, "Journey to Pennsylvania," quoted in Edwin McMinn, *A German Hero of the Colonial Times of Pennsylvania* (Moorestown, Pa., 1886), p. 253.
3. Shortly before his death, Franklin suggested that the Bohemian Deists "appear to resemble in some Points our Friends [Quakers]." Franklin to Abel James, March 19, 1786, Franklin Papers, Library of Congress.

paid clergy. As we have seen, he commended the Quakers also for avoiding lawsuits and determining all problems of equity at their own meetings without cost. To Franklin's practical mind, they were quite right in saving the expense of both lawyers and clergymen.

Most colorful of Franklin's early Quaker associates was Benjamin Lay, a dwarf scarcely over four feet tall, whom Franklin described as a "Pythagorean-cynical-christian Philosopher." Lay, a native Englishman, who had been brought up in the African slave trade, became a planter at Barbados but eventually abandoned his plantation because of the horrors which he witnessed toward the Negro slaves. He moved to Philadelphia, became a Quaker, and devoted the rest of his life to preaching and writing against slavery.

Since Franklin was sympathetic to Lay's humanitarian reforms, it was at his house that Lay propounded his most grandiose scheme, the converting of the entire human race to Christianity. Lay felt that this could be brought about through the instrumentality of three witnesses: himself, Michael Lovell, and Abel Noble, with the support of Franklin. At the first meeting, "the three chosen vessels" fell to wrangling over doctrinal points. Franklin, an amused observer, finally suggested that the three apostles develop the patience to tolerate each other before setting out to convert all mankind.[4]

Lay once paid Franklin to print fifty copies of Ralph Sandiford's antislavery treatise, *The Mystery of Iniquity* (1731), which he then proceeded to distribute gratuitously.[5] Six years later Lay published a treatise of his own on the same subject written with great fervor. When he took his work to the printing shop, Franklin told him that it was not paged and that there was no order or arrangement in it. "It is

---

4. *The Journal of John Woolman*, with an Introduction by J. Greenleaf Whittier (London, 1900), p. 12 n.
5. G. S. Eddy, *Account Books Kept by Benjamin Franklin* (New York, 1928), I, 24.

of no matter," said Lay, "print any part thou pleasest first."[6] Franklin did his best to impose his order upon Lay's chaos and printed 271 pages of crackling prose. The marathon title denounces slave-keeping as filthy leprosy and an apostasy which the friends of pure truth called Quakers have borne testimony against for many years. Since some Quakers were also slave owners, the Yearly Meeting of Friends at Burlington proceeded to denounce the book as containing "gross abuse" against their society and to advertise the author as not a member of their religious community.

When Franklin was elected to the colonial assembly, many Quakers gave him their support—even when he advocated armed defense of the colony. At one time Franklin called in "the Aid of Religion" to revive flagging interest in the voluntary militia of Pennsylvania, called the Association. He proposed the proclaiming of a fast day in December, 1747, "to promote Reformation, and implore the Blessing of Heaven" on the volunteer soldiers. Drawing upon his education in New England, where a fast was held every year, Franklin phrased his proclamation in the conventional religious style. "It was," he reported in his autobiography, "translated into German, printed in both Languages and divulg'd thro' the Province. This gave the Clergy of the different Sects an Opportunity of Influencing their Congregations to join in the Association; and it would probably have been general among all but Quakers if the Peace had not soon interven'd."[7]

In one sense Franklin's proclamation may be construed as a cynical attempt to use the religious beliefs of other people to promote a political goal. His blunt admission that he accomplished his purpose by "calling in the Aid of Religion" supports this interpretation. As a matter of fact, only two years previously he had ridiculed organized public prayers in

---

6. "Biographical Anecdotes of Benjamin Lay," *Annual Monitor*, I (1813) , 7.
7. Leonard W. Labaree *et al.* (eds.) , *Autobiography of Benjamin Franklin* (New Haven, 1964) , pp. 184–185.

an ironical letter to his brother, which one commentator has labeled immoral and irreligious.[8] The occasion was a New England prayer and fast day held to promote the taking of Cape Breton during one of the campaigns of King George's War. Franklin computed that five hundred thousand special petitions were offered in New England, "which added to the petitions of every family morning and evening, multiplied by the number of days since January 25th, make forty-five millions of prayers; which, set against the prayers of a few priests in the garrison, to the Virgin Mary" gave a vast balance in favor of the British.[9] Franklin added that if the British forces did not succeed, he would henceforth have "an indifferent opinion of Presbyterian prayers in such cases." It would be more logical, he suggested, to depend upon works rather than on faith in attacking strong towns, for "like the kingdom of heaven, they are to be taken by force and violence; and in a French garrison I suppose there are devils of that kind, that are not to be cast out by prayers and fasting, unless it be by their own fasting for want of provisions. I believe," he concluded, "there is Scripture in what I have wrote, but I cannot adorn the margin with quotations, having a bad memory, and no Concordance at hand."

When he wrote his Philadelphia proclamation, however, Franklin probably wrote with an open Bible, for he deliberately emulated "the different Ways of Writing and Expression used by the different Sects of Religion."[10] Although not addressed specifically to the Quakers but to the ministers and people of all sects, Franklin's proclamation reveals his mastery of liturgical language.

Even though this evidence of contrivance undoubtedly suggests a lack of plain dealing, one should bear in mind that the proclamation was a precursor of Franklin's famous mo-

8. H. W. Smith, *Life . . . of the Rev. William Smith* (Philadelphia, 1880), I, 342.
9. L. W. Labaree *et al.* (eds.), *Papers of Benjamin Franklin,* III (New Haven, 1961), 26.
10. *Ibid.,* I (1959), 331.

tion calling for prayers in the Constitutional Convention (1787), which is usually interpreted as a sincere appeal for divine guidance, or at least as a personal recognition of providence. It is quite possible that both proposals represented Franklin's bona fide desire at a time of crisis to extend his system of personal worship to embrace the community at large.

Some of Franklin's friends were alarmed lest his advocacy of strong military preparation lose him the political support of the Quakers in the assembly, but Franklin succeeded in keeping their good will during most of his career.

Although there are hundreds of references to Quakers in Franklin's writings, most of them concerned with the political repercussions of pacificism, they contribute very little to an understanding of his religion. By and large his attitude was favorable, epitomized by a panegyric in Voltaire's *Treatise on Toleration,* which he once quoted in French: "The name alone of their city of *Philadelphia,* which reminds them every moment that men are brothers, is the example and the shame of those peoples who are not yet acquainted with toleration."[11]

In his autobiography Franklin testified to a high regard for another of the typical sects of Philadelphia, the Dunkards. They were a kind of anabaptists, the term *dunkard* coming from the German *duncken* or *tunchen,* to dip. Franklin particularly commended the sincerity of one of their number, Michael Welfare or Wohlfahrt, a "Christian philosopher" just as eccentric in his way as Benjamin Lay. One autumn morning Franklin saw Welfare appear in the midst of the busy Philadelphia market "in the Habit of a Pilgrim, his Hat of Linnen, his Beard at full Length, and a long Staff in his Hand."[12] In a vehement tirade he declared himself sent by Almighty God, "to denounce Vengeance against the Iniq-

11. Translated from Albert Henry Smyth (ed.), *Writings of Benjamin Franklin* (10 vols., New York, 1905–1907), IV, 268.
12. *Pennsylvania Gazette,* Sept. 25, 1734.

uity and Wickedness" of the city. Franklin later printed Welfare's harangue as a pamphlet, *The Wisdom of God crying and calling to the Sons and Daughters of Men for Repentance* (1737), in both English and German versions.

Welfare once complained to Franklin that the Dunkards had been grievously calumniated by other sects and accused of "abominable Principles and Practices to which they were utter Strangers."[13] Franklin replied that it was traditional for established religions to disparage new ones and advised him in order to offset such abuse "to publish the Articles of their Belief and the Rules of their Discipline." Welfare modestly replied that he and his fellow believers were acutely conscious of their fallibility and therefore reluctant to commit themselves to a creed. They had already discovered that some doctrines they had esteemed truths were errors and some they had esteemed errors were truths. They feared that "if we should once print our Confession of Faith, we should feel ourselves as if bound and confin'd by it, and perhaps be unwilling to receive farther Improvement." This intellectual honesty naturally appealed to Franklin.

Early in the century a group of Dunkards formed a religious community outside Philadelphia which they called Ephrata Cloister. Franklin printed hymn books for their use in 1730 and 1732 as well as a tract in German by their leader, Conrad Beiser, *Mystical and very secret maxims which are learned in the heavenly school of the Holy Ghost* (1730).

Franklin had close personal relations with another key figure, Johann Peter Miller, who had been licensed to preach by the Philadelphia Presbytry but affiliated with Ephrata in 1735 and adopted the name Brother Jaebez or Agrippa. Jedidiah Andrews wrote of him: "he speaks Latin as we do our vernacular tongue."[14]

13. Labaree (ed.), *Autobiography*, p. 190.
14. *Church Music and Musical Life in Pennsylvania in the Eighteenth Century* (No. 4, Publications of the Pennsylvania Society of the Colonial Dames of America, Philadelphia, 1927), II, 79.

In 1771, when Franklin was in London, Miller sent him a manuscript book of 150 pages, setting forth the theological system of Ephrata as well as an English translation of the mystical maxims which Franklin had published for Beiser in 1730.

With this material Miller sent a beautifully illuminated manuscript hymnal of the Ephrata, a priceless treasure. According to Miller, this book, containing "musical Concerts" by Beiser, "did cost three Brethren three Quarters of a Year Work to write the same: by the Imbellishment thereof it will appear, what a great Regard we had for our Superior."[15] Known as the Codex Ephratensis, 1746, the manuscript is now in the Library of Congress. A note in the handwriting of John Wilkes, one of Franklin's associates at Wycombe, a member of the Hell Fire Club, and Lord Mayor of London, explains: "April 1775. This curious book was lent me by Doctor Franklin just before he set out for Pennsylvania." Just why Franklin would leave such a valuable rarity in the profane hands of Wilkes has never been explained. He seems to have been equally cavalier with Miller's manuscript book. Now in the American Philosophical Society, it bears the inscription in the hand of Jonathan Shipley, Bishop of St. Asaph, "These letters and manuscript belong to Doctor Franklin of Pennsylvania who gave them to me."

Franklin also observed the growth in Pennsylvania of another German sect, the Moravians, who went under the alternate names of Unitas Fratrum or United Brethren. Like the Dunkards, the Moravians had no creed or formal system of worship apart from a belief in the divine inspiration of the Scriptures, but this was enough to make them fundamentalists. Eventually they developed an ecclesiastical organization, including clergy and bishops. Their guiding principle became "in essentials unity, in non-essentials liberty, and in all things charity." They had originally come together in

15. Miller to Franklin, June 12, 1771, in Library of the American Philosophical Society.

Saxony on the estate of Count Nicholaus Ludwig von Zinzendorf, but the innovations of their communal pietistic economy had aroused the suspicions of civil and religious authorities, and they were driven out of their European haven. In 1734 many of them went to the new colony of Georgia and ultimately worked their way northward to the Lehigh River in Pennsylvania, where they established the community of Bethlehem. In December, 1741, Count von Zinzendorf himself came to Pennsylvania "to organize the Germans of all sects into some form of evangelical religion, which he called the Church of God in the Spirit."[16] In Europe the paradoxical combination of his noble birth and aristocratic privileges together with his advocacy of the simple piety of primitive Christianity had subjected him to a good deal of abuse and mockery. To avoid this in the New World, he called himself simply Mr. Von Thürnstein and "made it every where known, that he would not, and could not, makes use of his titles in Pennsylvania."[17] At a solemn convocation at the home of the governor in Philadelphia, May 26, 1742, he delivered a Latin address formally explaining his reasons for giving up his rank. Franklin was present on this occasion along with the other "principal people in the country, both clergy and laity."[18] Franklin was probably a sympathetic listener since he later collaborated with Mirabeau in denouncing aristocracy in a work which had a considerable influence upon the French Revolution, *Considerations on the Order of Cincinnatus* (1785).[19]

In 1742 Franklin printed a number of books in German relating to the Moravians, including six written by Zinzendorf himself. He also printed various defenses of Zinzendorf, including one in which he was exonerated from charges of close association with George Whitefield. In the *Gazette*

16. J. J. Sessler, *Communal Pietism* (New York, 1933), p. 21.
17. August Gottlieb Spangenberg, *The Life of Nicholas Count Zinzendorf* (London, 1838), p. 295.
18. *Ibid.*, p. 295.
19. A. O. Aldridge, *Franklin and His French Contemporaries* (New York, 1957), pp. 80–86.

Franklin printed much newsworthy material about Zinzendorf, including a translation of one of his Latin sermons.[20]

Three Moravian converts to Christianity, two young men and a young woman, natives of Greenland, visited Philadelphia in 1749. Franklin described them in the *Gazette* (June 15, 1749) as "clad in Seal Skins, with the Hair on, after the manner of their own Country, their Eyes and Hair black, like our *Indians*, but their Complexion somewhat lighter." In Bethlehem the Moravians brought these Greenlanders face to face with some Delaware and Mohican Indian converts. According to Franklin, "tho' their native Lands are so vastly remote ; . . . yet what they observ'd of each others Hair, Eyes and Complexion, convinc'd them that they were all of the same Race." Almost forty years later Franklin recalled that he had asked them when they were readying their homeward journey "whether, now they had seen how much more commodiously the white People lived by the help of the Arts, they would not choose to remain among us; their Answer was, that they were pleased with having had an Opportunity of seeing so many fine things, *but they chose to* LIVE *in their own Country.*"[21]

Another minor sect in Philadelphia, the Baptists, involved Franklin through his friendship with one of their lay ministers, Ebenezer Kinnersley, who was also an early experimenter with electricity, second only to Franklin in the American colonies. One of the Baptists' heated controversies raised issues similar to those of the Hemphill case and involved Franklin as editor of the *Pennsylvania Gazette*.

During the early years of Franklin's editorship, Kinnersley, "a gifted brother on tryal," served as assistant to the regular Baptist minister, the Reverend Jenkin Jones. In the midst of the Great Awakening, a Presbyterian evangelist, John Rowland, friend and supporter of George Whitefield, preached two highly emotional mid-week sermons at the Baptist church while the pastor was occupied in another

20. April 7, 1743.   21. Smyth (ed.), *Writings*, IX, 337.

community. During the second of these sermons, "the audience was sadly overcome by his description of their wholly-ruined condition as sinners; and the distress rose to such a pitch that Gilbert Tennant went to the pulpit stairs and cried out, 'Oh, brother Rowland, is there no balm in Gilead?' "[22] Kinnersley, who was present, considered Rowland's "horrid harangues" and "enthusiastick ravings" unbecoming to a minister of the gospel "and a reproach to that sacred character." This he affirmed in a sermon which he preached in the Baptist church on the following Sunday, July 6, 1740. In denouncing Rowland, he was carrying out his conviction of the "duty incumbent on every Christian Minister, publickly to oppose such distractive preaching, and the dangerous delusions that are propagated by it."

The congregation, more inclined to Rowland's evangelical fervor than to Kinnersley's moderation, listened with steadily mounting anger. "Some of them shewed their resentments by running out of the Place of Worship in a most disorderly and tumultuous manner."

When Jenkin Jones returned to Philadelphia, the congregation persuaded him to join in denouncing Kinnersley, and on the next Saturday Kinnersley was tried at a church meeting and found guilty of improper conduct. Because he refused to confess that he was in the wrong, the meeting further condemned him as unworthy to communicate with them in future.

Seeking vindication in a broader arena, Kinnersley wrote a bristling "Letter . . . to a Friend in the Country," which he induced Franklin to publish in the *Pennsylvania Gazette* (Postscript to No. 606, July 15, 1740). Franklin undoubtedly sympathized with Kinnersley, a rationalistic minister the victim of the intolerance of an ecclesiastical court. Although doctrine was not at stake—the issue being that of reason versus emotion in preaching—Kinnersley's relation to the

22. *Pennsylvania Gazette*, July 24, 1740. See also J. A. Leo Lemay, *Ebenezer Kinnersley, Franklin's Friend* (Philadelphia, 1964).

Baptist meeting was exactly parallel to Hemphill's situation vis à vis the Presbyterian synod.

Franklin, nevertheless, did not personally take up the defense of Kinnersley. First of all, he was not a member of the Baptist congregation—and Kinnersley, unlike Hemphill, wielded a fiery pen of his own and was perfectly capable of defending himself. Also Whitefield and the Great Awakening had then descended upon Philadelphia, and Franklin probably no longer dared to represent himself as a symbol of theological liberalism. He even felt it necessary, when printing Kinnersley's letter, to justify himself for doing so. Once again, he paraphrased Lord Shaftesbury. "It is a principle among printers, that when truth has fair play, it will always prevail over falsehood; therefore, though they have an undoubted property in their own press, yet they willingly allow, that any one is entitled to the use of it, who thinks it necessary to offer his sentiments on disputable points to the publick, and will be at the expense of it." The good, when printed, benefits the public; the bad exposes itself and disgraces the author.

Franklin wrote this editorial a mere two months after he had published Obadiah Plainman's strident apology for the closing of the dancing school. He complained, therefore, that "the printers of this city have been unjustly reflected on, as if they were under some undue influence, and guilty of great partiality in favour of the preaching lately admired among us [Whitefield's], so as to refuse printing anything in opposition to it, how just or necessary soever." This gave Franklin the means of construing his printing of Kinnersley's letter as merely maintaining his post of neutral arbiter and defender of the freedom of the press. He was safe from attack on either side.

The controversy continued throughout the summer in other advertisements and letters in the *Gazette* but finally wore itself out. Kinnersley was not only reinstated in the Baptist church but eventually ordained as well. He retained

strong ties of friendship with Franklin despite the half-heart-
edness of the support given him in the *Pennsylvania Gazette,* and whatever measure of fame he now enjoys came to
him from his association with Franklin's electrical experiments.

A few years before the Kinnersley affair, Franklin became
a Mason; he subsequently took an active part in both the
Philadelphia lodge and the Parisian lodge of the Nine Sisters.
Since eighteenth-century Masonic doctrines were almost inseparable from deism, there is little purpose in detailing this
segment of Franklin's religious history. In his Masonic rites
he referred to God as "the Supreme Architect" and to his
fellow members as "brothers," but otherwise Masonic ritual
had little to contribute to his spiritual life.

Some of Franklin's friends in Philadelphia once subjected
a weak-minded pharmacist's apprentice to a mock Masonic
initiation ceremony during which some burlesque ritualistic
elements of the black mass were introduced.[23] Franklin
laughed at accounts of the ceremony and asked for a copy of
an oath to Satan which had been part of the ceremony and
passed it around as a joke to some of his acquaintances. In a
subsequent stage of the initiation, the hapless apprentice was
fatally burned by a glass of brandy which had been ignited
to provide a ghastly decor. When knowledge of the affair
reached Franklin's parents in Boston, he felt a need to justify
his Masonic connections. He reassured them, therefore, that
"the Freemasons . . . are in general a very harmless sort of
People; and have no principles or Practices that are inconsistent with Religion or good Manners."[24]

It is evident by this time that the religious pattern which
Franklin followed throughout his public life in Pennsylvania consisted of private worship and deistical speculation
coupled with conformity in public to the received ortho-

23. A. O. Aldridge, *Benjamin Franklin: Philosopher and Man* (New York,
1965), pp. 44–46.
24. Labaree (ed.), *Papers,* II, 204.

doxy. By the middle of the eighteenth century, the voice of orthodox respectability in the colonies was that of the Episcopal church—in New England as well as in the middle and southern colonies. We shall see that Franklin drifted into a tacit adherence to the Episcopal church and had a longer and more continuous association with it than with any other religious group—but his basic theology seems to have been in no way modified by the affiliation.

CHAPTER THIRTEEN

A PROFESSING "PROTESTANT OF THE CHURCH OF ENGLAND"

No record exists of Franklin's formally becoming a member of any Anglican congregation, but he made a number of financial contributions to Christ Church in Philadelphia and served it in other ways. Probably he and his wife Deborah switched their allegiance from the Presbyterian church to the Anglican soon after the Hemphill affair.

The first record of their Episcopalian connection is a humorous advertisement concerning Deborah in the *Pennsylvania Gazette,* July 7–14, 1737. "Taken out of a Pew in the Church some Months since, a Common-Prayer Book, bound in Red, gilt, and letter'd D F on each Cover. The Person who took it, is desir'd to open it and read the *Eighth* Commandment, and afterwards return it to the same Pew again; upon which no further Notice will be taken."

Franklin himself appears in the records of Christ Church on May 7, 1739, among 200 signatures to a subscription for furnishing and repairing the interior of the church. Then on March 18, 1750, and throughout 1751, he was listed as a subscriber to a fund for building a steeple and providing bells. Subsequently he was appointed one of thirteen managers of a lottery to raise a greater supply of money for the steeple.[1]

In 1750, Franklin took charge of negotiations to hire a president for the projected College of Philadelphia and engaged in lengthy correspondence with Samuel Johnson, D.D., a leader of the Church of England in the New England colonies. His immediate problem was to overcome a scruple of Johnson's about moving to Philadelphia without first consulting the attitude of the incumbent Episcopal minister, Dr. Jenney, rector of the United Churches of Christ Church and St. Peter's. Franklin found his "tenderness of the church's

1. Benjamin Orr, *A Historical Account of Christ Church* (New York, 1841), *passim.*

peace . . . truly laudable" but pointed out that "to build a new church in a growing place is not properly *dividing* but *multiplying;* and will really be a means of increasing the number of those who worship God in that way. Many who cannot now be accommodated in the church, go to other places, or stay at home; and if we had another church, many who go to other places, or stay at home, would go to church."[2]

As he frequently did, Franklin clarified the situation by means of a fable. For many years in his youth he had owned a pigeon-box holding six pairs of birds. These bred constantly, but his total pigeon population never increased since the strong always drove out the weak. Eventually he put up an additional box with room for twelve more pairs, and it was soon filled with inhabitants. This Franklin took "to be a parallel case with the building of a new church."

In subsequent correspondence with Johnson, Franklin took pains to assure him that proper religious ceremonies were being observed at the college. A short form of prayers compiled by Richard Peters had been introduced for reading morning and evening in the Hall with all the masters and scholars present. These prayers were received, Franklin reported, July 11, 1751, with general approbation.

Johnson was pleased with this institution—but reminded Franklin nevertheless that he had omitted from his *Idea of the English School* the reading of the sacred classics. Franklin replied, December 24, 1751, that the Scriptures were already being read in the English School and that he would propose after the holidays, on Johnson's suggestion, "that the English Master begin and continue to read select Portions of them daily with the Prayers."[3]

A member of Franklin's own family, his daughter Sarah Bache, once asked his advice on the exact time in a child's life when he should be given instruction in religion. The

2. L. W. Labaree *et al.* (eds.) , *Papers of Benjamin Franklin,* IV (New Haven, 1961) , 42.
3. *Ibid.,* p. 222.

circumstances of the request, although completely irrelevant to the academy, are interesting in their own right. Sarah had raised the question after her son William had been frightened by a foolish girl who had predicted that someone was going to die in the house.

> He had not been long in bed before he came down in his shirt, screaming. I soon sent him up, and asking him in the morning how he could behave so, and what was the matter, he told me he thought death was coming. I was so frightened, says he, that I sweat all over, and I jumped out of bed and prayed up to Hercules. I asked him what he said? Down he went on his knees, with uplifted hands (I think I never saw such a picture of devotion), and repeated the Lord's prayer. Now, whether it is best to instruct him in a little religion, or let him pray a little longer to Hercules, I should be glad to have your opinion.[4]

All that Franklin said in reply was, "Teach him . . . to direct his worship more properly, for the deity of Hercules is now quite out of fashion," a cryptic answer indicating that Franklin believed firmly in religious instruction for the young but was still not sure exactly what direction it should take.

Certainly Franklin had no objection to the younger students of the Philadelphia Academy being given orthodox training, and he made every possible concession to persuade Johnson that all Christian formalities would be observed. He even appealed to Johnson's sense of moral obligation to engage him to accept the headship, arguing that "Ability with Opportunity manifestly pointed out Duty as tho it were [a] Voice from Heaven."[5] Johnson agreed to the principle but nevertheless declined the trustees' offer because he felt himself to be in the wane of life, both in body and mind. He must have had great powers of recuperation—or have received a stronger divine call in another direction, however,

---

4. [William Duane, ed.], *Letters to Benjamin Franklin* (New York, 1859), p. 93.
5. Labaree (ed.), *Papers,* IV. 260.

for in 1754 he accepted the presidency of King's College (later Columbia University), where he officiated for nine years.

Franklin's attention to the religious ceremonies of the college was more than a concession to Johnson. As a strong adherent of ceremony and ritual, he had earlier patterned his "Acts of Religion" after the Anglican service. And when he was en route to England during the sixties, he urged upon his daughter the importance of liturgical observances. "Go constantly to church, whoever preaches. The act of devotion in the Common Prayer Book is your principal business there, and if properly attended to, will do more towards amending the heart than sermons generally can do. For they were composed by men of much greater piety and wisdom, than our common composers of sermons can pretend to be; and therefore I wish you would never miss the prayer days; yet I do not mean you should despise sermons, even of the preachers you dislike, for the discourse is often much better than the man, as sweet and clear waters come through very dirty earth."[6] Franklin emphasized this point since Sarah had earlier seemed to entertain some inclination to leave the church, and Franklin was anxious to keep her from doing so. At about the same time he commended his wife for the way she spent her Sundays but added "I think you should go oftner to Church."[7]

Franklin, nevertheless, disapproved of strict Sabbatarianism both as a deist and an Anglican. On a vacation tour of Belgium in 1762, he contrasted the universal Sunday "singing, fiddling and dancing" with the New England observation of the day, where one could hardly travel without hazard of punishment.[8] Ironically he remarked that he looked around for signs of God's judgments but saw no signs of them. The health and prosperity of the people almost made

---

6. Albert Henry Smyth (ed.), *Writings of Benjamin Franklin* (10 vols., New York, 1905–1907), IV, 287.
7. *Ibid.*, p. 202.   8. *Ibid.*, p. 185.

him suspect "that the Deity is not so angry at that offence [Sabbath-breaking] as a New England Justice."

In the next year Franklin humorously approved the situation in Pittsburg, which could not afford to maintain both a parson and a dancing master. As a makeshift, he reported, "the Dancingmaster reads Prayers and one of Tristram Shandy's Sermons every Sunday."[9]

But when writing propaganda in the British press in favor of the colonies, Franklin made a determined defense of the New England Sabbath. In reply to a journalist who had attempted to trace American Sunday observance to Scottish law, Franklin indignantly retorted: " 'The Americans, like the Scots (you say) observe what *they call* the Sabbath.' Pray, Sir, you who are so zealous for your church (in abusing other Christians) what *do you call* it? and where the harm of their *observing* it? If you look into your prayer-book, or over your altars, you will find these words written, *Remember to keep holy the* SABBATH *Day*. This law, tho' it may be observed in Scotland, and has been *countenanced* by some of your statutes, is, Sir, originally one of *God's Commandments:* a body of laws still in force in America, tho' they may have become *obsolete* in *some other* countries."[10] Although this passage by itself represents an extreme fundamentalist attitude, Franklin published it for political rather than religious motives, concerning himself less with vindicating strict Sabbath observance that with disengaging such observance from Scottish tradition.

One of Franklin's closest friends in England was Joseph Shipley, bishop of St. Asaph, at whose country residence at Twyford Franklin spent three weeks in the summer of 1771, writing the first part of his famous autobiography. Although Franklin served as scientific mentor to the Bishop's daughters and he and the Bishop collaborated on a number of political

9. Carl Van Doren (ed.), *Letters and Papers of Benjamin Franklin and Richard Jackson* (Philadelphia, 1947), p. 94.
10. Verner W. Crane (ed.), *Benjamin Franklin's Letters to the Press* (Chapel Hill, 1950), p. 51.

projects, they seem not to have engaged in religious discussions, probably because of eighteenth-century notions of propriety and good taste. Well-bred Anglicans considered one's spiritual life primarily a private matter.

The only religious affair in which Franklin and the Bishop seem to have been jointly involved concerned the efforts of a young preacher, Cornelius Winter, to obtain ordination. Winter, a young man brought up for a mercantile career, had been converted to evangelical Christianity by George Whitefield and had then served as a missionary in Georgia. He sailed with Whitefield on the latter's last voyage to America, September 2, 1769, and arrived in Georgia December 14. He was designated a "catechist," it being understood that his primary purpose was to preach to a congregation of Negroes. According to his own admission most of his audience slept through his services. Occasionally he preached to another Negro congregation twelve miles from Savannah, which was sometimes joined by whites.[11]

After Whitefield's death, Noble Wimberly Jones, Joseph Clay, and other leading citizens of Georgia recommended Winter to the Lord Bishop of London for ordination, but the rector at Savannah, Samuel Frink, would have nothing to do with the request. In England the Society for the Propagation of the Gospel reproached Winter for his previous connections with Whitefield, virtually saying, "Now that Whitefield is dead, you want to put yourself under our wing." The society concluded not to recommend him to the Bishop, giving as a reason that it was improper "to ordain any person brought up to business." His Lordship categorically refused to ordain Winter without the recommendation of the society, taking the attitude that Winter's preaching in Georgia had been illegal—that he had appropriated functions to which he had no right.

Winter thereupon sought to engage in his interest every

11. William Jay, *Memoirs of the Life and Character of the Late Rev. Cornelius Winter* (New York, 1811) , *passim.*

man in London who exerted influence in the church. Among the rest, he approached Franklin, who promised to work in his behalf among the members of a charitable organization to which he belonged, the Associates of the Late Dr. Bray. Winter noted in his memoirs,

> Some of my brethren have reflected upon me for trying, as they supposed, the whole bench to obtain ordination; but I never applied to any beside the Bishop of St. Asaph after the Bishop of London refused me. The interview with the former was short, but favourable; he told me he would be my friend under the rose, but I did not wait upon him a second time. Some of the clergy in Dr. Bray's association, required, in order to my having their interest, that I should renounce my present sentiments; but Dr. Franklin properly said he was persuaded I had too much honesty to do so; when he mentioned it to me, so I told him I had no sentiment to renounce.[12]

Winter's ecclesiastical difficulties are of no great significance in the story of Franklin's religious life except as an illustration of the influence which he possessed in the Anglican church. Noble Wimberly Jones, speaker of the Georgia House of Commons, in thanking Franklin for his intervention in Winter's behalf took it for granted that it would clear the way for his reception into the church. Apparently the Bishop of London refused to change his method of reasoning, however, for despite all that Franklin could do, Winter was never ordained. He finally accepted his fate and joined the ranks of the dissenting clergy.

Franklin probably assumed that motives of prestige and monetary advantage weighed heavily in Winter's desire to enter the Anglican hierarchical structure. Writing to one of his closest friends, William Strahan, about the desire of the latter's son George to become a minister, he once remarked, "I think you have more sense than to stick him into a priesthood that admits of no promotion. If he was a dull lad it might not be amiss, but George has parts, and ought to aim at a mitre."[13]

12. *Ibid.*, p. 162.
13. Smyth (ed.), *Writings*, IV, 200.

During the period of Franklin's intimacy with the Ship-
leys, he interested himself in the intellectual and spiritual
development of a bright English girl, Mary Stevenson, who
was just a few years older than his own daughter. Friend,
philosophical mentor, and guide, Franklin alternated the
roles of playful suitor and good-natured matchmaker as well.
And then on more somber occasions he discussed weighty
points of divinity. Mary apparently accepted all of his notions
on religion with the same enthusiastic devotion with which
she absorbed his instruction in science and literature. Indeed through his guidance, she declared, she had learned to
adore "the Great Creator whose Wisdom and Goodness are
so manifest in the Operations of Nature. I would not have
trusted myself in the Hands of a Philosopher who regards
only Second Causes. There are indeed I believe none who
entirely deny a First, but there are many who do not give
him the Honour due as my Friend and Preceptor does."[14]

In one of her letters she expressed entire agreement with
Franklin's opinion "that those who have multiplied the
duties of Christianity have been its most effective Enemies."
This important phase of the liberalism of Franklin's religion
does not appear in his writings which have survived. In his
early days as a printer he had asserted the principle that
morality is more important than doctrine; here he indicated
the related principle that the spirit is more important than
the law. No longer inculcating multitudinous precepts, as he
had done in his *Way to Wealth,* he was preferring broad
principles. Mary in assent expressed her own opinion that
Christianity "enhances and gives us motives for the performance of moral obligation, but I know no more that it requires of us; and I believe the Gospel precepts are equally
calculated to make us happy Here as Hereafter."[15]

On another occasion Franklin revealed his rational approach to the Scriptures by interpreting the fasting and
temptation of Christ in the wilderness as visionary. He held,

14. Labaree (ed.) , *Papers,* IX (1966) , 319.
15. *Ibid.,* pp. 264–265.

in other words, that the episode did not actually take place but that Christ experienced it in a dream. Franklin's young correspondent readily accepted this supposition, particularly since in the narrative the power is Satan's, "who performs miracles upon the Son of God."[16]

Apparently Mary was upset, however, by Franklin's irregularity in church attendance and other observances. She made no secret of her concern. "I wish all the Members of the Reform'd [i.e., Protestant] Church had your Piety, and I wish that we could boast of you for one of the Pillars of it. Forgive me my dear Friend! I have a little Zeal for Religion, and I know nothing that would promote the Cause of it so much as Dr. Franklin's adding the Performance of it's Rituals to that inward Devotion of his Heart and his truely Virtuous Conduct."[17]

Although to a conscientious girl like Mary Stevenson Franklin's attention to the obligations of Christian worship may have seemed somewhat lax, we must not conclude that he in any sense looked down upon public worship. All the evidence is to the contrary. He never ceased exhorting the younger members of his family to attend church, and in whatever city he lived he consistently affiliated himself with one or more congregations—even though the pressure of public business sometimes kept him from regular participation. Indeed, he wrote to Polly Stevenson herself that no rank in knowledge is equal to the dignity and importance of being a good Christian.[18]

Franklin was so positive in his insistence on religious observance that during his English residence he collaborated with an eccentric rake and nobleman in preparing and publishing a revised version of the Book of Common Prayer, a work which is still known as the Franklin Prayer Book. The idea was that of Sir Francis Dashwood, Baron Le Despencer, joint postmaster general of England, who in private life was a vigorous debauchee with a taste for spectacular sex, blas-

16. *Ibid.*, p. 266.
17. *Ibid.*, p. 353.
18. *Ibid.*, p. 121.

phemy, and the macabre. On his estate at West Wycombe, Despencer presided over meetings of a notorious secret society, the Order of Saint Francis, where the members allegedly took part in black masses and other blasphemous rites.[19]

As early as 1769 Dashwood's duties in the postal service, which he carried out seriously and efficiently, brought him into business relations with Franklin, who was American joint deputy postmaster general. Having been introduced by William Denny, former governor of Pennsylvania, who recommended Franklin as a source of progressive notions concerning government administration in the colonies, the two postmasters became good friends. Franklin more than once visited West Wycombe, where he probably witnessed the weird ceremonies of the Brothers of Saint Francis, known also as the Monks of Medmenham Abbey and the Hell Fire Club.

We have previously noted a relationship between philosophical materialism and eroticism. Dashwood and his associates illustrate a more common parallel between supernaturalism and obscenity. The nature of their weird ceremonies is illustrated by the following commentary of a horrified contemporary:

> Rites of a nature so subversive of all decency, and calculated, by an imitation of the ceremonies and mysteries of the Roman Catholic Church, to render religion itself an object of contumely, were there celebrated, as cannot be reflected on without astonishment. Sir Francis himself officiated as High Priest, habited in the Dress of a Franciscan Monk; engaged in pouring a libation from a Communion-cup, to the mysterious object of their homage. Churchill, in his poem of "The Candidate," has drawn him under this Character, at Medmenham: but I cannot prevail on myself to cite the passage.[20]

Following is the couplet which this delicate scribe could not bring himself to print:

19. Background may be found in Ronald Fuller, *Hell-Fire Francis* (London, 1939) and Donald McCormick, *The Hell-Fire Club* (London, 1958).
20. N. William Wraxall, *Historical Memoirs of My Own Times* (London, 1815), II, 19–20.

Whilst Womanhood, in habit of a nun,
At Mednam lies, by backward monks undone.

Charles Churchill, who wrote these lines, was himself a member of the brotherhood, along with his friend John Wilkes. Although there may be exaggeration in some accounts of the exotic vices practiced by Dashwood's apostles, there can be no question that the purpose of the organization was to combine sex and heavy drinking with the external appearances of religion. The members garbed themselves in habits resembling those of Catholic orders of the Middle Ages, as did the prostitutes and other female visitors, designated as "nuns."

Greatest notoriety has been accorded to the licentious activities at West Wycombe, but there can be no doubt that the monks also shared a serious deistical purpose. These rakes could have indulged in their sexual excesses separately without banding together in a religious (or irreligious) order. An anonymous contemporary "who described himself as 'A Monk of the Order of Saint Francis' told how Dashwood disapproved of foreign 'religious seminaries founded in direct contradiction of Nature and Reason,' and that he determined on returning to England to deflate such pretensions by means of a burlesque society which would mock their rites and not enforce celibacy on members."[21] One might even go further and suppose that Dashwood derived satisfaction from the traditions and ritual of the church. As one acute observer has put it, he was "a madcap prankster fascinated by a religion in which he could not believe."[22]

Franklin probably was never counted as a member of the order despite his several visits to West Wycombe. In August, 1773, he wrote to his son that he was as much at home at Dashwood's house as if it were his own. "But a pleasanter Thing is the kind Countenance, the facetious and very intelligent Conversation of mine Host who, having been for

21. McCormick, *The Hell-Fire Club*, p. 63.
22. L. C. Jones, quoted in *ibid.*, p. 45.

many Years engaged in publick Affairs, seen all Parts of Europe, and kept the best Company in the World, is himself the best existing."[23]

Dashwood had spent a good deal of time and effort in rebuilding the Church of St. Lawrence, an ancient edifice in West Wycombe. In his restoration he filled the church with trappings from the Middle Ages, thus giving the impression that he was designing an elaborate stage for the acting out of his religious farces.

It was probably a combination of pious buffoonery and genuine intellectual concern that led Dashwood to take up the revision of the prayer book. We may judge his appreciation of symbolic values by the fact that as part of his ecclesiastical trappings he filled Medmenham Abbey with "scurrilous novels bound as Books of Common Prayer."[24]

The problem now facing us is to decide whether Franklin as a collaborator in the prayer book should be associated with the eccentric behavior of Dashwood and the other monks. The only logical answer is that Franklin cannot be separated from the milieu in which the book originated. He accepted Dashwood's hospitality, he visited his church and Hell Fire Caves, and he kept up close relations with several members of the brotherhood. More important than all this is the evidence from Franklin's previous life and character: his sexual prowess and lubricious writings, his deistical attitude toward superstition and tradition, and his concern for practical worship.

We shall probably never know how far—if at all—Franklin involved himself in the masquerading at Medmenham. But he obviously discussed religion with Dashwood and the others. Undoubtedly it was a consequence of some kind of anthropological-sociological discussion, probably at Dashwood's estate, that Franklin gave John Wilkes the priceless illuminated manuscript hymnal of the Ephrata. Wilkes was

23. Smyth (ed.), *Writings*, VI, 111.
24. McCormick, *The Hell-Fire Club*, p. 124.

the heaviest drinker of the brotherhood, and he produced for its delectation the original version of his pornographic poem *An Essay on Women*. Franklin would not have entrusted Wilkes with a book costing "three Brethren three Quarters of a Year Work to write the same" if he were any more capable than Wilkes of reverence for tradition. Franklin was not as accomplished a rake as Wilkes and Dashwood, but they were certainly fellow spirits.

Before securing Franklin's collaboration in re-editing the Book of Common Prayer, Dashwood had already completed the revision of the liturgy, and Franklin was given as his task the rest of the book, that is, "the Catechism and the reading and singing Psalms."

We may find further details of their aims and procedures in the Preface, which is generally attributed to Franklin.[25] In the person of editor he professed to be "a Protestant of the Church of England," holding "in the highest veneration the doctrines of Jesus Christ." "He is a sincere lover of social worship, deeply sensible of its usefulness to society; and he aims at doing some service to religion, by proposing such abbreviations and omissions in the forms of our Liturgy (retaining everything he thinks essential) as might, if adopted, procure a more general attendance." As a profession of faith, this is extremely ingenious. Without doubt, Franklin was genuinely a "lover of social worship," and he actually claimed to be nothing more. To hold the doctrines of Jesus Christ in highest veneration does not necessarily mean that one believes the doctrines of Christianity—and to profess oneself a Protestant of the Church of England in the eighteenth century, a period of great division even among clergymen, certainly did not amount to asserting one's orthodoxy. The position of the latitudinarian wing, as summarized by one distinguished scholar, consisted of "the right of private judgement, reduction of necessary beliefs to a few fundamentals, and a tendency towards moralism (expressed as a con-

25. Smyth (ed.), *Writings*, VI, 165–171.

cern for 'virtue and holiness' rather than theological opinion)."[26] This fits Franklin exactly. His Preface cannot be called hypocritical even though he did not manifest his deistical beliefs as such. We shall see later in the chapter, however, that Franklin for political reasons probably made some other professions of religious faith which were not at all compatible with his private views.

Further in his Preface, Franklin carefully explained that the editors respected the liturgy and were implying in their revision no criticism of its excellence. The only changes they had made were those of condensation. Their object was not "to lessen or prevent the practise of religion, but to honour and promote it." Piety and propriety were their main considerations.

> It has often been observed and complained of, that the Morning and Evening Service, as practised in England and elsewhere, are so long, and filled with so many repetitions, that the continued attention suitable to so serious a duty becomes impracticable, the mind wanders, and the fervency of devotion is slackened. Also the propriety of saying the same prayer more than once in the same service is doubted, as the service is thereby lengthened without apparent necessity; our Lord having given us a short prayer as an example, and censured the heathen for thinking to be heard because of much speaking.

The most important grounds for abridgment, however, were utilitarian, the comfort of old people, the interest of the young, the convenience of the busy.

> Many pious and devout persons, whose age or infirmities will not suffer them to remain for hours in a cold church, especially in the winter season, are obliged to forego the comfort and edification they would receive by their attendance at divine service. These, by shortening the time, would be relieved, and the younger sort, who have had some principles of religion instilled into them, and who have been educated in a belief of the necessity of adoring their Maker, would probably more frequently, as well as cheerfully, attend divine service, if they were not detained so long at any

26. Roland N. Stromberg, *Religious Liberalism in Eighteenth-Century England* (Oxford, 1954), p. 92.

one time. Also many well disposed tradesmen, shopkeepers, artificers, and others, whose habitations are not remote from churches, could, and would, more frequently at least, find time to attend divine service on other than Sundays, if the prayers were reduced to a much narrower compass.

Franklin's previous experience as a newspaper editor had accustomed him to rigorous excisions. In tackling the liturgy, he slashed right and left. Gone completely were the Absolution and the Canticle—nearly all of the Exhortation, the Te Deum, the Venite exultemus—and a large section of the Confession. Over half of the Apostles' Creed went by the board, leaving the following:

> I believe in God the Father Almighty, Maker of Heaven and Earth:
> And in Jesus Christ his Son, our Lord.
> I believe in the Holy Ghost; The Forgiveness of Sins; And the Life everlasting. Amen.

In his Preface, Franklin went into greatest detail to vindicate his treatment of the Psalms, coating over with a show of literary criticism his deistical aversion to the Old Testament concept of the god of a chosen race. He had omitted or abbreviated many Psalms since as "a collection of odes written by different persons" they frequently treat the same subjects and "repeat the same sentiments"—that is, "complain of enemies and persecutors, call upon God for protection, express a confidence therein, and thank him for it when afforded." The historical parts repeat facts mentioned in previous books, "which, relating to the ancestors of the Jews, were more interesting to them than to us." Those Psalms which concern purely personal relations, "the particular circumstances of David or Solomon, as kings, . . . can . . . seldom be rehearsed with any propriety by private Christians." And most objectionable of all, "others imprecate, in the most bitter terms, the vengeance of God on our adversaries, contrary to the spirit of Christianity, which commands us to love our enemies, and to pray for those that hate us and despitefully use us."

Franklin revealed an even stronger sign of deistical anti-Biblicism in a terse reference to the Commination: this "and all cursing of mankind, is, we think, best omitted in this abridgment."

In France almost a century later, Sainte-Beuve, who otherwise greatly admired Franklin, adopted a patronizing tone in referring to his aim of making the Psalms more rational and moral. Admitting that Franklin in some of his original tales and parables had sensed and well imitated the style of the Scriptures, the French critic charged that he was incapable of understanding either Job or David.

> Their obscurities annoy him; their eloquence, which shines in part in the clouds, dazzles him; he wants everything to be comprehensible, and he does his best to bring Mt. Sinai down to earth. However from the moment that one admits, as he had the wisdom of doing, public adoration and worship, are there not emotions in the human spirit, mysteries and profundities in human destiny, which invoke and justify the storm of divine eloquence? Be that as it may, he did not admire sublime disorder, and he did his best to keep the thunders of Moses from approaching us, just as he had with the other thunder.[27]

Here Sainte-Beuve probably takes Franklin a little too seriously. Although the abridged prayer book certainly reflects Franklin's common-sense approach to the major issues of life, it should not be considered a complete and faithful measure of his spiritual vision. We must not forget his own far from prosaic "Articles of Belief and Acts of Worship." The circumstances of the publication of Franklin's prayer book indicate that it was partly a hoax (comparable to the monkish rites of the Brothers of the Hell Fire Club), partly a new application of Franklin's efficiency methods (comparable to a reformed phonetic alphabet, which he devised about the same time), and partly a serious attempt to improve organized worship.

One might find a clue to his motives for the abridgment

---

27. Translated from *Causeries du lundi* (Paris, n.d.), VII, 155.

by considering a well-known episode in his autobiography—his advice given to a Presbyterian chaplain, Charles Beatty, on the Pennsylvania frontier. When the latter complained that "the Men did not generally attend his Prayers and Exhortations," Franklin suggested that he act as steward of the rum and deal out each man's daily provision after prayers.[28] Beatty thought the idea was a good one, carried it out, and as a result "never were Prayers more generally and more punctually attended." To Franklin, dealing out the rum and abridging the prayers were alike efficient, practical means of increasing attendance at worship, a goal which he sincerely favored.

Since Franklin's abridged prayer book had been drawn up by two laymen without the aid or supervision of any clergymen, it is not surprising that it was never adopted for church use. It was printed in 1773 under the title *Abridgement of the Book of Common Prayer,* but, as Franklin later wrote, it was "never much noticed. Some were given away, very few sold, and I suppose the bulk became waste paper."[29] When the authors published their work, however, they had believed that it might become popular. At least they published two errata sheets containing emendations to be attended to, if the abridgment should have a second edition.

Nevertheless Franklin retained his conviction that a ritual of prayer and praise, such as that in his liturgy, was a more important function in a religious service than a sermon or other discourse. We will remember that he advised his daughter that "the act of devotion in the Common Prayer" was her principal business at church—that if properly attended to, it would "do more towards amending the heart there than sermons generally can do." Franklin probably felt that most Anglican sermons were beyond the intellectual capacities of the ordinary worshipers, who were more com-

28. Leonard W. Labaree, *et al.* (eds.), *Autobiography of Benjamin Franklin* (New Haven, 1964), p. 235.
29. Smyth (ed.), *Writings,* IX, 358.

fortable with ritual than philosophy. One day he attended an Anglican service near Lord Despencer's with his lordship and heard a bright young man deliver a sensible discourse in elegant language, which, nevertheless, did not seem to have much effect upon the congregation. This led Franklin to reflect that the Quakers probably were wiser in their system of religious instruction: simply listening "to some plain sensible man of their sect, whose discourse they all understand."[30]

Shortly after his experiments with the prayer book, Franklin decided to revise the Lord's Prayer—and produced but did not publish what he considered an improved version.

1. Heavenly Father,
2. May all revere thee,
3. And become thy dutiful Children and faithful Subjects.
4. May thy Laws be obeyed on Earth as perfectly as they are in Heaven.
5. Provide for us this Day as thou hast hitherto daily done.
6. Forgive us our Trespasses and enable us likewise to forgive those that offend us.
7. Keep us out of Temptation, and deliver us from Evil.[31]

In preparing his earlier prayer book, Franklin had made no verbal emendations—"not even to substitute *who* for *which* in the Lord's Prayer, and elsewhere, although it would be more correct." In revising the Lord's Prayer, however, Franklin made sweeping changes. He reduced the address "Our Father which art in Heaven" to the terse "Heavenly Father," which he justified as "more concise, equally expressive, and better modern English." In most of his other changes, Franklin was motivated not only by a desire for clarity and brevity but by the deistical conviction that the earlier form of the prayer reflected the political and theological notions of the ancient Jewish kingdom, notions which had become obsolete in modern society.[32]

He changed "Hallowed be thy Name" to "May all revere

30. *Memoirs of the Life of Sir Samuel Romilly Written by Himself* (London, 1842), I, 450.
31. Smyth (ed.), *Writings*, VII, 427.   32. *Ibid.*, pp. 428–430.

thee" because the earlier expression was a vestige of the Jewish taboo "not to pronounce the proper or peculiar Name of God, they deeming it a Profanation so to do. We have in our Language no *proper Name* for God; the Word *God* being a common or general Name, expressing all chief Objects of Worship, true or false. The Word *hallowed* is almost obsolete. People now have but an imperfect Conception of the Meaning of the Petition."

Franklin changed "Thy Kingdom come" to "And become thy dutiful Children and faithful Subjects" because the earlier petition revealed the dissatisfaction of the Jewish nation with a theocratic state. The Jews had considered that God as a ruler was too remote and "desired a visible earthly King in the manner of the Nations round them." Franklin made no reference whatsoever to the Christian millennial concept of the creation of a kingdom of God on earth after the second coming of Christ, even though this doctrine was widely discussed by eighteenth-century theologians and poets and Franklin had himself alluded to it in his writings on the Hemphill affair. Whether or not he accepted the millennial interpretation himself, it is doubtful that he had any knowledge from contemporary New Testament scholarship concerning what this petition was thought to have meant at the time it was incorporated into the Gospels.

Ezra Stiles, however, wondered whether Franklin may have been a millennialist or revelationist because in his will he left the city of Boston a legacy of 1,000 pounds and instructions for administering it for the next two hundred years. That he made no provision for any later period might indicate, Stiles thought, that Franklin accepted a contemporary doctrine that the millennium would commence about 2000 A.D.[33] But since Franklin was not a believer even in the inspiration of the Bible, it is doubtful that he accepted its eschatology.

33. F. B. Dexter (ed.), *Literary Diary of Ezra Stiles* (New York, 1901), III, 395.

Franklin objected to the phrase "Give us this Day our daily Bread" because of its presumptuousness. "Give us what is *ours,* seems to put us in a Claim of Right, and to contain too little of the grateful Acknowledgment and Sense of Dependance that becomes Creatures who live on the daily Bounty of their Creator."

He detected the same presumptuousness in "Forgive us our Debts, as we forgive our Debtors." This, he felt, "has the Air of proposing ourselves as an Example of Goodness fit for God to imitate. *We hope you will at least be as good as we are;* you see we forgive one another, and therefore we pray that you would forgive us. Some have considered it in another sense, *Forgive us as we forgive others;* i. e. If we do not forgive others we pray that thou wouldst not forgive us. But this being a kind of conditional *Imprecation* against ourselves, seems improper in such a Prayer." In this reasoning, we notice a striking resemblance to one of the *Colloquies* of Erasmus entitled "The Shipwreck," where his spokesman, disgusted with voyagers who make extravagant promises to the saints on condition of their being rescued from the sea, repudiates such dealing. "For what else is that but a bargain according to the form, 'I'll give this if you do that' or 'I'll do this if you'll do that.' "[34]

Franklin traced the metaphor concerning debtors to the ancient Jewish state, where offerings were due to God on many occasions. When people could not pay or "had forgotten as Debtors are apt to do, it was proper to pray that those debts might be forgiven." Franklin remarked that the liturgy used the phrase "those that trespass against us" instead of "Debtors," as it appears in Matthew, or "the indebted" as it appears in Luke. Humorously he suggested that "perhaps the Considering it a Christian Duty to forgive Debtors, was by the Compilers thought an inconvenient Idea in a trading Nation." Franklin preferred "Forgive us our Trespasses, and enable us likewise to forgive those that offend us." "This

34. Craig R. Thompson (trans.), *Ten Colloquies* (New York, 1957), p. 8.

instead of assuming that we have already in & of ourselves the Grace of Forgiveness, acknowledges our Dependance on God, the Fountain of Mercy for any Share we may have in it, praying that he would communicate of it to us."

The expression "lead us not into Temptation," Franklin rejected as a vestige of primitive superstition. "The Jews had a Notion, that God sometimes tempted, or directed or permitted the Tempting of People. Thus it was said he tempted Pharaoh; directed Satan to tempt Job; and a false Prophet to tempt Ahab, &c. Under this Persuasion it was natural for them to pray that he would not put them to such severe Trials. We now suppose that Temptation, so far as it is supernatural, comes from the Devil only, and this Petition continued conveys a Suspicion which in our present Conception seems unworthy of God."

Although in these comments Franklin appears in the light of a Bible expositor, his emendments actually had no real reference to Christian theology. What he was really presenting was a petition to God completely abstracted from the milieu of Christianity. The Lord's Prayer had become a deist's prayer, parallel in abbreviated form to the petition which Franklin had inscribed in his youthful "Articles of Belief and Acts of Religion." His revised Lord's Prayer can be compared almost point by point with the earlier composition.

Because of his concise, unadorned style, it is even doubtful that Franklin intended his revised prayer for his own or anyone else's actual use. He may have conceived the project merely as a device for introducing philosophical explanations for his verbal changes, which have less relevance to the historical tradition of Christianity than to the deistical notion of disparaging the doctrines of the Jews as a chosen people.

In this sense, Franklin's revisions are hardly susceptible to the scathing remarks of critics, who condemn "his bland shallowness in treating weighty and intricate religious matters."[35] One should not solemnly point at Franklin's "smugness" as exposing his "irreverence for the subject matter" without being certain of Franklin's purpose. And nobody today has that certainty. His serious "Articles of Belief and Acts of Religion," revealing decorum and sensitivity in style, were obviously intended for his private worship, and his revision of the Book of Common Prayer was intended for use in churches. His revision of the Lord's Prayer, if it is to be compared to his other works, has most resemblance to his bagatelles—minor compositions with a serious moral purpose but presented in a manner wholly or partly facetious.

35. Ralph L. Ketcham, *Benjamin Franklin* (New York, 1966), p. 181.

CHAPTER FOURTEEN

THE CHURCH OF AMERICA

FRANKLIN had important relations with the Anglican church which were historical rather than literary and came about as a consequence of the American Revolution. He figures in the history of the Protestant Episcopal church of America in connection with the ordination of bishops and with the drawing up of an American revised Book of Common Prayer.

Even before the Revolution the problem of the ordination of American clergymen had been a vexing one. Since there were no bishops in America, it was necessary for candidates for holy orders to make a long and expensive trip to England. The obvious solution would be to provide an American bishop.

A complicating element, however, was the suspicion with which other denominations, particularly the Presbyterians, looked upon the establishment of a bishop in America. Since bishops in England automatically took seats in the House of Lords, American non-Anglicans feared that the advent of an American bishop would give the Church of England political advantages. Franklin wrote to Jane Mecom, February 23, 1769, expressing concern over American religious squabbling. "I do not conceive," he wrote, "that Bishops residing in America, would either be of such advantage to Episcopalians, or such Disadvantage to Anti-episcopalians as either seems to imagine.—Each Party abuses the other, the Profane & the Infidel believe both sides, and enjoy the Fray; the Reputation of Religion in general suffers, and its Enemies are ready to say, not what was said in the primitive Times, *Behold how these Christians love one another,* but *Mark how these Christians hate one another!* Indeed when religious People quarrel about Religion, or hungry People about their Victuals, it looks as if they had not much of either among them."[1]

1. Carl Van Doren (ed.), *Letters of Benjamin Franklin and Jane Mecom* (Princeton, 1950), p. 109.

The Revolution was fought and won and still no bishop was appointed. To make matters more complicated, political independence for America meant the breaking of all ties between the Church of England and the congregations in America. The College of Philadelphia as an organization affiliated with the Church of England was also cut adrift. Fearing that control might be forfeited to the state or to other denominations, a group of Anglican "gentlemen interested in the inviolability of religious and scientific corporations" met in 1776 at the home of Dr. William Smith. Franklin, the president of the convention which framed the first republican constitution of Pennsylvania, was present on request.[2] He "cheerfully promised to propose to the body an article drawn up by Dr. Smith, securing all chartered rights" to the incumbent trustees of the college, but despite this precaution Smith was soon dismissed in favor of a Presbyterian provost.

Immediately after the close of the war two young divinity students from Maryland went to England to petition the Archbishop of Canterbury for ordination. These were Mason Locke Weems, later to be famous as the author of a romantic biography of George Washington, and Edward Gant, later chaplain of the United States Senate. The archbishop refused to grant them holy orders unless they would take the customary oath of allegiance to the British crown.

After soliciting in vain for over a year, the disappointed candidates wrote to Franklin, who was then American minister in France, acquainting him with the situation—all the more grave, they remarked, because out of sixty churches in their state the pulpits of over thirty were vacant. Since orders in the Roman Catholic church were valid, they asked Franklin to inquire whether the proper authorities in Paris would consent to their ordination there.

The Danish church had already suggested to John Adams, American minister in London, that it would be willing to

---

2. Bird Wilson, *Memoir of the Life of William White* (Philadelphia, 1839), p. 69.

ordain American clergy, but the offer was never accepted. Weems and Gant explained to Franklin that "the Orders from Denmark are not so good as we wish them to be."

Franklin upon receiving the request of the young divinity students immediately went to work to see whether they could be ordained through the Roman Catholic church. He first of all asked one of his clerical acquaintances, probably the abbé André Morellet, whether the Catholic rites could be extended to his Protestant countrymen. Franklin's friend expressed great doubt and affirmed that in any event the candidates would be required to vow obedience to the Archbishop of Paris. Franklin next asked the papal nuncio whether the Roman Catholic superior in America, the Bishop of Quebec, could be empowered to ordain them, but the answer was, "The Thing is impossible, unless the Gentlemen become Catholics."[3]

Franklin reported his lack of success to Weems and Gant (July 18, 1784) and then proceeded to offer other suggestions, which he admitted might be improper or impractical. He pretended an almost total ignorance of church politics and the doctrine of apostolic succession—probably writing with his tongue in cheek.[4] "What is the necessity of your being connected with the Church of England? Would it not be as well, if you were of the Church of Ireland? The Religion is the same, tho' there is a different set of Bishops and Archbishops." If this resource failed, Franklin felt that the best expedient of the Episcopalian clergy of America, unless they became Presbyterians, would be to follow the example of the first clergy of Scotland, whose method he reported from Holinshed's *Chronicles*. Soon after the conversion of the country to Christianity, the clergy requested the King of Northumberland to lend them his bishops to ordain one of them so that their future clergy could be spared the journey

3. Albert Henry Smyth (ed.), *Writings of Benjamin Franklin* (10 vols., New York, 1905–1907), IX, 238.
4. *Ibid.*, pp. 239–241.

to Northumberland for orders. When this request was refused, they elected one of their own brethren. In appropriate ceremonies the King of Scotland said to him, *"Arise, go to the Altar, and receive your Office at the Hand of God."* "His brethren led him to the Altar, robed him, put the Crozier in his Hand, and the Mitre on his Head, and he became the first Bishop of Scotland."

If the British Isles were to sink in the sea, Franklin continued, "you would probably take some such Method as this; and, if they persist in denying you Ordination, 'tis the same thing. An hundred years hence, when People are more enlightened, it will be wondered at, that Men in America, qualified by their Learning and Piety to pray for and instruct their Neighbors, should not be permitted to do it till they had made a Voyage of six thousand Miles out and home, to ask leave of a cross old Gentleman at Canterbury." Revealing his exasperation with English national selfishness, Franklin told an anecdote of a clergyman from Virginia in the early days of the colony who appealed to a court official for funds to educate young men to be ministers of the gospel. The minister crowned his appeal with the earnest reminder "that the People of Virginia had souls to be saved, as well as the People of England." *"Souls,"* replied the court official, *"damn your Souls. Make Tobacco!"*

A modern church historian has objected to the injustice of this indictment of the English episcopate. Franklin "could not, and evidently Weems did not, know that while this letter was being written an action was already under way to open the door to American candidates."[5] A law was passed in Parliament in August, 1784, giving temporary permission for the Bishop of London to ordain deacons or priests without requiring the Oath of Allegiance.

While Weems and Gant were in England seeking holy orders, a number of clergymen in America were agitating for

5. Richard G. Salomon, "British Legislation and American Episcopacy," *Historical Magazine of the Protestant Episcopal Church,* XIX (1951), 282.

the installation of a native American bishop. In Connecticut ten missionaries of the Society for Propagating the Gospel selected Samuel Seabury in March, 1783, for the honor and sent him to England to be ordained.[6] When he arrived in England, the Anglican bishops raised legal objections. The enterprising Seabury then took his case to Scottish non-juring bishops, who belonged to a succession which out of original loyalty to the Stuart kings had never taken an oath to the Hanoverian dynasty. These bishops readily agreed to perform the rite, and Seabury on November 14, 1784, became the first American bishop.

Franklin in London was presumably not aware of these developments, for in July, 1785, he wrote to Claudius Crigan, bishop of Sodor and Man, who had entertained thoughts of going to America. Franklin pointed out that American Episcopalians might not necessarily welcome having a bishop of their own. After explaining the autonomy of the thirteen states and the complete lack of authority of the Congress over ecclesiastical matters, Franklin expressed his private opinion that Congress would "do nothing either to encourage or discourage the Introduction of a Bishop in America."[7] Franklin recognized that an American bishop might improve church government and prevent the risk and expense of sending young men to England for ordination (and he even suggested that a bishop, if appointed, be authorized to consecrate other bishops) , but he cautioned that it would be extremely difficult for Americans to support a bishop. The state governments would not be inclined to do it and individuals could not be depended on for sufficient contributions. According to Franklin, Episcopalians represented a small minority in most states and even where they were a majority they not only failed to see the utility of a resident bishop but feared some inconveniences. He gave as an example the unanimous vote of censure in the Virginia

6. Arthur L. Cross, *The Anglican Episcopate and the American Colonies* (New York, 1902) , p. 264.
7. Smyth (ed.) , *Writings*, IX, 354.

House of Commons in 1772 against a proposition of their own clergy for introducing a bishop. Franklin concluded that the Virginians felt apprehensions of the expense to "maintain a Bishop suitable to his Dignity, and of Attempts to oblige the Laity to defray such Expence by Taxes, or Tythes, or at least of their being solicited for voluntary Contributions." All that Franklin could then say to encourage his correspondent was that if the laity had changed their minds and now wished to have a bishop, "I imagine none of the Governments would forbid it, but the Support would probably be too small and too precarious to be a sufficient Encouragement." Although Franklin outlined the earlier American opposition to episcopacy in such a way as to avoid offending his reverend correspondent, there is no doubt that it had been extremely strong in most of the colonies. Indeed, historians consider it as one of the contributing causes of the American Revolution.

After independence had been won, however, the climate of opinion changed. When the clergy and laity of seven states met in a convention on September 27, 1785, under the new name of Protestant Episcopal Church, fear of political domination had given way to alarm over depletion of the ranks of the clergy. The convention altered the Book of Common Prayer so that it would conform to the new political situation and composed an address to the English bishops asking them to consecrate American candidates for holy orders. Oddly enough, the subsequent deliberations of the bishops were influenced by the correspondence of three men completely outside of the Anglican clergy. These were Franklin, Granville Sharp, and Dr. James Manning, an American Baptist minister, president of Rhode Island College (later Brown University).

Early in 1785 Sharp had sent Manning some books for the college as well as some remarks "concerning the popular right of electing bishops." Manning communicated these remarks to local Episcopalian ministers and informed Sharp that they would be circulated at the convention in Philadelphia. These remarks Sharp had printed in a pamphlet on episcopacy, which he had not yet released for general circulation. He sent a copy also to Franklin, June 17, 1785. In his accompanying letter he expressed the view that he and Franklin shared the opinion that "true Religion is more compendiously Efficacious for the forming of useful Citizens & sincere Patriots in every State, than any other Principle that can be inculcated."[8] The best means, he felt, of maintaining "Sound Doctrine & purity of Manners in a Christian Society" would be to restore "the *primitive Apostolic form of Episcopal Government*" including "the ancient Freedom of Election to Ecclesiastical Offices." Since Sharp included bishops among the elected offices, his views were similar to those which Franklin had expressed in his letter to Weems and Gant. Sharp had also been considering reforms in the liturgy, and he inquired about Franklin's prayer book.

Two weeks before the convention at Philadelphia opened, Sharp showed the letters of Manning and Franklin to the Archbishop of Canterbury and received assurance "that the Administration would be inclined to give leave to the bishops to consecrate proper persons." Sharp, a bitter opponent of Jacobitism, urged that the Church of England immediately dispense with the oath of allegiance to the crown in consecrating American bishops so that the rite could be kept from passing into the hands of the Scottish non-juring bishops or the Methodists.

The circumstance which kept the bishops from immediately granting the petition of the convention was a revised Book of Common Prayer which the convention considered in 1785 and printed the next year. It had been drawn up by a committee as a "proposed book," the name by which it has since been known. Like Franklin's, the book omitted "the Nicene and the Athanasian Creeds, and . . . the Descent into Hell in the Apostles' Creed." For this reason church

8. Prince Hoare, *Memoirs of Granville Sharp* (London, 1820), pp. 216–218.

historians have suggested that Dr. William White, one of the members of the committee, had been influenced by Franklin in his liturgical emendations.

There is a legend that Franklin and White, in company with Francis Hopkinson, had once jointly engaged in a romantic episode. When White was eighteen and Franklin fifty-six, they are supposed to have assisted a young girl to elope from her father's house in Philadelphia. They smuggled a rope ladder into the house, and she used it to escape after dark. All three then rode until daybreak in a carriage to Chester where the young lady found her awaiting suitor, the painter Benjamin West, and embarked with him on a boat bound for England.[9]

Although this story may be apocryphal, there is no question that White knew Franklin's prayer book. One of the few extant copies contains the following note in White's handwriting: "This book was presented to me in the year 1785 while ye Liturgy was under review by Mrs. Sarah Bache, by direction of her father, Dr. Benjamin Franklin, who, with Lord Le Dispenser, she said, were the framers of it."[10]

But the excisions in Franklin's liturgy are so much more extensive than those in the "proposed book" that it is unrealistic to speak of any direct influence. Also Dr. William Smith, Franklin's personal enemy, was another powerful member of the committee to draw up the prayer book, and he certainly would not have been likely to use Franklin's work as a model.

The American editors justified the omission of "Christ's descent into hell" on the grounds that it did not appear in any creed until the fifth century and that it referred merely to "his burial or descent into the grave." This may possibly be one of the "deistical" tendencies which various writers attribute to the American prayer book.

9. Walter Herbert Stowe, *Life and Letters of Bishop William White* (New York, 1937), p. 23.
10. John Wright, *Early Prayer Books of America* (St. Paul, 1896), p. 398.

On the Fourth of July, 1786, when the "Form of *Prayer and Thanksgiving*" was used for the first time, Samuel Magaw dedicated a sermon, which he preached at St. Paul's Church, to Franklin and the members of the Supreme Executive Council.[11] Franklin undoubtedly approved of the sermon since it contained a quotation from Addison which Franklin had used many years previously in his own "Articles of Belief":

> Whatever he delights in must be happy.

When the American liturgy made its way to England, it aroused the alarm and drew the censure of the bishops, particularly because of the publication in the English newspapers of a note by an English Unitarian comparing the proceedings of the convention to those of an Episcopalian congregation with unitarian convictions in Boston. The latter had adopted a liturgy "formed after the manner of Dr. Clarke and Mr. Lindsey," a reformed prayer book carefully omitting all Trinitarian references.

Sharp wrote to Franklin, August 19, 1786, explaining the concern which the archbishops felt over the rumors of Socinianism in the convention and giving his own detailed opinion of the liturgy. Franklin thereupon transmitted Sharp's letter to Dr. White.

The convention reassembled June 20, 1786, and drew up an address to the English prelates in which they affirmed their intention not to depart from the doctrines of the English church and repeated their request for the succession. Parliament in the same year passed an act authorizing the consecration of bishops for America. Two candidates, White and Dr. Samuel Provoost of New York, immediately sailed for England, where they were consecrated February 4, 1787. Together with Seabury, this brought the number of bishops in America up to three, the necessary number for the perpet-

---

11. *A Sermon Delivered in St. Paul's Church on the 4th of July, 1786* (Philadelphia, 1786).

uation of the orders of the Anglican church. The American Protestant Episcopal church was now fully established, thanks in some measure to the good offices of Benjamin Franklin.

When Franklin returned from France to America in 1785, he renewed his affiliations with Christ Church. His name appears on a subscription list for repairs and for discharging the arrears due on recent improvements. Out of thirty-six subscribers, three others gave the same amount as Franklin, 60 shillings, and only three others gave more. He and his wife Deborah are buried in the churchyard with a simple inscription on their tomb giving only their names and dates.

George Washington was also nominally an Episcopalian, and it is almost inevitable that he and Franklin should be compared in regard to their religious observances. The nineteenth-century biographer of Bishop William White devoted thirteen pages to a well-documented discussion of Washington's religion.[12] His conclusion is brief: Washington attended service, but never communicated. This circumstance is subject to two contrary interpretations: one, that of White's biographer, that the sacrament was a rite so sublime that Washington never felt worthy to participate; the other, that of deists and free-thinkers, that Washington did not believe in the divinity of Christ and that he could not bring himself to make a hypocritical profession.

So far as is known, nobody has ever raised the question of whether Franklin was ever a communicant in the Anglican church, and there is absolutely no evidence on the point. The conclusion to be drawn, therefore, is that Franklin, like Despencer, who held similar views, was a communicant. Had he consistently refrained from the sacrament, there would probably have been some public discussion.

The eighteenth century in England, we remember, was the era of "occasional conformity," when unbelievers in the doctrine of the Church of England (chiefly dissenters and

12. Bird Wilson, *Memoir*, pp. 187–200.

deists), in order to exercise political functions which would otherwise have been denied, occasionally made a token acknowledgment of membership in the church by taking the sacrament.

Franklin, before entering upon any of the crown offices which he held in Pennsylvania prior to the Revolution, was required to take an oath subscribing to a belief in the Trinity as defined by the Athanasian Creed.[13] He undoubtedly regarded this oath as a type of occasional conformity rather than a literal profession of faith. With his fellow officeholders he was required to declare: "We . . . do profess faith in God the Father, and in Jesus Christ his Eternal Son the true God, and in the Holy Spirit, one God blessed for evermore; and we do acknowledge the Holy Scripture to be given by Divine inspiration."[14]

A deist, by definition, does not believe in any kind of direct supernatural inspiration of any scripture or of any individual or group. We cannot find any statement of Franklin's in which he specifically denies believing in the inspiration of all the Scriptures, but we hardly need one to know that he did not have such a belief. We remember his statement in the Hemphill controversy that in any conflict between Scripture and reason he would accept the authority of the latter. He once suggested, moreover, in a letter to Ezra Stiles, that the Christian revelations have no more authority than the Persian Zend-Avesta (January 13, 1772). With a touch of irony, he observed that among the writings deemed sacred by the followers of Zoroaster "there seems too great a Quantity & Variety of Ceremonies & Prayers, to be directed at once by one Man."[15] Extending the scope of his skepticism, he pointed out that sacred writings "in the Romish Church . . . have increas'd gradually in a Course of Ages to their present Bulk. Those who added new ones from time to

13. Charles J. Stillé, "Religious Tests in Provincial Pennsylvania," *Pennsylvania Magazine of History and Biography*, IX (1885), 405.
14. *Ibid.*, p. 392.   15. Smyth (ed.), *Writings*, V, 372.

time found it necessary to give them Authority by Pretences of their Antiquity. The Books of Moses indeed, if all written by him, which some doubt, are an Exception to this Observation." In order to keep from shocking his reverend correspondent, Franklin carefully kept from revealing whether he belonged to the group who doubt the inspiration of the Pentateuch, but Stiles probably assumed that he did belong.

In subscribing to the oath concerning Christian faith in the Pennsylvania Assembly, Franklin could only have been motivated by considerations of public relations and political expediency. He later confided to Joseph Priestley, August 21, 1784, that in the convention drawing up the Pennsylvania Constitution he had been opposed to the clause requiring assembly members "to declare their belief, *that the whole of it was given by divine Inspiration.*" But realizing that he was outnumbered by advocates of the clause and fearing that in the future even more might be "grafted on it," he "prevailed to have the additional Clause, 'that *no further or more extended Profession of Faith should ever be exacted.*' " Franklin comforted himself that "the Evil of it was the less, as *no Inhabitant,* nor any Officer of Government, except the Members of Assembly, were oblig'd to make that Declaration."[16] He had protected most of his fellow citizens but had not secured exemption for himself.

Franklin added his opinion "that there are several Things in the Old Testament, impossible to be given by *divine* Inspiration," a forthright statement to be compared with his equivocal one to Stiles. He explained to Priestley that he balked particularly at "the Approbation ascribed to the Angel of the Lord, of that abominably wicked and detestable Action of Jael, the wife of Heber, the Kenite. If the rest of the Book were like that, I should rather suppose it given by Inspiration from another Quarter, and renounce the whole."

According to a French historian personally acquainted with Franklin, when the latter was presiding at a session of

16. *Ibid.,* IX, 266–267.

the Pennsylvania Constitutional Convention, he made a penetrating observation concerning the required oath. He remarked that if there were in the state an atheist who was an honest man, he would not take this oath, which would deprive the state of the intelligence and assistance of a good citizen; and if there were an atheist who was dishonest, he would not hesitate, he would take the oath—and the lawmakers would have accomplished nothing.[17]

Franklin opposed religious oaths and tests in the body politic not only because they made deists profess doctrines which they rejected intellectually, but also because they supported the economic power of ecclesiastical organizations. "They were invented," he believed, "not so much to secure Religion itself, as the Emoluments of it."[18] He told a dissenting minister, Richard Price, October 9, 1780, that "If Christian Preachers had continued to teach as Christ and his Apostles did, without Salaries, and as the Quakers now do, I imagine Tests would never have existed. . . . When a Religion is good, I conceive that it will support itself; and, when it cannot support itself, and God does not take care to support, so that its Professors are oblig'd to call for the help of the Civil Power, it is a sign, I apprehend, of its being a bad one."[19]

But no matter the extent or the foundation of Franklin's opposition to oaths of religious conformity, he found them no barrier in his public career.

Probably he regarded them in the light of formalities, comparable to responses in the Anglican ritual, which a practical man could overlook or take in his stride. His grandson, William Temple Franklin, repeated an anecdote concerning the liturgy, which may be apocryphal but still illustrates Franklin's common-sense approach to conventional observances.

In one of the assemblies in America, wherein there was a majority of Presbyterians, a law was proposed to forbid the

17. Hilliard d'Auberteuil, *Essais historiques et politiques sur les Anglo-Américains* (Bruxelles, 1782), II, 135.
18. Smyth (ed.), *Writings*, VIII, 154.   19. *Ibid.*

praying for the King by the Episcopalians; who, however, could not conveniently omit that prayer, it being prescribed in their Liturgy. Dr. Franklin, one of the members, seeing that such a law would occasion more disturbance than it was worth, said, that he thought it quite *unnecessary;* for, added he, "those people have, to my certain knowledge, been praying constantly these twenty years past, that *God would give to the King and his counsel wisdom,* and we all know that not the least notice has ever been taken of that prayer; so that it is plain they have no interest in the court of Heaven."[20]

Even though Franklin rejected the divinity of Christ, he probably would not have considered any form of Christian worship as a hypocritical gesture. His early "Acts of Religion" is sufficient evidence of his need for external manifestation of inner devotion. Also he clearly affirmed in his autobiography that he had "kept several Lents most strictly."[21] Although this he may have done partially for the sake of good diet or self-discipline, he was nevertheless adhering to a positive ordinance of the church to which he belonged. Since Franklin kept Lent faithfully, he would presumably have taken communion in the same spirit, probably considering the act merely as a symbolic gesture of reverence toward God.

As a matter of fact, there exists an explicit assertion of this conclusion by William Duane, a close friend of Franklin's grandson Benjamin Franklin Bache, who married the latter's widow. Duane's relations with Franklin's family were so intimate that we must accept the following affirmation as authoritative. "Like Cicero and Sir William Jones, he acquiesced without accepting the dogmas of the prevailing systems, and even conformed in his exterior deportment, and in his family, to the usages of some one or other sect, unbiassed by any."[22]

20. *Memoirs of the Life and Writings of Benjamin Franklin* (London, 1818), I, 448.
21. Leonard W. Labaree *et al.* (eds.), *Autobiography of Benjamin Franklin* (New Haven, 1964), p. 89.
22. *Memoirs of Benjamin Franklin* (New York, 1861), I, xxiv.

Franklin in this sense resembled his friend the abbé André Morellet, who remained a Roman Catholic ecclesiastic all his life while disbelieving the entire Christian system and even attacking parts of it in his literary work. Despite his contempt for religious prejudice, Morellet died at the age of ninety-three still a virgin. "How is it," his physician asked him on his deathbed, "that an unbeliever like you still remained true to your vow of chastity?" "It was not because of superstition," the abbé replied. "Here is the whole mystery: when I had temptations, I had no opportunities; and when I had opportunities, I had no temptation."[23]

23. Translated from Gilbert Stenger, *La Société française pendant le consulat* (Paris, 1905), p. 214.

CHAPTER FIFTEEN

THE JUDAIC TRADITION

IN one sense, Franklin's preoccupation with the language of the Old Testament shows the influence of Jewish as well as Anglican tradition. At various times during his life he showed his respect and sympathy for the Jewish Scriptures by imitating them to inculcate some moral lesson. His most famous imitation of the style of the Old Testament is an object lesson concerning tolerance based upon the character of the patriarch Abraham. Purportedly a chapter from Genesis, his *jeu d'esprit* was published scores of times in the eighteenth century under the title of *A Parable Against Persecution*.

Before his imitation became well known, Franklin amused himself in social groups by presenting it as a genuine passage of Scripture. At one time he introduced it in a conversation with a literary gentleman of considerable genius ostensibly to illustrate his admiration of "the simplicity and beauty of the *Oriental* style of composition."[1] According to Priestley, who was present, Franklin opened his Bible and appeared to read, but actually quoted his own text from memory. After the literary gentleman concurred in praising the passage, Franklin revealed that it was a hoax. Then to demonstrate that people of his time were ignorant of the Scripture, Franklin again took up his Bible and read aloud the first chapter of the authentic Book of Job. This time the gentleman once more admired the style, but insisted that the chapter was no more part of the Bible than the other.

Franklin's parable, containing fifteen verses, concerns Abraham in his extreme old age. He had offered hospitality to another old man, who was passing by his tent in the evening. When the traveler refused to join him in worshiping God, Abraham drove him back into the wilderness with blows. God then appeared to Abraham, as we see in the last five verses:

1. Joseph Priestley, *Theological and Miscellaneous Works* (Hackney, n.d.), XVII, 79–80.

11. And God said, Have I born with him these hundred ninety and eight Years, and nourished him, and cloathed him, notwithstanding his Rebellion against me, and couldst not thou, that art thyself a Sinner, bear with him one Night?

12. And Abraham said, Let not the Anger of my Lord wax hot against his Servant. Lo, I have sinned; forgive me, I pray Thee:

13. And Abraham arose and went forth into the Wilderness, and sought diligently for the Man, and found him, and returned with him to his Tent; and when he had entreated him kindly, he sent him away on the Morrow with Gifts.

14. And God spake again unto Abraham, saying, For this thy Sin shall thy Seed be afflicted four Hundred Years in a strange Land:

15. But for thy Repentance will I deliver them; and they shall come forth with Power, and with Gladness of Heart, and with much Substance.[2]

The story had been told by Jeremy Taylor and other authors before Franklin, and he has as a result been accused of plagiarism. Franklin, however, never claimed the narrative itself as his own, but merely the idea of casting it into scriptural language. Literary historians who have traced the story back to ancient Jewish sources have in so doing indirectly indicated a positive link between Franklin and Judaism. "Were it really a chapter of Genesis," Lord Kames wrote, "one is apt to think, that persecution could never have shown a bare face among Jews or Christians. But alas! that is a vain thought."[3]

Another of Franklin's friends, William Strahan the printer, sent a copy of the parable to the *London Chronicle*, where it was printed April 17, 1764. In introducing it, Strahan related it to Christian traditions, particularly to the season of Easter, when the church called upon its members "to commemorate the Amazing love of HIM, who possessing the divine virtue of Charity in the most supreme degree, laid down his life EVEN FOR HIS ENEMIES."[4]

Franklin wrote another Old Testament-inspired parable

2. L. W. Labaree *et al.* (eds.), *Papers of Benjamin Franklin*, VI (New Haven, 1963), 123.
3. *Ibid.*, p. 118 n.   4. *Ibid.*, p. 117.

—one on brotherly love—but it never attained the popularity of its forerunner. Reuben bought an axe but refused to allow his brothers Simeon, Levi, or Judah to use it. Subsequently each of the three brothers bought an axe for himself, and Reuben in the meanwhile lost his. Reuben then went in turn to ask each brother whether he might borrow his axe. Simeon curtly refused; Levi rebuked him pharasaically, saying, "I will be better than thou, and will lend thee mine"; but Judah, exemplifying true brotherly love, freely offered to give Reuben his own axe. Judah's noble action proved that he had the soul of a king and that he deserved to rule over his brethren. Franklin declared that his parable was "taken from an ancient Jewish tradition" and later scholars have traced it to the Babylonian Talmud, but it still is not known where Franklin found it. The editors of the Franklin *Papers* have pointed out in regard to his version of the narrative that "his insight into the characters and relative status of the brothers and the close relation of his text at several points to particular Biblical passages . . . are evidence . . . of Franklin's thorough familiarity with the Old Testament."[5]

In a humorous vein Franklin once appealed to the authority of the Old Testament to support a favorite theory of the salutary effect of fresh air. "It is recorded of Methusalem," he wrote to Catherine Shipley, ". . . that he slept always in the open air; for, when he had lived five hundred years, an angel said to him; 'Arise, Methusalem, and build thee a house, for thou shalt live yet five hundred years longer.' But Methusalem answered, and said, 'If I am to live but five hundred years longer, it is not worth while to build me a house; I will sleep in the air, as I have been used to do.' "[6]

The perplexed Catherine searched the Bible in vain for this intriguing passage which is a parody of the Scriptures,

5. *Ibid.*, p. 126.
6. Albert Henry Smyth (ed.), *Writings of Benjamin Franklin* (10 vols., New York, 1905–1907), X, 133–134.

unlike Franklin's two parables which imitate the moral seriousness as well as the style of the Scriptures. The intention of parody is to ridicule or at least to produce a comic effect. We have seen that Franklin used it very effectively in the *Pennsylvania Gazette* in his ridicule of lugubrious religious meditations. But he seems never to have permitted himself any public disparagement of the Scripture. In his autobiography he expressed his disapprobation of one of his acquaintances, a Pennsylvania quack named Browne, for using his literary abilities to bring reproach upon the Scriptures. This man, Franklin explained, "wickedly undertook . . . to travesty the Bible in doggrel Verse as Cotton had done Virgil. By this means he set many of the Facts in a very ridiculous Light, and might have hurt weak minds if his Work had been publish'd."[7] Later in the century Franklin specifically denounced ridicule of the Scripture as a "species of profaneness." He expressed the theory to Priestley that this form of jest had become extinct because the Scriptures "were no longer read by such persons as were used to take that liberty with them."[8]

Franklin himself, however, certainly took liberties with the Book of Job, preparing during his London sojourn two brief commentaries, one interpreting it as a political allegory and the other suggesting a translation in modern idiom to support the political interpretation.

Observing in the latter piece that over 170 years had passed since the King James translation of the Bible, Franklin pointed out that "the language in that time is much changed, and the style, being obsolete, and thence less agreeable, is perhaps one reason why the reading of that excellent book is of late so much neglected."[9] His illustrations from the first chapter were designed to show how the sense may be

---

7. Leonard W. Labaree *et al.* (eds.), *Autobiography of Benjamin Franklin* (New Haven, 1964), p. 74.
8. John Towill Rutt, *Life and Correspondance of Joseph Priestley* (London, 1831), XVII, 30.
9. Smyth (ed.), *Writings*, VII, 432–433.

preserved while the turn of phrase and manner of expression are modernized. Following is the sixth verse:

OLD TEXT: Now there was a day when the sons of God came to present themselves before the Lord, and Satan came also amongst them.

NEW VERSION: And it being *levée* day in heaven, all God's nobility came to court, to present themselves before him; and Satan also appeared in the circle, as one of the ministry.

Franklin's companion political allegory, entitled "The Levée," presents Job's dialogue with God in the light of a discussion between a modern king and his courtiers and can be considered in part propaganda for the American colonies in the Revolution.[10] The moral which Franklin deduced from the Book of Job as a whole, "Trust not a single person with the government of your state," is undoubtedly designed to illustrate the superiority of republican to monarchical government.

According to Franklin, the dialogue of the first chapter of Job takes place at the court or levee "of the best of all possible princes, or of governments by a single person, viz. that of God himself." The "sons of God" were assembled at this levee, and Satan also appeared. It is usual at such gatherings for those who are enemies to each other to "seek to obtain favor by whispering calumny and detraction, and thereby ruining those that distinguish themselves by their virtue and merit." The king asks familiar questions of everyone in the group merely to show his benignity.

If a modern king, for instance, finds a person in the circle who has not lately been there, he naturally asks him how he has passed his time since he last had the pleasure of seeing him? the gentleman perhaps replies that he has been in the country to view his estates, and visit some friends. Thus Satan being asked whence he cometh? answers, "From going to and fro in the earth, and walking up and down in it." And being further asked, whether he had considered the uprightness and fidelity of the prince's servant Job, he immediately displays all the malignance of the designing courtier,

10. *Ibid.*, pp. 430–432.

by answering with another question: "Doth Job serve God for naught? Hast thou not given him immense wealth, and protected him in the possession of it? Deprive him of that, and he will curse thee to thy face." In modern phrase, Take away his places and his pensions, and your Majesty will soon find him in the opposition.

The result of this whispering was to deliver Job into the power of his adversary and eventually to bring about his total ruin. The theme of Franklin's new interpretation is the revelation of the danger inherent in an excessive concentration of power "in a mere man, though the best of men, from whom the truth is often industriously hidden, and to whom falsehood is often presented in its place, by artful, interested, and malicious courtiers."

Franklin knew, of course, the traditional interpretation of the narrative as an explanation of evil in the universe and alluded to it briefly by concluding that "the Deity himself . . . may for a time give way to calumny, and suffer it to operate the destruction of the best of subjects." Many years before in his ridicule of melancholy meditations in the *Pennsylvania Gazette,* he had condemned what he considered a logical fallacy in the entire narrative as an allegory of evil. "I never thought," he had written, "even *Job* in the right, when he repin'd that the Days of a Man are *few* and *full of Trouble;* for certainly both these Things cannot be together just Causes of Complaint; if our Days are full of Trouble, the fewer of 'em the better."[11]

Even though we accept "The Levée" as a serious interpretation of the allegory of Job, we may see in it also an expression of Franklin's pique at his treatment at the hands of the British lords. As a colonial agent, he was required to submit to a considerable amount of heel-cooling in the precincts of the British Parliament, and he may have been comparing Satan to some of the courtiers who received precedence over him.

11. A. O. Aldridge, "A Religious Hoax by Benjamin Franklin," *American Literature,* XXXVI (1964), 204–209.

Also, Franklin's project to discard the obsolete language of the King James translation for modern idiom may have been intended to encourage an actual undertaking to convert "the bold and barbarous language of the old vulgar version" into "the elegance of modern English." Edward Harwood in 1768 —approximately the presumed period of Franklin's squibs— published a *Liberal Translation of the New Testament: Being an Attempt to translate the Sacred Writings with the same Freedom, Spirit and Elegance with which other English Translations of the Greek Classics have lately been executed.* Franklin's proposals for Bible translation, whether facetious or serious, were at any rate not unique.

Franklin later treated Old Testament Scriptures less respectfully in a commentary on the obstructionist tactics of the opponents of the new Constitution of the United States. In an essay filled with parallels from Mosaic history comparing "The Conduct of the Ancient Jews and of the Anti-Federalists in the United States of America" (1788), he revealed a disdainful attitude toward the theory of a chosen people, particularly in a summary of the history of the thirteen tribes before the appointment of the theocracy.[12] According to Franklin, the Supreme Being nourished this "single Family" by continued acts of favor until it became a great people. Then he delivered to his servant Moses "a Constitution and Code of Laws," appointing Aaron and his sons together with Moses to govern under it. Yet discontented, restless spirits in each of the tribes continually stirred up opposition to the new government. By copious references to Numbers and Exodus, Franklin outlined the motives for dissension. Some still retained an affection for Egypt; others preferred idolatry. Those who were afraid that Moses would engross all the government sinecures for his own family accused him of ambition and peculation. Moses denied the charge, but his enemies gained headway with the populace, "for no kind of Accusation is so readily made, or easily

12. Smyth (ed.), *Writings*, IX, 698–703.

believ'd, by Knaves as the Accusation of Knavery." Two hundred and fifty of the principal men of the congregation, "heading and exciting the Mob, worked them up to such a pitch of Frenzy, that they called out, 'Stone 'em, stone 'em, and thereby *secure our Liberties.*' " This was not a pretty picture of the Israelites—and Franklin did not intend it to be.

Although his primary purpose may have been to ridicule opponents of the federal Constitution, his method was the method of Shaftesbury, Peter Annet, Voltaire, and other deists who sneered at the vices of God's "chosen people." If the anti-Federalists were made to look ridiculous in Franklin's parallel, the Old Testament characters were equally so. Franklin was not ridiculing the Scriptures as such. We have already seen that he opposed parodies of the Bible, but he was certainly portraying Old Testament characters in an unfavorable light. This was as far as he ever allowed himself to go in public, but in private he did not disguise his barbs. One of his contemporaries reported that "in his conversation with some intimates, the miracles of the Old Testament have frequently employed the sallies of his wit and humour."[13]

In the conclusion of his essay, Franklin drew attention away from the ancient Jews by affirming his belief that the federal Constitution was in some degree divinely inspired. Because of his faith "in the general Government of the world by *Providence,*" he could hardly conceive that "a Transaction of momentous Importance to the Welfare of Millions now existing, and to exist in the Posterity of a great Nation, should be suffered to pass without being in some degree influenc'd, guided and governed by that omnipotent, omnipresent, and beneficent Ruler, in whom all inferior Spirits live, and move, and have their Being."

Echoes of both Old and New Testament language and symbols in Franklin's other writings are almost as numerous

13. James I. Wilmer, *Memoirs of the Late Dr. Benjamin Franklin* (London, 1790) , p. 90.

as the sum of all the congregation of the children of Israel. During his days as an editor in Pennsylvania he constantly called in "the Aid of Religion" by couching in scriptural language his appeals for defense of the colony or for charitable projects. Like Thomas Paine in *Common Sense*, Franklin appealed to the authority of the Bible, not because he believed it himself but because most of his readers did.

His habit of using scriptural quotations and phraseology was so ingrained that even in his old age he kept it up with correspondents as skeptical of divine inspiration as himself. In writing to John Adams about his governmental borrowing at the French court, for example, he revealed that he was "quite sick of my Gibeonite office—that of drawing water for the whole congregation of Israel."[14] And to justify deducting his own salary and expenses from funds passing through his hands, he remarked to Robert Morris that he supposed "it not intended to *muzzle* immediately *the mouth of the ox that treadeth out the corn.*"[15]

Even more impressive evidence of Franklin's Biblical knowledge appears in connection with one of his minor editorial activities in France. In an edition of Samuel Cooper's sermons which he was editing for European readers, he noted in the margins the sources of scriptural verses and phrases.[16]

We have already noticed that some of Franklin's proposed changes in the Lord's Prayer were designed to eliminate alleged Jewish taboos and superstitions as well as political complaints of the Israelites. But these apparently unfavorable references to Jewish tradition reflect merely the deistical theme of ridiculing the concept of the "chosen seed of Israel's race." Franklin came close to actual anti-Semitism, however, in negotiations during the American Revolution with a greedy financier of Amsterdam, John de Neufville. Franklin allowed his resentment of this man's profiteering to reflect upon Jews in general. His animosity was first aroused when

14. Smyth (ed.), *Writings*, VIII, 378. 16. *Ibid.*, p. 257.
15. *Ibid.*, p. 584.

Neufville held back delivery of some supplies for America until he was reimbursed for minor damages suffered in the transaction. "Tho' I believe him to be as much a Jew as any in Jerusalem," Franklin wrote to John Adams (November 26, 1781), "I did not expect that with so many & such constant Professions of Friendship for the United States with which he loads all his Letters, he would have attempted to inforce his Demands (which I doubt not will be extravagant enough) by a Proceeding so abominable."[17]

In the next month Franklin reported to Adams his negotiations with the same person for a loan to America in which an exorbitant interest had been demanded. Franklin let loose his fury. "By this time, I fancy, your Excellency is satisfy'd, that I was wrong in supposing J de Neufville as much a Jew as any in Jerusalem, since Jacob was not content with any per cents, but took the whole of his Brother Esau's Birthright, & his Posterity did the same by the Cananites, & cut their Throats into the Bargain; which, in my Conscience, I do not think Mr. J de Neufville has the least Inclination to do by us,—while he can get any thing by our being alive."[18] Here Franklin allowed his principles of toleration to be overcome by exasperation but was saved from outright anti-Semitism by his knowledge of the Old Testament. In condemning an unscrupulous individual by means of that person's own Scripture, Franklin was using the Jewish tradition to criticize offensive behavior rather than criticizing the tradition itself.

The notion has been rather widely held on other grounds, however, that Franklin held anti-Semitic opinions—and this erroneous notion should be refuted here. It grew out of a piece of racist propaganda circulated throughout the United States in the 1930's. The document consists of a purported anti-Jewish speech or prophecy by Franklin allegedly taken from a transcription by "Charles Pinckney of South Carolina, of the proceedings of the Constitutional Convention of

17. *Ibid.*, p. 332.   18. *Ibid.*, p. 345.

1789." The speech accused the Jews of a depraved moral level, of predatory financial conduct, and of unwillingness to be assimilated. It predicted, moreover, that the Jews would overrun and destroy America unless excluded by the Constitution. The piece was issued in several versions, the most common of which asserts that the original manuscript of Pinckney's journal is deposited in the Franklin Institute in Philadelphia.

A number of reputable historians have proved that this "prophecy" is a forgery. There is no original in the Franklin Institute or anywhere else. The fraud has been traced to an Asheville, North Carolina, periodical, *Liberation,* where the speech appeared for the first time, February 3, 1934, as a deliberate weapon of Nazi propaganda.

Not only is Franklin guiltless of the fanatical hatred of the forged attack, but he also took a positive stand in favor of the Jewish people of Philadelphia. Along with many other public-spirited citizens of the city, he helped to keep the Synagogue of the Congregation Mikveh Israel from being auctioned for debt. Franklin contributed five pounds toward a subscription fund of 800 pounds drawn up on April 30, 1788.[19]

Yet there is no use pretending that Franklin's principles of tolerance enabled him to treat all religions on the same footing. As we have seen, he combined Puritan and deistic strains in his intellectual life. In his day, the Puritans—oriented toward the Old Testament—by and large held very favorable opinions of the Jews, whereas the deists considered the Biblical tales of Jewish heroes as subjects of scorn and derision. Franklin certainly shared deistical antipathies against sects which professed exclusiveness of any kind, the Catholics in one way, the Jews in another.

Although tolerance is one of the primary themes in Franklin's religious life, his toleration was moral and political rather than intellectual. And his intellectual deism always

19. Labaree (ed.), *Autobiography,* pp. 146–147 n.

took precedence over his social toleration. Even in his most tolerant moments, Franklin never went as far as Thomas Paine's declaration "Every religion is good that teaches man to be good; and I know of none that instructs him to be bad."

In his autobiography he affirmed that he respected all the religions in Philadelphia, although with different degrees of respect. He highly approved those which tended "to inspire, promote or confirm Morality" and had little use for those which tended "to divide us and make us unfriendly to one another." Franklin's respect to all churches "with an Opinion that the worst had some good Effects" led him "to avoid all Discourse that might tend to lessen the good Opinion another might have of his own Religion."[20] With slightly less exactitude and considerably more complacence, he revealed to Ezra Stiles that "All Sects here, and we have a great Variety, have experienced my good will in assisting them with Subscriptions for building their new Places of Worship; and, as I have never opposed any of their Doctrines, I hope to go out of the World in Peace with them all."[21]

Franklin supported all varieties of religious belief because he believed that in the long run all had a salutary influence upon society. This is why he was reputed to have wished for the establishment of a sect of Musselmans in Philadelphia— particularly so that they might influence their fellow citizens to drink less wine. Purportedly, he advised the city of Philadelphia, "Encourage the makers of religions—in this domain nothing but competition is salutary."[22]

20. *Ibid.*, p. 146.
21. Smyth (ed.), *Writings*, X, 85.
22. Translated from *La Clef du cabinet des souverains,* November 18, 1797, p. 2818.

CHAPTER SIXTEEN

UNITARIANS AND DEISTS

So far we have had little to say about Franklin's actual attendance at religious services, concerning ourselves primarily with the intellectual and historical foundations of his belief. It is important to emphasize, however, that his concern for worship was more than theoretical and that he always felt a need for active participation in organized worship.

He disliked long, empty, and pretentious displays of piety but respected the symbols of religious homage. He once explained that he could not bring himself to rescue his character from the imputation of irreligion "by attending the long tedious services of the church, yet he never passed a place of public worship on a Sunday, without feeling some regret, that he had not an opportunity of joining in a rational form of devotion."[1] The publication of his liturgy did practically nothing to help his religious life, for, as we have seen, the revised prayer book was never used in churches— except possibly at Le Despencer's Church of St. Lawrence. Franklin was forced to go beyond the Church of England in his quest for the form of group devotion which would be compatible with his mind and personality.

In the early fall of 1772 he wrote to a well-known dissenting preacher, Richard Price, remarking that Sir John Pringle had asked where he could "hear a preacher of *rational* Christianity." Franklin knew several of them, but not the location of their churches in town. He proposed that they attend Price's services in Newington on the following Sunday. But so that on subsequent Sundays Pringle "could take a round" among various churches, Franklin asked Price for a list of liberal preachers in all parts of London.[2]

Franklin's personal acquaintance with ministers was exten-

1. Thomas Morris, *General View of the Life and Writings of the Rev. David Williams* (London, 1792) , p. 11.
2. Albert Henry Smyth (ed.), *Writings of Benjamin Franklin* (10 vols., New York, 1905–1907) , V, 440.

sive, for he belonged to a number of social and philan-thropic organizations. One of these was the Honest Whigs, a social literary club, which embraced in its membership a number of liberal clergymen, including Price, Priestley, and Theophilus Lindsey.[3] The meetings of the Honest Whigs were originally held at a coffee house in St. Paul's Church-yard and later moved to the London Coffee-house at Ludgate Hill.

Although the Honest Whigs was a social rather than a political group, the members subscribed to the principles associated with the liberal wing of the Whig movement. To be sure, distinctions between Whigs and Tories in the sec-ond half of the eighteenth century were rather nebulous, but Whigs in general considered themselves as exponents of religious toleration. Franklin himself is said to have written a character sketch of a Whig in which he indicated the rela-tionship between advanced political thinking and religious liberalism.

> The Whig lives in every state, but wishes to live only in a free state. He claims no right to himself, but what he is willing to give to his neighbour. He is not listed in sects by sounds, nor kept in them by prejudice; his mind is not contracted by systems, nor soured by bigots; it is open to God and nature. He is not attached to person or faction; but to things, to justice, to liberty, to virtue, to his country. He adheres to the men who adhere to these; and adheres to them no longer than they adhere to these. Not lurking, as a drone, to reap what others sow, he chearfully acts his part in society; he does what he can; he endeavours within his sphere to promote the general welfare. No matter what you call him; what his rank, his profession, or the title of his religion, this is the Whig; and many such, to their immortal honor, has Providence raised up for the defence of Liberty.[4]

Among the members of the Honest Whigs, Franklin con-sidered Priestley as an intimate friend, and his relations with Lindsey were more than casual, for he supported Lindsey's

---

3. Verner W. Crane, "The Club of Honest Whigs, Friends of Science and Liberty," *William and Mary Quarterly,* 3rd ser., XXIII (1966), 210–233.
4. *Gazetteer and New Daily Advertiser,* July 21, 1790.

attempt to establish the first Unitarian chapel in England.

Lindsey, known as the "father of Unitarian Churchmanship," had been ordained in the Church of England shortly after being elected a Fellow of St. John's College, Cambridge, in 1747. He held various livings in the Church of England until the latter part of 1773, when he resigned his benefice and withdrew himself from the communion of the Church of England.[5] Under the influence of Priestley, whom he had met in 1769, he had become "persuaded that there was but One God, the Father, the sole object of prayer and religious worship."[6]

Because of his excessive modesty and diffidence, however, Lindsey was singularly unfit to be the rallying point of Arianism. His strong-minded friends, nevertheless, organized to provide a chapel where he could expound his unitarian principles. The publisher Joseph Johnson found a suitable assembly room on the second floor of a house in the Strand, and on April 11, 1774, made application to the Westminster Justices "for the registration of Essex Chapel as a place of dissenting worship."

Franklin seems to have been one of Lindsey's enthusiastic patrons, for on opening day, April 17, 1774, he sent brief notes to two of his friends, inviting them to meet him at the service. One was sent to his collaborator on the revised prayer book. "Dr. Franklin presents his respects to Lord Le Despencer, and acquaints him, that Mr. Lindsey's Church opens this Day at 11 o'clock, in Essex House, Essex Street, Strand; and that if his Lordship continues his intention of being there, Dr. F. will be ready to attend him." The other was sent to George Whatley, treasurer of the Foundling Hospital and a close friend of Lord Le Despencer. "I have just sent my Lord Le Despencer Word, that the Place is Essex House, in Essex Street, Strand: the Hour Eleven.—I shall be

5. H. McLachlan, *Letters of Theophilus Lindsey* (Manchester, 1920), *passim.*
6. "Introduction" to *Two Dissertations. I. On the Preface to St. John's Gospel. II. On Praying to Jesus Christ* (London, 1779).

glad to meet you there.—Thanks for the Pamphlet, &c." These notes conjure up an intriguing picture: Dr. Franklin and his friends seated with a small group of worshipers in the converted auction hall.

Lindsey took as text for his sermon Ephesians 4:3, "Endeavouring to keep the unity of the Spirit in the bond of peace."[7] He defined unity of spirit as kindness and harmony among Christians and argued that mankind in their religious observances are subject only to the authority of God and their own consciences. We may suggest reasons to other men to persuade them to adopt our opinions, but that is as far as we may legitimately go. The words of Christ and the Scriptures may be variously interpreted, and it would be ridiculous for anyone to insist that his own sense be adopted as authority. Peace and unity do not depend upon bringing all Christians to the same opinion in religion. Certainly God never designed that Christians be formed into one great church. Uniformity of opinion is not required—nor can it be obtained. The difference of sects in a country does not disturb public peace and quiet but develops better Christians and more useful citizens.

The design of the congregation at Essex Chapel, Lindsey concluded, was "to join together in the public worship of Almighty God." They had separated from the national church so that they could be "at liberty *to worship God alone,* after the command and example of our Saviour Christ."

This sermon was delivered before an audience "as respectable for rank and character as were ever collected together upon a similar occasion." Franklin attended in company with Le Despencer, who subscribed handsomely to the expenses of the enterprise. Lindsey did not use the Franklin-Despencer liturgy but another reformed version by Samuel

7. *A Sermon preached at the Opening of the Chapel in Essex House . . . to which is added, A summary account of the Reformed Liturgy, on the plan of the late Dr. Samuel Clarke, made use of in the said Chapel* (London, 1774).

Clarke to which he had made further alterations of his own.

Although the Unitarianism of the twentieth century may have much in common with the deistical creeds of Franklin and Paine, that of the eighteenth century looked upon deism with horror. Priestley and Lindsey believed in the divine inspiration of the Scriptures and differed from orthodox Anglicans and dissenters only by denying the doctrine of the Trinity.

In his memoirs Priestley lamented that a man of Dr. Franklin's general good character and great influence should have been an unbeliever in Christianity and also have done so much as he did to make others unbelievers. Somewhat pretentiously, Priestley affirmed that Franklin had once asked him to recommend some treatises on the evidences of Christianity, acknowledging that he had not given as much attention to the subject as he ought to have done.[8] Priestley had recommended the relevant sections of Hartley's *Observations on Man* and his own *Institutes of Natural and Revealed Religion*. Unfortunately, according to Priestley, the American war broke out soon after and Franklin consequently lacked sufficient leisure to pursue his investigation.

In conversing with Benjamin Rush, Priestley more modestly portrayed himself merely as an observer of Franklin's religion. From Franklin's often saying "he should like to peep out of his grave a hundred years hence," Priestley concluded "that he did not believe in a future state." Franklin acknowledged "a belief only in the Being of a God and a particular providence" and he also "said that he had made many Deists."[9]

Priestley was giving way to his own vanity when he sought to give the impression that Franklin would not have had deistical opinions had he met Priestley earlier in life—or that he would have changed them had providence given him the

8. John T. Rutt (ed.), *Life and Correspondence of Joseph Priestley* (London, 1831), I, 212.

9. Benjamin Rush, Commonplace Book, June 4, 1794, in George W. Comer (ed.), *The Autobiography of Benjamin Rush* (Philadelphia, 1948), p. 231.

time to profit by his association with the great Joseph. It was just as preposterous for him to suggest that Franklin lacked knowledge of either the Scriptures or Christian theology. Franklin's deism certainly was not a result of his being deprived of Christian evidences. As we have seen, he had pursued the question from many aspects long before meeting Priestley.

Although Priestley made no attempt to claim Franklin as a Unitarian, a member of a kindred sect, the Universalists, looked upon him as a fellow spirit. In the year of his death, Mrs. John Murray, wife of a leading Universalist clergyman, affirmed on the authority of Franklin's daughter that the philosopher believed "that no system in the Christian world was so effectually calculated to promote the interests of society, as that doctrine which shows a God reconciling a lapsed world into himself."[10] The key phrase in this sentence, "to promote the interests of society," certainly has the ring of Franklin.

During the same year that Franklin was listening to the unitarian doctrine of Lindsey, he collaborated with a political philosopher, David Williams, in preparing another system of public worship. Openly deistical, it was far more radical than the order of service in his own and Le Despencer's prayer book or that of Clarke and Lindsey.

Williams in 1773 had published a book, *Essays on Public Worship, Patriotism and Projects of Reformation,* in which he expressed the need for a new liturgy and advocated that the language of the Book of Common Prayer be used as a model. He affirmed that "all disputed opinions should be excluded from public worship, and all honest, pious men, Calvinists, Arians, Socinians, Jews, Turks and Infidels, might and ought to worship God together in spirit and in truth." A suitable liturgy, therefore, would contain only those universal principles upon which all men could agree. Those wor-

10. *The Life of Rev. John Murray . . . Written by Himself* (Boston, 1870), p. 353 n.

shiping on this plan could hold whatever doctrines they wished privately, but in public worship they would join in affirming the essentials. The Trinitarian would make no reference to the particular form in which he felt that the deity existed—nor indeed would the Christian even describe himself as a Christian.

This is exactly the theory of Franklin's scheme of virtue which is outlined in his autobiography. Franklin explained, "tho' my Scheme was not wholly without Religion there was in it no Mark of any of the distinguishing Tenets of any particular Sect. I had purposely avoided them; . . . that it might be serviceable to People in all Religions."[11]

Franklin was very favorably impressed with Williams' idea, and he bought and distributed a number of copies of the pamphlet. When he gave one to Colonel Dawson, lieutenant governor of the Isle of Man, the colonel said, "I suppose you know the Author, Doctor."[12] Franklin replied that he did not but would like to. The colonel promised to arrange the introduction, and on the appointed day, Franklin, Williams, Dawson, and Thomas Bentley, an associate of the potter Josiah Wedgwood, met at the Old Slaughter Coffee House "over a Neck of Veal and Potatoes." Here they formed another of the ubiquitous philosophical clubs of the century, the Society of Thirteen. Some of its other distinguished members were Daniel Charles Solander, eminent botanist; Sir Joseph Banks, later president of the Royal Society; James Stuart, painter and architect; and Thomas Day, novelist and exponent of Rousseauistic doctrines.

The purpose of the club, according to Thomas Morris, Williams' eighteenth-century biographer, "was an unlimited freedom of conversation; and it continued the great delight of the members until Franklin departed in 1774."[13] Williams

11. Leonard W. Labaree *et al.* (eds.), *Autobiography of Benjamin Franklin* (New Haven, 1964), p. 157.
12. Williams' autobiography quoted in David Williams, "More Light on Franklin's Religious Ideas," *American Historical Review*, XLIII (1938), 810.
13. *General View*, p. 10.

later affirmed that *"Franklin, Stuart,* and *Bentley,* have left no men in this country to be compared with them in the 'delicate and difficult art of conversation.' "

At one of the meetings of the club which happened to fall on a religious festival, somebody observed "that the members in general, though very good men, much beloved by their friends, and some of them much admired by the public, were under the imputation of irreligion, because they never went to church."[14] Franklin, who was expected to be flippant on the subject, expressed his regret at the lack of an organized rational form of devotion. According to Williams, "he thought it a reproach to Philosophy that it had not a Liturgy and that it skulked from the public Profession of its Principles."[15]

At a subsequent meeting eight of the members including Franklin gave lengthy opinions in favor of adopting a philosophical liturgy, and Williams "was requested either to compile or to draw up a Specimen for the consideration of those Members of the Club, who would attend its first reading on a given day, at the Lodgings of Dr. Franklin."

Williams produced the desired specimen in a short time and tried it on the members on the agreed occasion. Twelve of the thirteen members were present for the reading and rereading of the liturgy, after which it was sent to the press. After correcting it six times, the members ordered an edition of fifteen hundred or two thousand copies. Such a large number was not excessive, according to Williams, "if the Period be considered in which this Project was conceived, when the Press governed everything, and the reputation of Dr. Franklin was at a height which scarcely any Talents or Morals could deserve. . . . Multitudes of Demi-Philosophers would have flocked to have the honor of associating with Dr. Franklin in any form of Worship." Had it not been for the approach of the American Revolution which restricted

14. *Ibid.,* p. 11.
15. Williams, "More Light on Franklin's Religious Ideas," p. 810.

Franklin's public activities, the effects of the liturgy "would have been extensive and important."

At the first reading of the liturgy, Franklin is supposed to have named Williams "Priest of Nature," a term by which he was commonly known thereafter.

The projectors envisaged the putting of their liturgy into use in regular services in a deistical chapel—on a plan similar to that of Lindsey's unitarian scheme of worship. Williams described the liturgy as a "form of social worship composed on the most enlarged and general principles" in which all men may join, including Jews, Christians, and Mohammedans.

Originally the founders proposed to form a society which would cover the expenses of the services by subscription. At the last moment, however, some of the members partially backed out. They expressed a willingness "to subscribe or to take Pews, but not to form a body, as had been first proposed, to conduct the Undertaking and to be responsable for the expence." Williams decided to go ahead on his own responsibility. He rented a chapel on Margaret Street, Cavendish Square, for one part of the Sunday—the Methodists using it on the other—and issued a public advertisement for the first meeting. According to Williams' autobiography, "no Person gave me ostensible assistance, a hired clerk alone opened the book of Subscriptions in the Vestry, and told the People who crowded into it my name."

The weak-hearted members of the society were apparently afraid that the authorities would oppose the meeting on political grounds. According to Thomas Holcroft, *"Banks and Solander acted with great shyness, if not hypocrisy, and instead of countenancing Williams, and promoting the plan, they now and then peeped into the chapel, and got away as fast as they decently could."*[16] When it was finally apparent that the project would offend no one, a new organization

16. Elbridge Colby (ed.), *The Life of Thomas Holcroft Written by Himself* (London, 1925), II, 198.

was formed, and Williams conducted services and delivered sermons, or lectures, for four years.

Despite Franklin's warm interest in the preparation of the liturgy, there is no evidence that he ever attended a service in which it was used. He returned to America eleven months before the opening of the Margaret Street Chapel in April, 1776.

During that year Williams sent Franklin copies of the liturgy, but they were presumably lost in transit. In September, 1778, when Franklin was in France, Williams sent him a circumstantial account of the launching of the chapel.

> I was assured of a large subscription by a Society consisting mostly of my provincial Neighbours & Acquaintance; some of whom accompanied me to your house. On your departure I lost them wholly, as well as several others who had appeared sanguine in supporting the Design. Some of the Gentlemen who met at the Coffee house & at your Room to read the Liturgy, were disposed to become Subscribers, if I chose to hazard the Undertaking. I opened the Chapel therefore, on the seventh of April as an Adventure. Great Numbers came to it out of Curiosity; some behaved indecently; & all with a shy timidity; excepting two or three of my particular friends.[17]

Williams planned to publish the lectures he had delivered at the chapel and sent Franklin printed proposals with the request that he procure subscriptions in the intervals of his more important business at the French court. He asked also that Franklin send "that little *moral work* which you had thought of finishing when you left England; to which there was *not much to be done;* and which you wished to have distributed with the Liturgy at the Chapel. It was written in a little Pocket-Book." This is a highly important reference to Franklin's "Art of Virtue," which he eventually included in the second part of his autobiography written in France in 1784. Williams' letter shows that Franklin had apparently considered publishing it as an addendum to the liturgy. The

17. Nicholas Hans, "Franklin, Jefferson and the English Radicals at the End of the Eighteenth Century," *Proceedings of the American Philosophical Society*, XCVIII (1954), 409.

combination of liturgy and ethical system would presumably have represented Franklin's mature conception of a deistical religious handbook.

Another member of the society, Dr. William Hodgson, learned of Williams' aspersions on members of his congregation—his insinuation that all those who had met at Franklin's lodgings to prepare the liturgy had later slunk off—"conveying the idea that he had been ill treated and deceived." Hodgson wrote to Franklin, May 12, 1780, affirming that this was "a gross falsehood," since almost every man had subscribed to the chapel and supported Williams.[18] Hodgson further informed Franklin that he had complained to Williams of this misrepresentation and declared that he would explain to Franklin the true circumstances of the affair. Hodgson's remonstrance "lay brooding" upon Williams' mind until he vented his spleen in an abusive letter in the London press, a copy of which Hodgson enclosed. "You will see that in order to blacken me you are introduced and others to whose principles at least he professed attachment but revenge knocks down all these barriers." This episode may explain the disparaging references to Franklin in some of Williams' later publications. Apparently his liturgy had no effect in developing sweetness of temper.

In his autobiography, Williams stated that he was obliged to give up his deistical services after four years because of "many causes, of a public and private nature." For one thing, the finances were inadequate and badly managed. Also, dissensions arose concerning the doctrine to be preached. According to Williams,

> those who associated, at the first preparation of the Liturgy were Shaftesburyists, i. e. Deists, acknowledging a Supreme Being, having moral attributes and holding the Immortal spirits of men accountable in a future state. But these Persons were soon superceded by the Disciples of Helvétius, and the admirers of the *Système de la Nature*. Controversies therefore took place, and introduced in new forms the spirit of

18. *Ibid.*, p. 411.

Hostility and Intolerance which the general Nature of the Public Service was intended to remove. I had no person, like Franklin, to assist me in that species of meditation which the occasion required, and in recalling all Parties to the first principles of Universal Toleration, on which the Society had been formed. [The deistical and atheistical factions] contended for the public acknowledgment of what it denominated the Truth, as religious Sects contend for Orthodoxy, whereas the Society had been originally formed to recognise those principles and maxims of Morals on which all Philosophical and Religious Sectaries had been always united.[19]

Thomas Holcroft reported another internal controversy: Bentley urged Williams to insist on the immortality of the soul in his lectures, but *"Williams* replied he could and would teach no other doctrines than such as agreed with the original plan." Holcroft did not attribute the failure of the chapel to dissensions among the members, however, but to deficiencies in Williams' preaching.

Williams in his autobiography left a detailed statement of the principles upon which his liturgy and lectures were based. Presumably these were accepted by Franklin as well.

> The God of Newton was probably the regulating Principle or Good of the Solar System. The God of a Nation or of a Sect is always the Spirit of that Nation or Sect, whatever be its nature. These are local Gods.
>
> What Principles may govern or preserve other Systems we know not, and therefore know not their Gods. It is probable that all the Systems of Nature are governed and preserved by a relative Principle or Law, and that governing Principle is the Universal God.
>
> It is to local Gods, those of various Nations, Sects and Parties that Theologists have generally ascribed the dominion of the Universe, and the ministers of these Gods have imputed to them their own Properties, to sanctify their own Views, and they have justified the imputation by the Sophism "that causes and effects are similar."
>
> It was my wish to direct the attention of the Society to the universal Good, not to the spirit of a Nation or a Party, to the general feelings of our Nature, and the general results of our Organisation, which are ever in harmony with those Circumstances we call Good.

19. Williams, p. 811.

The moral Sense, the principle of Universal Virtue, seems to precede all those comparisons and calculations by which afterwards the preference of Goodness may be demonstrated.[20]

Most unusual in this statement is the reference to the gods of other systems and the local gods of our own system. This is a direct link, of course, to the polytheism of Franklin's youthful "Articles of Belief."

The reference to Newton becomes quite significant in the light of our previous suggestion that Franklin's notion of subordinate gods is based upon Newtonian science.

While Williams was holding services at Margaret Street, he was satirized in a long mock-heroic poem, *Orpheus, Priest of Nature, and Prophet of Infidelity; or, the Eleusinian Mysteries Revived.* Franklin plays an important part in the action as he throws open his house for "The first Experiments of the Priest of Nature, in developing the Mysteries of Infidelity." During the rites Franklin approaches the throne of Orpheus and addresses him with deference:

> All hail illustrious ORPHEUS! erst my Friend!
> Deliverer from *Old Gods!* to thee I bend!
> To crown this *sapient aera* thou wert born,
> This *aera,* which so nobly *I* adorn
> To combat *old religious whims,* is thine,
> To overturn *old Governments,* is mine.
> To laugh at *Heaven's dread fires* I teach mankind,
> From *fires below* do Thou set free their Mind!
> Or say, We join our powers? what *infant Sect*
> Can without *wonders* its weak head erect?
> My magic *Kite,* all my *Electric* skill
> Shall be subservient to thy guiding will.
> Compose, harangue, procure the melting lay;
> While I work *miracles,* and *signs* display.
> Besides, thy plan to consecrate, what name
> Can vie with *mine,* in dignity and fame?

After this address, several eminent members of the Royal Society appear but quarrel among themselves and abandon the group.

20. Williams, p. 812.

But now amid the *Philosophic croud*
All was rude clamour, and disorder loud.
Not FRANKLIN'S art th'obstreperous *mob* could awe,
For *mobs* are still averse to *sense* and *law*.

In concluding our discussion of Franklin's pleasure in belonging to a congregation, his feeling of well-being through participating in a communion of praise and thanksgiving which was lacking from purely rational forms of devotion, we must not overlook an important source of this pleasure. Like Peter Miller and the Pennsylvania Dunkards, Franklin recognized the appropriateness of music as an avenue of approach to God. In his autobiography he said nothing about this form of spiritual satisfaction, and in his Junto lecture on providence he even complimented his audience for believing "a Thing to be no more true for being sung than said." But his own church attendance was undoubtedly at times inspired not by the doctrine, "but the music there." Franklin himself invented one of the musical novelties of the eighteenth century, an instrument known as the harmonica or glass-organ, based on earlier instruments utilizing glasses filled with varying amounts of water to give out notes on the musical scale. The instrument attained an enormous vogue, and such musical giants as Beethoven and Mozart composed for it.

Peter Miller wrote to Franklin in 1786 that he was of the opinion "that among all musical Instruments none would insinuate itself better with human Voices than Your Excellency's new-invented Glass-Organ. The human Voice is a most noble Instrument, by which a Man may reveal his most intimate Recesses, even as God Himself made known by His eternal Word."[21]

And another clergyman, Nathaniel Evans, several years earlier wrote a poem "To Benjamin Franklin, Esq., L.L.D. Occasioned by hearing him play on the HARMONICA,"

21. *Church Music and Musical Life in Pennsylvania in the Eighteenth Century* (No. 4, *Publications of the Pennsylvania Society of the Colonial Dames of America*, Philadelphia, 1927), II, 82.

asserting that a spirit of worship was fostered by Franklin's music.[22]

> And sure if aught of mortal-moving strain,
> Can touch with joy the high angelic train,
> 'Tis this enchanting instrument of thine,
> Which speaks in accents more than half divine!

Franklin once amused himself with the abbé Morellet by making an exhaustive list of all the passions and sentiments which could be expressed by music.[23] Included were "consolation" and "reverence or veneration."

22. *Poems on Several Occasions* (Philadelphia, 1772), p. 109.
23. "List of Musical Passions," manuscript *ca.* 1772 in Franklin Papers, American Philosophical Society.

CHAPTER SEVENTEEN

FRENCH CATHOLICS

OF all the religions with which Franklin came into close
contact there is no doubt that the Roman Catholic was
farthest away in spirit and form from the basic deism
which he held and professed throughout his life. Like most
Americans born into a Puritan environment, Franklin grew
up with strong prejudices against the sect which his contemporaries described pejoratively as Popish or Papistical.

Probably his first actual contact with Catholics came at
the age of nineteen during his first residence in London. He
lodged "in Duke-street opposite to the Romish Chapel" with
a widow who had been converted from Protestantism to
Catholicism by her husband. In the garret of the house
lived a maiden lady in her seventies who gave Franklin a
practical illustration of the asceticism of the Catholic faith.
"A Priest visited her, to confess her every Day. I have ask'd
her, says my Landlady, how she, as she liv'd, could possibly
find so much Employment for a Confessor? O, says she, it is
impossible to avoid *vain Thoughts.*"[1] Franklin was once allowed to visit. "The Room was clean, but had no other
Furniture than a Matras, a Table with a Crucifix and Book,
a Stool, which she gave me to sit on, and a Picture over the
Chimney of St. Veronica, displaying her Handkerchief with
the miraculous Figure of Christ's bleeding Face on it."
Franklin stressed the "great Seriousness" with which she explained the veronica. Her life impressed him primarily, however, "as another Instance on how small an Income Life and
Health may be supported."

Later in life on a visit to Belgium in 1761, Franklin and
his son William were allowed to visit a convent for high-
born English ladies. Although they were unable to converse
with any of the nuns, who were at devotions, William re-

1. Leonard W. Labaree *et al.* (eds.) , *Autobiography of Benjamin Franklin*
(New Haven, 1964) , p. 103.

marked disdainfully, "Indeed they did not look very inviting and on the contrary appeared like Cross Old Maids who had forsaken the World because the World had first forsaken them."[2]

As editor of the *Pennsylvania Gazette* Franklin published various derogatory remarks concerning Catholics, particularly during King Phillip's War, when Popery and the iniquity of the French enemy were generally equated. Also, during the Hemphill controversy, Franklin particularly denounced the persecutions of the Spanish Inquisition.

In 1757 when he landed in England after an extremely hazardous voyage, he was attracted by the sound of church bells and went to worship with his heart full of gratitude. "Were I a Roman Catholic," he wrote to his wife, "perhaps I should on this occasion vow to build a chapel to some saint; but as I am not, if I were to vow at all, it should be to build a *light-house*."[3]

Although Franklin moved in broad and tolerant circles during the next few years in London and on the Continent, it is doubtful that his acquaintance with Catholics was wide enough to change his prejudices, either puritanical or deistical. James Boswell, who at the time was far more tolerant of Rome than was Franklin, recorded that Franklin once raised the question in company, "whether Infidels or Protestants had done most to pull down Popery."[4]

While visiting the country estate of Lord Shelburne at Wycombe, near London, in the spring of 1772, Franklin first made the acquaintance of the abbé Morellet. In his company, Franklin carried out an experiment of calming troubled waters by spreading some oil concealed in the tip of his cane on a windy pond. A superstitious farmer who was also a witness, thinking he had seen a sign of the supernatural,

2. Spelling modernized from L. W. Labaree *et al.* (eds.), *Papers of Benjamin Franklin*, IX (New Haven, 1966), 366.
3. *Ibid.*, VII (1963), 243.
4. *Private Papers of James Boswell* (Mount Vernon, 1930), VII, 193–194.

asked Franklin, "Tell me, what am I to believe?" "Nothing except what you see," he replied.[5]

It does not appear that Franklin and Morellet discussed religion very widely at this time, but they laid the basis for a friendship which flourished a few years later when Franklin became a commissioner in France.

The French intellectual with whom Franklin first had extensive personal contact was Dr. Jacques Barbeu Dubourg, a physician who translated and edited a French collection of Franklin's works entitled *Œuvres de M. Franklin* (1773). In the same year, Franklin arranged the publication in London of a deistical handbook by Dubourg with many resemblances to Franklin's "Art of Virtue," and later Franklin also brought out an expanded edition on his own Passy press.[6] Dubourg dedicated his work, *A Brief Code of Human Reason (Petit code de la raison humaine)*, to Franklin, explicitly indicating that Franklin had been his chief inspiration and intellectual source: "You recognized in the first sketch of this Little Digest the simple and naive expression of your own heart. I have developed it as much as I am able, and I hope that you will perceive in it only the best of yourself."

When Franklin went to France as American commissioner late in 1776, his reputation had preceded him. According to a contemporary observer, "our free thinkers have adroitly sounded him on his religion, and they maintain that they have discovered that he was of their own, that is, that he had none at all."[7] In public, however, he tried to give the impression that he was a Quaker because of the high reputation for moral probity and religious simplicity which that sect had acquired in France, due primarily to the plaudits of Voltaire and Montesquieu. In order to advance his diplomatic aims, Franklin adopted a grave demeanor and assumed Quaker

5. A. O. Aldridge, *Franklin and His French Contemporaries* (New York, 1957), p. 189.
6. A. O. Aldridge, "Jacques Barbeu-Dubourg, A French Disciple of Benjamin Franklin," *Proceedings of the American Philosophical Society*, XCV (1951), 332–392.
7. Aldridge, *Franklin and His French Contemporaries*, p. 61.

garb. So successful was his pose as a "Quaker philosopher" that after his return to America a controversy took place in the *Journal de Paris* concerning whether he was or was not actually a member of the Society of Friends.[8]

Probably through the abbé Morellet, Franklin was introduced to the household of the widow of the materialistic philosopher, Claude Adrien Helvétius, who had been a symbol of atheism for a large part of the eighteenth century. Morellet lodged on the estate of Mme Helvétius along with another priest, l'abbé Lefebvre de la Roche, and a young medical student, Pierre Jean Cabanis. All four considered themselves warm friends of Franklin and looked forward to the days when he came to visit. Franklin fancied himself as a suitor for the favors of Mme Helvétius and joined with the others in addressing her as Notre Dame d'Auteuil.[9]

The abbé de la Roche was an ex-Benedictine whom Helvétius had secularized after a fashion in obtaining a brief from Rome. The young medical student Cabanis later became an eminent doctor, a friend of Mirabeau and Condorcet, and a senator under Napoleon.

According to Morellet, he, la Roche, and Cabanis shared essentially the same political and philosophical opinions, "liberty, tolerance, horror of despotism and superstition, the desire of seeing abuses reformed." It is quite likely that association with these enlightened Catholics helped to diminish Franklin's prejudices against the Roman faith. Accounts of Franklin's disbursements indicate that on one occasion in 1781 he went so far as to buy an expensive gold cross, probably either a present for one of his personal friends or a diplomatic gift for some member of the French court.[10] But this was merely worldly politeness and nothing more. One of Franklin's scientific friends in Paris wrote to him in the same year, remarking in part, "Vous n'êtes pas un mangeur de

8. Nov. 26 and 29, 1786.
9. Aldridge, *Franklin and His French Contemporaries*, pp. 161 ff.
10. Accounts of W. T. Franklin, Dec. 31, 1781, in Library of the American Philosophical Society.

messes." ("You are not a glutton for the Mass.") [11] It must not be overlooked, moreover, that the abbés Morellet and la Roche were not typical Catholics. Their close association with Helvétius and the admitted similarity of their philosophical notions with those of the free-thinking Cabanis indicate that they most certainly would not have expressed any sentiments which Franklin would have considered bigoted or superstitious.

All three men left extensive recollections of their friendship with Franklin, but only Cabanis, the acknowledged materialist, discussed Franklin's religious beliefs. Cabanis in his memoirs repeated from Franklin's autobiography the accounts of his early vegetarianism, his skepticism from reading Shaftesbury, and his scheme for attaining moral perfection.[12] He also supplied information concerning Franklin's reading, which Franklin himself had not disclosed in his writing. Greatly impressed by Bacon's essay "Of Atheism," Franklin loved to quote two passages, "one that it requires more credulousness to be an atheist than to believe in God; the other, 'that a little philosophy inclineth man's mind to atheism; but depth in philosophy bringeth men's minds about to religion.' " Cabanis also attributed to the Bible a greater influence upon Franklin than Franklin himself admitted. "In reading the Bible, which he did often, the Book of Proverbs attracted his attention in a particular manner. One notices in those books called wisdom books a great knowledge of the human heart and of society. The Proverbs contains excellent lessons applicable to common life and compressed in energetic and piquant phrases. Franklin there read: 'Length of days is in her right hand, and in her left hand riches and honor.' "

Cabanis also reported that the only form of superstition which touched Franklin was a credence in dream visions. According to Cabanis, Franklin believed that he had more

11. Le Roy to Franklin, Oct., 1781, in Library of the American Philosophical Society.
12. Aldridge, *Franklin and His French Contemporaries*, pp. 203 ff.

than once received a revelation in his dreams of the outcome of his affairs—and despite his otherwise strong mind devoid of prejudice, he could not give up faith in these inner voices.

Franklin's relations with Morellet, who was closer to his own age, seem to have been more relaxed. At one time they had discussed the practice of adding water to wine, and Franklin wrote him a sparkling letter of protest filled with whimsical interpretations of Biblical passages.

Starting with the maxim *in vino veritas,* Franklin explained that before the time of Noah men turned to wickedness because they lacked the truth of wine; they knew only water and were justly destroyed by it. Although we speak of the turning of water into wine at Cana as a miracle, the same operation takes place every day, although at a slower rate, when rain from the skies enters the roots of vines and produces grapes. God out of his great love has also taught man the reverse process—to make brandy *(eau de vie)* out of wine.

Since God has created wine to make man happy, it is churlish ingratitude to put water into it—and thus to adulterate the truth. We read in the Holy Scriptures "that the apostle Paul counselled Timothy very seriously to put wine into his water for the sake of his health; but that not one of the apostles or holy fathers ever recommended *putting water to wine.*"

Franklin concluded his "religious observations" by pointing out the efficient cause of the elbow in human anatomy: it is placed precisely in such a way as to allow the wine glass to be raised to the mouth. "Let us, then, with glass in hand, adore this benevolent wisdom;—let us adore and drink!"[13]

This pleasantry is in some measure an appreciation of good wine, for both Franklin and Morellet had composed drinking songs. But it is also a parody of the physico-theology of the eighteenth-century philosophers, which consisted in

13. Translated from Albert Henry Smyth (ed.), *Writings of Benjamin Franklin* (10 vols., New York, 1905–1907), VII, 436–438.

proving the existence of God and purpose in the universe by rhapsodies over the stars in the heavens or the structure of the human body. Franklin had himself used physico-theology in his youthful "Articles of Belief," but the method had gone out of fashion and he now saw its ridiculous aspect.

One day in a conversation with Morellet, Franklin discussed the witch trials which had disgraced New England in the seventeenth century and made a shrewd observation on the reason they were finally abandoned. "They proceeded to hang the pretended witches, particularly old women who were very thin and ugly. As they pardoned those who confessed and divulged their accomplices, the accusations and the tortures multiplied until some of the allegedly guilty began to accuse some of the judges. Then and only then did the latter decide that these unfortunates could only be imbeciles or have made their accusations only to save themselves. The prosecutions dropped off markedly and soon ceased altogether."[14]

In a manuscript collection of anecdotes, Morellet relates this story along with another of his own which Franklin borrowed from him. "Two very loquacious men were in the same company. One of them, taking over the conversation, a third party said to the other, 'What is going to become of us, this man will never finish.' 'Leave it to me,' replied the other, 'if he spits, he is lost.' " When Franklin returned to Pennsylvania in his old age, he told the same story but gave it additional piquancy by applying it to two French bishops.

Another clergyman with whom Franklin had close contact in France was the abbé Jean Louis Soulavie, who corresponded with him extensively on scientific questions. One day in August, 1781, Franklin pointed out to Soulavie an article in *Le Courrier de l'Europe* complimenting a historical work by the abbé in which he had exposed the alleged efforts of the English to establish an independent Protestant

14. Translated from "Ana" manuscript in the British Museum.

republic in the Cevennes region in southern France. Soulavie was surprised that Franklin, a Protestant, would agree
with him in condemning the British policy. Franklin
replied: "Were I a Frenchman, a Cévegnol, a mountaineer, a
protestant, subject of Lewis XVI, and harassed by his dra-
goons, I should prefer the safety of my country to the disa-
greeable alternative of seeking in a foreign land the protection of an English or Prussian monarch."[15] According to
Franklin, England would be guilty of a grave injury by
"raising up a religion in the state which dissents from the
head of the state." If there is a principle involved here, it
would certainly seem to be that of loyalty to one's country
over one's religious sect.

According to published reports while Franklin was in
France, part of his mission consisted in healing the breach
between Protestants and Catholics and persuading the
French government to adopt a more lenient policy toward
the Protestants. A newsletter dated December, 1778, remarked that he was shrewdly stressing the value to France of
the liaisons which would be formed between France and
America in the wake of independence, "the alliances, the
marriages, the family mixtures, the reciprocal emigrations to
which the difference of religions would place an invincible
obstacle if the Protestant religion did not find the same
tolerance in France as the Catholic in America."[16] According
to this source, Franklin's arguments could not help producing a good effect for the new republic; if they were successful, the French Protestants would be grateful for his efficacious pleading, and, even if his solicitations bore no fruit in
France, these people would realize that they would be welcome immigrants in America. Largely because of Franklin,
therefore, the French government had set itself to examining
the important political questions of religious toleration.

15. Aldridge, *Franklin and His French Contemporaries*, pp. 68 ff.
16. Translated from *L'Espion anglais, ou correspondance secrète entre milord all'eye et milord all'ear* (London, 1782), X, 94.

Perhaps in some measure because of the influence of Franklin, a decree in favor of non-Catholics was promulgated in France shortly before the outbreak of the French Revolution. Franklin explained to a minor French official, June 8, 1788, that this measure pleased Americans as "a good step towards general toleration, and to the abolishing in time all party spirit among Christians, and the mischiefs that have so long attended it. Thank God, the world is growing wiser and wiser; and as by degrees men are convinced of the folly of wars for religion, for dominion, or for commerce, they will be happier and happier."[17]

Since members of the Catholic clergy constituted a major part of the French intelligentsia, it is not surprising that many of Franklin's closest associates should have been priests. One of his correspondents, the abbé Joseph André Brun, dedicated to Franklin a sociological treatise and then sent several additional pages as manuscript inserts, which would have been too compromising had they been printed in his book. In these unusual pages, now in the library of the American Philosophical Society, the abbé proposed a system of companionate marriage and indicated various legitimate reasons for divorce.

Although other clergymen whom Franklin knew in France were even less orthodox, it is not true that his acquaintance was limited to skeptics and atheists. John Adams gave a completely false impression in his diary when he reported a conversation he allegedly had with Marbois when they were crossing the Atlantic.[18] Adams hinted that Franklin had no religion at all. " 'No,' said M. Marbois, 'Mr. Franklin adores only great Nature, which has interested a great many people of both sexes in his favor.' 'Yes,' said I laughing, 'all the atheists, deists, and libertines, as well as the philosophers and ladies, are in his train,—another Voltaire, and thence—.' " Adams was here more flippant than accurate. It is true that

17. Smyth (ed.) , *Writings,* IX, 657.
18. C. F. Adams (ed.), *Works of John Adams* (Boston, 1851), III, 220.

such skeptics as Condorcet and Voltaire were among Franklin's friends, but most of the liberal clergymen whom we have mentioned cannot be considered complete rebels to the Catholic tradition. Certainly Franklin had much more to do with a number of dedicated church dignitaries including the papal nuncio than with libertines or atheists either in or outside of the church.

Even though Franklin was included in the *Dictionnaire des athées anciens et modernes* published in Paris in 1800, he appears merely as "the Pythagoras of the new world and the second founder of American liberty," and nothing whatsoever is said to indicate that he was not a Christian believer.

One of the ladies in his train to whom John Adams referred was a beautiful and talented matron, still in her thirties, Mme d'Hardancourt Brillon, who professed to love Franklin as a daughter loves a father. In an extensive correspondence Franklin made it clear that he would have preferred another kind of intimacy.[19]

Mme Brillon had a daughter of marriageable age—and Franklin entertained hopes that she might accept for a husband his grandson, William Temple Franklin, who was then in Paris as his secretary. Unfortunately, one of the two major objections which Mme Brillon and her husband raised against Franklin's proposal was the difference in religion.

Franklin wrote earnestly to Mme Brillon, April, 1781, attempting to prove that the differences between Protestants and Catholics are superficial, not fundamental.

> In each religion there are some essential things and others which are only forms and modes. As a lump of sugar, which can be wrapped in brown, white or blue paper & tied with string of flax or wool, red or yellow, it is always the sugar which is the essential thing. Now the essentials of a good religion consist, it seems to me, in these 5 articles, namely:
> 1) That there is a God who made the world & who governs it by his providence.

19. This correspondence, in large measure still unpublished, is in the Library of the American Philosophical Society.

2) That he should be worshipped and served.
3) That the best service toward God is doing good toward men.
4) That the soul of man is immortal &
5) That in a future life, if not in the present, vice will be punished, & virtue punished.[20]

This is the essence of the religious system which Franklin propounded more frequently than any other. He incorporated it almost verbatim, for example, in two separate passages in his autobiography.

Mme Brillon agreed that "there is but one religion and one moral law common to all wise men," but she, nevertheless, opposed the marriage. She and her husband needed a son-in-law "skilled in the knowledge of the laws and customs of our country and of our religion." They were obliged to submit to the usages of their country, which would countenance Temple as a friend to the family but not a member of it. "An isolated being, keeping silent and leaving to others their prejudices, can do as he wishes. Married people, belonging to a large family, owe it some account of their doings."

Franklin was regretfully forced to accept the decision of the Brillons and give up his cherished dream of seeing his family united with theirs. Human reason, he felt, had been overcome by practical considerations. Nevertheless, he did not interpret Mme Brillon's rejection of his grandson as religious prejudice. Indeed he had used reasoning similar to hers in choosing the religious milieu for his other grandson, Benjamin Franklin Bache. Having taken young Benny to France at the age of seven, Franklin was obliged to look after his education. Instead of keeping Benny with him at Passy, however, he sent him to Geneva in Switzerland. The Swiss schools were as good as the French, he believed, and they would offer the additional advantage of educating Benny as "a Republican and a Protestant, which could not be so

20. Translated from Smyth (ed.), *Writings*, X, 419.

conveniently done at the Schools in France."[21] Both Franklin
and the Brillons tolerated each other's religion but were
reluctant to admit an alien faith to the inner family circle.

Before leaving for Geneva, little Benny played a mute but
central role in a scene which later became famous, his receiving the blessing of Voltaire at the latter's sickbed in the
company of his grandfather. The French sage, laying his
hand on the lad's shoulder, pronounced the grave benedic-
tion, "God and Liberty."[22] It is hard to decide exactly what
Voltaire implied by this cryptic formula, but he was reputed
by his contemporaries to hold that a simple belief in God
was a religion sufficient to provide tranquillity and social
stability. Although "certain fanatics" interpreted his blessing of little Benny as a gesture of "derisive impiety," Franklin himself probably accepted it as a genuinely religious act.

Voltaire's sentiments "God and Liberty" in a sense represent the concepts which many French people associated with
Franklin. L'abbé Claude Fauchet, for example, in a public
eulogy of Franklin which he delivered July 14, 1790, in the
name of the Commune of Paris, described Franklin as "the
philosopher *par excellence* of protestantism." This address
represents one of the most glowing tributes ever accorded to
Franklin's religion.

Fauchet, a Catholic priest, praised the Quaker city of Philadelphia with such fervor that he felt called upon to defend
himself for extolling the virtues of Protestants. He had done
so, he explained, because he accepted the principles of
Franklin concerning universal tolerance—and he admired
the Quakers because their city had produced Franklin, who,
lacking the perfection of Catholic belief, still possessed the
perfection of evangelical benevolence.

Fauchet considered Franklin's religious beliefs so admirable that he gave a rhapsodic summary. Toleration is the

21. Carl Van Doren (ed.), *Letters of Benjamin Franklin and Jane Mecom*
(Princeton, 1950), p. 191.
22. A. O. Aldridge, "Benjamin Franklin and the *philosophes,*" *Studies on
Voltaire and the Eighteenth Century,* XXIV (1963), 46.

theme of his exposition, a virtual echo of Lindsey's opening sermon at the Unitarian Chapel on the diversity of opinion. Fauchet considered the following to be a faithful précis of Franklin's doctrine:

> Men cannot be brothers and consequently social when some condemn others for their private opinions and, because of the diversity of views, conceive of themselves as separated from their fellow men by the distance between heaven and hell. No one can judge conscience but God himself. The man who asserts that every one is free to believe or not to believe any doctrine is often guilty of injustice and always guilty of temerity. . . . The greatest genius in the universe, even though he feels the most ardent love of truth, may embrace a religious error and find himself bound to it by the severity of his conscience. Who is the audacious mortal who will pretend to have the power to calculate all the lights and shadows which affect the most simple or the most sublime spirits and who will dare say, "it was possible for him to believe as I do"? There are ingrained prejudices . . . which can invincibly imprison the most honorable and the most just of men in an inherited religion filled with errors. The sage himself who by the force of his reflection and the activity of his great soul raises himself, by imploring divine assistance, above vulgar thoughts and common superstitions, succeeds only in floating in the immensity of eternal conceptions and redescends with a holy fear to the elements of his primitive faith. Doubtless, mental laziness, guilty passions, or the free abuse of our faculties can, in matters of religion, restrain us or impel us into errors which are truly imputable to us. But it belongs only to him who reads our thoughts and who probes our hearts to note them in the book of conscience and to punish them at the day of judgment. Only those actions manifestly contrary to the laws of universal morality are submitted to the inspection of all men and to the sentence of society. The vicious or the wicked man, the man who corrupts—there is the enemy of humanity; the virtuous, the good, the beneficent man, even when his doctrine is in error—there is the friend of the human race.[23]

And there is the doctrine of Franklin, according to Fauchet. We do indeed find in it reminiscences of Franklin's thought extending from his early *Dogood Letters* to the liturgy in which he assisted David Williams.

23. Translated from *Eloge civique de Benjamin Franklin* (Paris, 1790).

CHAPTER EIGHTEEN

AMERICAN CATHOLICS AND
A SPANISH SERMON

FRANKLIN's relations with the Catholic clergy were public
as well as private. Immediately after the American Revolution, when the same problems faced American Roman
Catholics which had faced their Episcopalian countrymen,
Franklin served as liaison between the American clergy and
the Holy See. As a result of the independence of the United
States, it no longer seemed appropriate for American clergymen to receive their ordination from English superiors or to
profess allegiance to them, even though no political ties were
involved. The Holy See recognized this problem and
through the agency of the papal nuncio in Paris directly
sought the aid of the French court and of Dr. Franklin,
America's most distinguished citizen.

Even before the end of the war, rumor had linked Franklin with Rome. In March, 1782, facetious members of the
court of Louis XVI had amused themselves by inventing a
fictitious correspondence between Franklin and the Pope. In
it "His Holiness begged the doctor-minister to give his advice on the conduct that he should pursue in the crisis in
which the Roman power found itself," its temporal control
having been reduced in many European nations.[1] The doctor replied that the shortest and most certain measure
"would be to arm all the monks and priests and to substitute
a temporal power for the spiritual government, or at least to
support the one by the other. He advised the Pope to ally
himself with France, Spain, the King of Prussia and the
Americans, and to defend the rights of the Holy See as these
powers defended their liberty, and for this purpose to re-
place the canons of the church by canons firing balls of 12,
24, 36 or 48 pounds. Everything considered, he found that

---

1. Translated from M. de Lescure, *Correspondance secrète . . . sur Louis
XVI, Marie-Antoinette* (Paris. 1866), I, 469–470.

His Holiness could arm three hundred thousand men well nourished and well built which six hundred Prussian officers could train in very little time, and he believed that these methods would give respect to briefs, bulls, etc." This was, of course, a joke—but a plausible one.

In the actual historical situation brought on by the defeat of the English in America, it was logical for the Holy See to consult Franklin on the future of the Catholic church in the new nation. The English Catholic clergy no longer held any influence and their American brothers were numerically insignificant and politically obscure. To be sure, it was not without some misgivings that the Papacy looked toward Franklin as its liaison with the faithful in America. The papal secretary of state, Cardinal Leonardo Antonelli, admitted in no uncertain terms that he would have preferred negotiating with an American Catholic to "the present circumstances, in which the minister is heretical, possibly Presbyterian, or non-Conformist."[2]

Both Franklin and French authorities, civil and ecclesiastical, graciously and disinterestedly gave their advice and assistance in helping to arrange the future of American Catholics. Some American historians have charged the French with seeking to dominate the American church and have considered Franklin as overly willing to co-operate in compromising the independence of American Catholics. French historians, on the other hand, have pointed out that alarm over the possibility of French influence in America grew out of the sensibilities of English Jesuits. Smarting under the recent suppression of their order in response to the demands of European powers, they distrusted everything French and viewed the negotiations carried on in Paris with jealous eyes. It is now generally accepted that all French personalities involved were interested solely in resolving a pressing prob-

2. Details concerning Franklin's relations with the Papacy are taken from Jules A. Baisnée, *France and the Establishment of the American Catholic Hierarchy. The Myth of French Influence* (Baltimore, 1934) .

lem of concern only to American Catholics and the Holy See and that they had no view whatsoever of promoting French national interest. And since the French themselves had no selfish or sinister views, Franklin could not have been a party to them.

He did not immediately suggest the appointment of a bishop in America merely because he felt that American Catholics preferred not to be burdened with the support of a resident bishop. Franklin had good reason for such a view. In 1765, Father John Carroll, then a spokesman for a group of ex-Jesuits in Maryland left without supervision as a result of the disbanding of their order, had written to the Vicar-Apostolic of London: "For many years past attempts have been made to establish a Protestant Bishop on this continent, and . . . such attempts have been as constantly oppos'd thro the fixed avertion ye people of America in general have to a person of this character. If such is the avertion of Protestants to a Protestant Bishop, with w[ha]t an eye will they look upon an Apost[olic] Vicar?"[3]

Franklin had made the acquaintance of this Father Carroll shortly after the commencement of the American Revolution, when he was appointed one of three commissioners on a mission to Montreal to try to bring the Canadians into the war on the side of the Americans. Carroll, whom Franklin considered "a gentleman of learning and abilities," was asked to go along to persuade the Catholic population that they would receive complete religious liberty under the new government.

The commissioners reached Montreal in April, 1776, but were very coolly received. The Canadian spiritual leaders had no more faith in American pledges to respect the Catholic religion than the political leaders had in Continental credit. Neither Franklin nor Carroll was capable of changing the climate of hostility. Franklin realized the uselessness of

---

3. Details concerning Franklin's relations with John Carroll are taken from Annabelle M. Melville, *John Carroll of Baltimore* (New York, 1955).

his mission early in May and started back to Philadelphia alone. At this time he was in his seventies and apprehensive that the fatigue of the journey might prove too much for him. Father Carroll, concerned for the health and comfort of the venerable diplomat, soon overtook him and helped ease the rigors of the road. When they reached New York, Franklin expressed his gratitude in a letter to the other commissioners, "I find I grow daily more feeble, and I think I could hardly have got along so far but for Mr. Carroll's friendly assistance and tender care of me."

The Holy See itself took the initiative in arranging the spiritual direction of American Catholics. On January 15, 1783, Cardinal Antonelli, prefect of the propaganda, instructed Prince Doria Pamphili, papal nuncio in Paris, to request the assistance of the King of France. When the problem was broached to Vergennes, French minister of foreign affairs, that official declared that it would not be fitting for the French government to interfere in American internal policies. The nuncio thereupon ended his interview with Vergennes by begging him "to inform Mr. Franklin . . . that I would have spoken to him of this matter, as I will do, when I shall have heard from the Count of Vergennes what Mr. Franklin may have had to say on the subject."

On July 28, 1783, the nuncio informed Franklin in a formal note that the Congregation of the Propaganda had "determined to propose to congress the installation of one of their Catholic subjects, in some city of the United States of North America, with the powers of vicar-apostolic, and with the character of bishop or simply as prefect apostolic." In the event that at any time no native American could be found with the necessary qualifications, the nuncio hoped that Congress would consent to the choice being made among the subjects of a friendly foreign nation.

Franklin, after mature reflection, replied that it would be "absolutely useless" to send such a proposal to Congress, "which, according to its powers and its constitutions, can not, and should not, in any case, intervene in the ecclesiastical affairs of any sect or of any religion established in America. Each particular State has reserved to itself by its own constitutions the right to protect its members, to tolerate their religious opinions, and not to interfere with the matter, as long as they do not disturb civil order." As his own opinion, Franklin added that "the Court of Rome, in concert with the minister of the United States, may make [use] of a French ecclesiastic, who, residing in France, may regulate the spiritual affairs of the Catholics who live, or who may come to establish themselves, in those States, through a suffragan residing in America."

In all the negotiations for the establishment of an American church, this is the only document which suggests placing the American clergy under a French bishop. Franklin was undoubtedly governed by the opinion that Americans themselves would prefer not to have a bishop residing among them, and he naturally felt that a French superior would be better than an English one.

To supplement his opinion, Franklin prepared a note on American Catholics, pointing out that "in the greater number of the colonies, there is no endowment, no fixed revenue, for the support of a clergy of whatever denomination" and that there is also no "college or public establishment where a Catholic ecclesiastic may receive necessary instruction." There existed in France, however, "four establishments of English monks" with large revenues and practically no subjects to care for. Franklin thereupon proposed that "the king of France, to please the Court of Rome and to strengthen the bonds of friendship with the United States," would permit these establishments to be set aside "to train, instruct, and in part support the ecclesiastics who would be used in America." To forward this purpose, Franklin further proposed "that one of the bishops named by the Holy See should be a subject of the King, residing in France, in a position, always, to act in accordance with the Nuncio of His Holiness and the

American minister, and to adopt with them the means of training the ecclesiastics, which might be agreeable to Congress and useful to American Catholics."

The nuncio emphatically rejected Franklin's plan of confiscating English property in France but considered with favor the plan of appointing a French bishop with the duty of supervising the training of ecclesiastics. Vergennes and Talleyrand, then bishop of Autun, also approved this proposal and conferred on the means of carrying it out.

Franklin, in the meantime, changed his mind about the uselessness of transmitting the nuncio's note to Congress, and on September 13, 1783, he submitted it to that body.

Back in America, a committee of the Catholic clergy, of which Carroll was a member, drafted a petition to the Holy See in November, 1783, requesting permission to elect their own superior—but not to have him made a bishop because of the "republican jealousy" of American Protestants.

When the proposition of the papal nuncio, transmitted by Franklin, circulated in Congress, a number of congressmen, speaking privately to the Chevalier de la Luzerne, French minister in Philadelphia, gave him to understand that the subject of Catholic organization concerned the members of that sect alone, not the Congress, but they felt nonetheless that a Catholic bishop would be favorably received in Pennsylvania and Maryland. La Luzerne passed on these sentiments to Vergennes with the additional suggestion, "The Catholics would not be pleased with a foreign Bishop, but they could very well choose the worthiest of their priests and present him to His Holiness for consecration, if he judges him qualified for the episcopal functions."

Congress took the position Franklin had predicted. On May 11, 1784, it requested him to notify the apostolic nuncio at Versailles "that Congress will always be pleased to testify their respect to his sovereign and state; but that the subject of his application to Doctor Franklin, being purely spiritual, it is without the jurisdiction and powers of Congress, . . .

these powers being reserved to the several states individually."

Franklin, in the meantime, had written two further letters supporting his proposal that the superior of the American clergy be a Frenchman; one of these was to Vergennes, the other to Jerôme Marie Champion de Cissé, archbishop of Bordeaux. Franklin was on friendly terms with both men, and he and the archbishop had a mutual friend in the abbé de la Roche, whom both loved and esteemed. Although Franklin had recommended a French superior, when the Holy See independently reached the decision that a native American would be the best choice and the nuncio asked Franklin his opinion of John Carroll, Franklin "recommended him . . . with great solicitude." The nuncio reported to the cardinal prefect (May 17, 1784) that Franklin had given him "favorable information . . . of the merits and good reputation of Mr. Carrol" and that if he should be selected as the vicar-apostolic to be sent to Maryland he "would be very welcome to many members of Congress, and especially, to Mr. Franklin."

Shortly afterward the cardinal prefect informed Carroll that he had been appointed "Superior of the Mission in the thirteen United States of North America" both because he had presented "conspicuous proofs of piety and zeal" and because his selection would "please and gratify many members of that republic, and especially Mr. Franklin." Carroll was not entirely happy with this turn of affairs, now deeming the rank to which he was appointed somewhat of an affront to the honor of the American clergy. He had changed his mind about the reception which a bishop would meet with in the United States and now felt that his coreligionists deserved a national bishop rather than a vicar-apostolic. "To govern the spiritual concerns of this country as a mission," he wrote, "is absurd, seeing there is a regular clergy belonging to it." He resented also the fact that the Roman authorities had negotiated "with Dr. Franklin, without ever deigning to apply for information to the Catholic clergy in this country."

At the urging of Charles Plowden, an English ex-Jesuit, two or three American members of the same disbanded order subsequently wrote to Franklin urging that no further proposals be entertained without the participation and consent of the American clergy.

For all practical purposes Franklin's personal intervention in the affairs of the Catholic church came to an end on July 1, 1784, with the visit of the papal nuncio, who came to tell him that the pope on Franklin's recommendation had appointed Carroll "Superior of the Catholic Clergy in America, with many of the Powers of a Bishop; and that probably he would be made a Bishop *in partibus* before the End of the Year."[4]

The nuncio asked Franklin whether it would be preferable for Carroll to receive his ordination in France or Santo Domingo rather than in Quebec, but Franklin favored the Canadian city. The American government would take no offense at Carroll's going to an English province, he affirmed, provided that ordination would not give the English bishop any authority over the American. The conversation then drifted to more general topics, and Franklin introduced the subject of the Inquisition, which in the past had been his greatest obstacle in the way of cordial feelings toward Rome. The nuncio assured Franklin that he would "find that the Catholics were not so intolerant as they had been represented; that the Inquisition in Rome had not now so much Power as that in Spain; and that in Spain it was used chiefly as a Prison of State."

Franklin also discussed with the nuncio the question of whether the Anglicans Weems and Gant could be ordained by a Catholic bishop, possibly in order to embarrass the nuncio by putting to the test his affirmation of Catholic

4. Albert Henry Smyth (ed.), *Writings of Benjamin Franklin* (10 vols., New York, 1905–1907), X, 349.

tolerance. Perhaps Franklin knew in advance that the nuncio would be forced to refuse the request, but it is just as possible that Franklin's motives were sincere—that he was giving the nuncio an opportunity of demonstrating good faith. As a practical politician, Franklin probably realized that the situation held political potentialities of great value for the Roman Catholic church and assumed that the hierarchy might be willing to exploit it by making certain concessions. His close personal contacts with liberal French ecclesiastics may well have given him the impression that the proposal would be at least considered.

During the conversation about Carroll the nuncio made another attempt to impress Franklin with his tolerance. He "spoke lightly" of John Thayer, a Bostonian who had recently been converted to Catholicism.[5] Thayer had been for some time a real thorn in Franklin's flesh—and the nuncio presumably wanted to show Franklin that he had no great opinion of the new convert.

Thayer had received an honorary A.B. at Yale in 1779 and had been licensed, but not ordained, as a Congregational minister. After serving during the next two years as chaplain at Castle William in Boston, he set off to learn languages in Europe. He was a smooth talker, and for months before sailing he had teased Jane Collas, Franklin's niece, for a letter of recommendation to Franklin. Thayer would not leave her in peace until she wrote him a few lines of introduction, which she gave him unsealed. A week later he was back again to appeal for a warmer statement, and she could not help laughing in his face. Yet at his request she gave him pen and paper so that he could write out a letter for her to copy. When Jane read his text she flatly refused to alter her original letter. As she explained to Franklin years later: "I told him . . . as I had no reason to doubt, the truth of what he had writen I would oblig him by signing my Name and beg the favor of Mamma to do the same which would put an

5. *Ibid.*, p. 350.

end I hoped to all further trouble, Mamma laughed very hartily at the drolery and the poor fellow with all his Assurance look'd greatly mortified."[6]

Jane relented enough to allow Thayer to plead his cause with her mother—Jane Mecom, Franklin's sister—which he did very ingeniously by heaping praise on a recent work by Franklin which had just come off the press, *Political, Miscellaneous, and Philosophical Pieces,* and which Franklin's sister then heard about for the first time. Thayer ran on so prettily about the collection of Franklin's works that Jane Mecom thought he must be very clever. She gave him a letter, describing him as a gentleman of liberal education. "I have no personal Acquaintance with Him," she wrote, "but hear He is much Esteemed in Boston."[7]

When Thayer arrived in France, he attempted to foist himself on Franklin by the same arts he had used in America. He tried to persuade Franklin to appoint him chaplain to the American legation, but Franklin would have nothing of it. Thayer was aggressive, impudent, and demanding, and he even occasioned Franklin a good deal of expense. Although he claimed to be in easy circumstances, Thayer contrived to make Franklin pay his tailor's bill. When Jane Mecom heard this, she could not help calling him a "worthless little animal."[8]

Thayer moved on to Rome, where he was converted to Catholicism, and returned to France to study theology. An English priest reported, September 2, 1784: "He is noticed by the archbishop of Paris and other dignified clergymen of the greatest merit, and much commended by the superior of Navarre college, in whose house he lives gratis. He appears to be sincere and zealous for the promotion of religion in America, and we hope he will not be misled."[9]

When Franklin first learned that Thayer had changed his

6. Carl Van Doren (ed.), *Letters of Benjamin Franklin and Jane Mecom* (Princeton, 1950), p. 303.
7. *Ibid.,* p. 211.   8. *Ibid.,* p. 217.
9. Baisnée, *France and the Establishment,* p. 145.

Presbyterianism for Catholicism, he wrote to his sister, September 13, 1783, "I hope he got something to boot, because that would be a sort of Proof that they allow'd our Religion to be, so much at least, better than theirs.—It would be pleasant, if a Boston Man should come to be Pope! Stranger Things have happened."[10]

The nuncio in speaking lightly of Thayer's conversion told Franklin that he had advised the new convert "not to go to America, but settle in France. That he wanted to go to convert his countrymen; but he knew nothing yet of his new religion himself, etc."

Somewhat later to Jonathan Williams, Franklin commented with some acerbity, April 13, 1785, "Our ancestors from Catholic became first Church-of-England men, and then refined into Presbyterians. To change now from Presbyterianism to Popery seems to me refining backwards, from white sugar to brown."[11]

When Franklin returned to Philadelphia he retained his doubts concerning Catholic political powers and challenged a Spanish priest to defend the Inquisition in much the same spirit in which he had broached the subject with the nuncio. A young clergyman, Don Antonio José Ruiz de Padrón, had been shipwrecked in a furious storm off the coast of Pennsylvania in 1788 and had taken refuge in Philadelphia. There he was invited to the informal meetings of a group of twenty Protestant ministers who assembled frequently at Franklin's home. The others all called Don Antonio "the Papist." The conversation, which was managed amicably and very methodically, although with warmth and energy, nearly always turned on the subject of religion.[12] Ruiz de Padrón, despite his youth and limited experience, was able to uphold

10. Van Doren (ed.), *Letters*, p. 224.
11. Smyth (ed.), *Writings*, IX, 303.
12. The remaining discussion is based upon Miguel Villalba Hervás, *Ruiz de Padrón y su tiempo* (Madrid, 1897). The material concerning Philadelphia in that book is in turn based on *Dictamen del Doctor Don Antonio José Ruiz de Padrón . . . sobre el tribunal de la inquisición* (Cadiz y reimpreso en Mexico, 1813).

to the satisfaction of many of his listeners the primacy which the Bishop of Rome claimed by divine right in all the church. Nor was it difficult for him to refute other points of controversy, and he replied with some dexterity to the assaults of the Protestants. There lived in Philadelphia a nephew of the famous John Francis Budé, in Ruiz de Padrón's eyes, one of the most weighty of "Lutheran" theologians. Leaning on the system of his uncle, this man denied the traditional basis of the Catholic faith by impugning the Council of Trent. The group discussed this dogmatic point with more heat than any other, some of the ministers even dissenting from the Lutheran and coming to the defense of the priest. Without exception, however, the group joined in attacking the Spanish Inquisition.

The Roman church, they argued, cannot be the true church of Jesus Christ. Why, they demanded, does it harbor in its bosom the dreadful tribunal of the Inquisition—despotic, bloody, cruel, and contrary to the maxims of the Gospel? Its divine author, who is the God of peace and charity, detested the violent compulsions and horrible punishments which the Inquisition used against the dissidents. All the pages of the New Testament paint the religion of Jesus Christ as compassionate, attractive, kind—as stemming from the bosom of the celestial Father. But the Inquisition has made it intolerable and odious, and instead of attracting Protestants, repels them more and more from the society of the Roman church, particularly in Spain.

Ruiz de Padrón was at first much troubled by these objections, but after mature reflection he gave the direct and forthright answer that he also deplored the Inquisition—but that the Inquisition did not represent an inherent or essential part of the Catholic church. He maintained that it was a tribunal of purely human establishment, involving not only the court of Rome but also the politics of the Spanish monarchy. He admitted its enormous abuses, its despotic domination contrary to the spirit of the Gospel, but insisted that its evils were evils of men which could not in any way prejudice the purity of doctrine, the sanctity and the primacy of the Roman church, mother and teacher of all the churches.

George Washington appeared for several days in Philadelphia, and Ruiz de Padrón carried on similar discussions in the general's home. Like every one else, Ruiz de Padrón was unable to penetrate Washington's religious beliefs or even to find out what sect he belonged to. With Franklin though, he thought he had more success. He asserted positively that Franklin subscribed to the Arminian principles of Philipp Van Limborch. If this is all that the Spanish priest was able to discover about Franklin's religion, it indicates that the aged deist had not fully exposed his own beliefs to the company of ministers. The Arminian doctrine that man is a free moral agent is certainly quite compatible with deism—but for that matter so is the contrary doctrine that all human behavior is inevitably fixed. Possibly Franklin expressed notions concerning free will comparable to those in his early Junto discourse. That he should have given the ministers no further indication of his fundamental conceptions is not surprising, considering his reputation for taciturnity. At a similar discussion group founded in the previous year, The Society for Political Inquiries, of which he was president, Franklin gave no greater insight into his views on politics. According to the recollections of another member, Franklin, although very attentive, "said but little after the subject was broached."[13] In keeping with his theories of tolerance, Franklin enjoyed religious discussion but deplored controversy. It was his practice to reconcile his own religious views with those of his associates wherever he happened to be. He could hardly be expected to try to convert the assembled clergy of Philadelphia to his own system of rational deism.

When Franklin heard Padre Antonio disassociate the Roman church from the evils of the Inquisition, however, he

13. T. I. Wharton, "A Memoir of William Rawle," *Memoirs of the Historical Society of Pennsylvania*, IV, Pt. I (1840), 57.

challenged the priest to express the same sentiments in public as a proof of his sincerity. Perhaps he expected Ruiz de Padrón to back down, as the nuncio had previously responded negatively about ordaining Weems and Gant, but the good priest boldly preached a sermon in the Catholic church of Philadelphia in which he incorporated the same doctrine he had professed at Franklin's house. The entire Spanish colony—consisting of the crews of two Spanish frigates of war and of eight or ten boats from Florida—attended this service. Franklin was directly responsible for this significant event in the history of the church—the first sermon in Spanish delivered in the vast northeastern regions of America.

At the request of the English-speaking Catholics, the sermon was translated and read in English on the following Sunday by the Reverend Francis Beeston, one of the two curates of the parish of St. Joseph's and St. Mary's. On this no less significant occasion, sectaries of every persuasion packed the church. The attendance was so great that Ruiz de Padrón himself could scarcely squeeze himself into the presbytry, despite his friendship with the two curates. The Protestant ministers wished no doubt to test the sincerity with which a Spaniard would speak about the Inquisition, and they were convinced.

As a result of the courageous priest's frank disavowal of the Inquisition, more than eighty Protestant families subsequently presented their children for baptism in the Catholic parish. Here is another paradox in the history of Franklin's religion. The arch-deist, intellectual ally of Shaftesbury and Voltaire, not only played a major role in organizing the Catholic hierarchy in the United States but also indirectly contributed to the growth and extension of the spiritual influence of that church.

When Ruiz de Padrón returned to Spain, he became a member of the legislative body of the country, the Cortes, and then attempted to enlist other progressive thinkers in his struggle against the Inquisition. He was indeed one of the few enlightened Spaniards of his time, a leader in the liberal cause who would probably have enunciated even more radical views had he lived in a more congenial environment. It is matter for speculation as to how much influence his association with Franklin and other Philadelphians had upon the development of his advanced views.

Despite the delaying tactics in the Cortes of the proponents of the Inquisition, Ruiz de Padrón and his supporters succeeded in opening a formal debate, January 5, 1813, on the subject: "The tribunal of the Inquisition is incompatible with the Constitution." In the session of January 15, the secretary read aloud the valiant priest's *Dictamen sobre la Inquisición,* in which he described his experiences in Philadelphia and Franklin's role in drawing his attention to the evils of the Inquisition. After this, Ruiz de Padrón himself delivered a *Discurso contra la Inquisición,* repeating the same sentiments in his own voice. In the ensuing voting, 90 members voted in favor of the proposition condemning the Inquisition and 60 against. Thanks, therefore, in considerable measure to the influence of Benjamin Franklin, the notorious Spanish Inquisition was finally dissolved.

CHAPTER NINETEEN
LAST THOUGHTS

DURING his life, Franklin was mindful enough of the actual approach of his own death to prepare a series of wills, but he did not in his final one follow the common eighteenth-century practice of using the document as a means of declaring his personal religious opinions. He came closest to doing so in his earliest will, drawn up in June, 1750, in which he sought to preserve the appearance of Christianity for the benefit of his orthodox townsmen who might read it.[1] For all the mercies and favors he had been granted, he blessed that "BEING OF BEINGS who does not disdain to care for the meanest of his Creatures," a reference which suggests "the *Supremely Perfect*" of his "Articles of Belief" and recalls his polytheistic speculation. Also in this document, he hoped for continued acquiescence in the divine will —submission "to resign my Spirit chearfully into his Hands whenever he shall please to call for it; reposing myself securely in the Lap of God and Nature as a Child in the Arms of an affectionate Parent." However this may have been interpreted by Franklin's associates, it was far from an affirmation of Christianity—merely a tactful gesture to keep from giving offense.

In his final will, Franklin set forth a number of his political and social opinions but said not a word about his religious beliefs. He delivered a partial testimony to the world, however, by means of his posthumously published autobiography. It has never been pointed out that when Franklin wrote an outline for his memoirs in 1771, he made no provision for a statement of his religious creed. Yet when he wrote Part II in 1784 and Part III in 1788, he included his creed in both parts in virtually identical language. At both times, moreover, he had a copy of his outline before him, and both

1. L. W. Labaree *et al.* (eds.), *Papers of Benjamin Franklin*, III (New Haven, 1961), 480–482.

additions were, therefore, in deliberate disregard of his first intention. Both statements of his creed are substantially identical with that in his letter to Mme Brillon in 1781 on the occasion of his unsuccessful proposals for the marriage of his grandson. A warranted conclusion would seem to be, therefore, that in the ten years between the first part of his autobiography and his proposal to Mme Brillon the subject of his formal religious beliefs came to occupy an important place in his thinking.

Also, Franklin made another formal statement three months before his death in a letter to Ezra Stiles, president of Yale College, who had queried Franklin on his "religious sentiments," particularly his opinion of Jesus. Franklin made the somewhat surprising statement that Stiles was the first who had ever questioned him about his religion. Since Franklin's reply represents his most comprehensive single statement on the subject and also his most authoritative, written virtually at the end of his life, it merits printing in full.

> Here is my Creed. I believe in one God, Creator of the Universe. That he governs it by his Providence. That he ought to be worshipped. That the most acceptable Service we render to him is doing good to his other Children. That the soul of Man is immortal, and will be treated with Justice in another Life respecting its Conduct in this. These I take to be the fundamental Principles of all sound Religion, and I regard them as you do in whatever Sect I meet with them.
>
> As to Jesus of Nazareth, my Opinion of whom you particularly desire, I think the System of Morals and his Religion, as he left them to us, the best the World ever saw or is likely to see; but I apprehend it has received various corrupting Changes, and I have, with most of the present Dissenters in England, some Doubts as to his Divinity; tho' it is a question I do not dogmatize upon, having never studied it, and think it needless to busy myself with it now, when I expect soon an Opportunity of knowing the Truth with less Trouble. I see no harm, however, in its being believed, if that Belief has the good Consequence, as probably it has, of making his Doctrines more respected and better observed; especially as I

do not perceive, that the Supreme takes it amiss, by distinguishing the Unbelievers in his Government of the World with any peculiar Marks of his Displeasure.

I shall only add, respecting myself, that, having experienced the Goodness of that Being in conducting me prosperously thro' a long life, I have no doubt of its Continuance in the next, though without the smallest Conceit of meriting such Goodness.[2]

In his autobiography where he twice repeated the essence of this creed, Franklin described it as a statement of universal application, containing "the Essentials of every known Religion" and nothing "that might shock the Professors" of any one of them.[3] Ignoring the brief period when he was writing his *Dissertation on Liberty and Necessity,* he also affirmed that he had never doubted these principles throughout his life.

Most scholars have taken Franklin's letter to Stiles as the final statement of his religious belief, and Franklin himself probably expected that it would be so considered. We have already investigated his concept of providence, his spirit of worship, and his gospel of good works. And we have also seen that in all phases of his religious life, Franklin used social utility as the final measure of the value of belief and conduct —a principle upheld in his letter to Stiles, by his willingness to support the doctrine of the divinity of Christ if it has good consequences.

There remains for our consideration Franklin's final fundamental principle of religion, "that the soul of Man is immortal." Did Franklin really believe it or did he profess to believe it because of its social utility?

Not long after his youthful necessitarian tract, which denied immortality, Franklin composed his famous printer's epitaph, a *jeu d'esprit* which reappeared in countless manuscript and printed versions throughout the eighteenth century.

2. Albert Henry Smyth (ed.), *Writings of Benjamin Franklin* (10 vols., New York, 1905–1907), X, 84.
3. Leonard W. Labaree *et al.* (eds.), *Autobiography of Benjamin Franklin* (New Haven, 1964), pp. 146, 162.

The Body of
B. Franklin,
Printer;
Like the Cover of an old Book,
Its Contents torn out,
And stript of its Lettering and Gilding,
Lies here, Food for Worms.
But the Work shall not be wholly lost:
For it will, as he believ'd, appear once more,
In a new & more perfect Edition,
Corrected and amended
By the Author.[4]

Throughout his life Franklin frequently reaffirmed a faith in immortality and never again completely denied its possibility. Yet it cannot be denied that these statements, like the epitaph, were by and large an expression of hope rather than a reasoned account of unwavering conviction. Instead of trying to examine all the passages in Franklin's works which reflect his belief in another state, we shall look only at those which give some reason for the belief.

One of his comments strongly suggests the principle of social utility—a common view of many deists that even though there may not in reality be another life, it is a good thing to have the sanction of future rewards and punishments to regulate the conduct of ordinary mortals. In regard to a man who, Franklin thought, was guilty of "atrocious Wickedness" in stealing funds intended for the relief of American prisoners of war, he argued: "If such a Fellow is not damn'd, it is not worth while to keep a Devil."[5]

A moral argument widely used by Christian apologists against the deists ever since the seventeenth century concerned the demonstratable lack of a principle of justice in this world. Some of the noblest and most virtuous people seem to undergo extreme suffering, whereas some of the most wicked seem to prosper in every possible way. If the moral universe is founded upon justice, therefore, there must be a

4. Labaree (ed.), *Papers*, I (1959), 111.
5. Smyth (ed.), *Writings*, VIII, 231.

future life in which the wicked will be punished and the virtuous rewarded. Franklin knew this argument since as a young man he had refuted it indirectly in his necessitarian pamphlet, but late in his life he adopted it as his own after hearing of abominable wholesale murders of peaceful Indians committed by cruel frontiersmen. "The Dispensations of Providence in this World puzzle my weak Reason," he admitted. "I cannot comprehend why cruel Men should have been permitted thus to destroy their Fellow Creatures. Some of the Indians may be suppos'd to have committed Sins, but one cannot think the little Children had committed any worthy of Death." At that time Franklin regarded George III of England as the greatest villain of the century and even suggested that he could have been indirectly responsible for the Indians' being slaughtered. The more Franklin thought of King George's enjoying all the good things of this world, the more he saw "the Impossibility, from the number & extent of his Crimes, of giving equivalent Punishment to a wicked Man in this Life," and so the more he was "convinc'd of a future State, in which all that here appears to be wrong shall be set right, all that is crooked made straight."[6]

Another conventional argument, the teleological, we have already alluded to in connection with the abbé Morellet. Franklin gave the notion of divine perfection a typical twist by associating the scientific concept of the conservation of matter with the wisdom of God. "When I observe," he wrote,

> that there is great Frugality, as well as Wisdom, in his Works, since he has been evidently sparing both of Labour and Materials; for by the various wonderful Inventions of Propagation, he has provided for the continual peopling his World with Plants and Animals, without being at the Trouble of repeated new Creations; and by the natural Reduction of compound Substances to their original Elements, capable of being employ'd in new Compositions, he has prevented the Necessity of creating new Matter; so that the

6. *Ibid.*, pp. 561–562.

Earth, Water, Air, and perhaps Fire, which being compounded form Wood, do, when the Wood is dissolved, return, and again become Air, Earth, Fire, and Water; I say, that, when I see nothing annihilated, and not even a Drop of Water wasted, I cannot suspect the Annihilation of Souls, or believe, that he will suffer the daily Waste of Millions of Minds ready made that now exist, and put himself to the continual Trouble of making new ones. Thus finding myself to exist in the World, I believe I shall, in some Shape or other, always exist.[7]

The remainder of the letter in which this passage occurs indicates that Franklin was completely sincere in his reasoning. His correspondent, George Whatley, was neither a clergyman nor a pious believer. In a prior letter to Franklin, Whatley had queried Franklin's comfortable assurance of "the sweet sleep of death," and Franklin was attempting to convince him that there was a real possibility of immortality. Perhaps he was also trying to convince himself. At about the same time he wrote to another old friend, Jonathan Shipley, bishop of St. Asaph, obviously trying to look at the approach of death with maximum cheerfulness and at the same time please his correspondent by orthodox sentiments. He affirmed a growing curiosity to be acquainted with some other world as well as his entire readiness to resign his spirit "to the conduct of that great and good Parent of Mankind, who created it, and who has so graciously protected and prospered me from my Birth to the present Hour."[8]

Other letters written about the same time, however, not only fail to reflect this exuberant confidence but reveal implicit doubts concerning any worthwhile kind of afterlife. In August, 1785, he admitted to Jan Ingenhousz that he was not at all certain "if Consciousness and Memory remain in a future State."[9] This is an obvious vestige from his necessitarian pamphlet in which he had argued that since continued consciousness is necessary for immortality, "to cease to *think* is but little different from *ceasing to be*." He revealed the

7. *Ibid.*, IX, 333–334.   9. *Ibid.*, p. 442.
8. *Ibid.*, p. 491.

same undercurrent of doubt at just about the time of his quasi-formal statement to Stiles. He wrote to George Washington that "in whatever State of Existence" he should be placed hereafter, if he retained "any Memory of what has pass'd here," he would also retain his respect and affection for Washington.[10] The element of doubt is too apparent to be overlooked.

Indeed, there were also moments when he did not even believe that the doctrine was pragmatically desirable. Because of the tendency of some sanctimonious Christians to gloat in anticipation of their own salvation and the damnation of friends and acquaintances, Franklin reacted in the vein of Swift's bitter poem, "The Day of Judgment."

> You who in different sects were shamm'd,
> And come to see each other damn'd
> (So some folk told you, but they knew
> No more of Jove's designs than you)
> —The world's mad bus'ness now is o'er,
> And I resent these pranks no more.
> —I to such blockheads set my wit!
> I damn such fools—Go, go, you're *bit*.

Franklin, shortly before his own death, wrote to a correspondent: "And with regard to future Bliss I cannot help imagining, that Multitudes of the zealously Orthodox of different Sects, who at the last Day may flock together, in hopes of seeing [mutilated] damn'd, will be disappointed, and oblig'd to rest content with their own Salvation."[11] This seems to mean that if Franklin accepted the doctrine of resurrection at all, he did so, as the Universalists claimed, in their sense that nobody would be damned.

Another subject about which we notice an incompatibility between Franklin's public statements and his private conviction is that of the efficacy of prayer. In one of the final public acts of his life, Franklin made a speech in the Constitutional Convention calling for daily prayers in that body—

10. *Ibid.*, X, 41.   11. *Ibid.*, IX, 683.

probably his most famous testimony in favor of religion.

At the end of June, 1787, after four or five weeks of "close Attendance and continual Reasonings" resulting in deadlock or indecision on important questions, Franklin asked why the delegates had not "hitherto once thought of humbly applying to the Father of Lights to illuminate our Understandings." During the war with England they had held daily prayers in the same room—prayers which were heard and graciously answered. The hand of providence had been frequently extended in their protection—indeed the convention itself was an instance of divine favor. Had they now forgotten their "powerful Friend"? Or did they imagine they no longer needed its assistance? "The longer I live," Franklin affirmed,

> the more convincing proofs I see of this Truth, *that* GOD *governs in the Affairs of Men.* And if a Sparrow cannot fall to the Ground without his Notice, is it probable that an Empire can rise without his Aid? We have been assured, Sir, in the Sacred Writings, that "except the Lord build the House, they labour in vain that build it" I firmly believe this; and I also believe, that, without his concurring Aid, we shall succeed in this political Building no better than the Builders of Babel; we shall be divided by our little, partial, local Interests, our Projects will be confounded, and we ourselves shall become a Reproach and a Bye-word down to future Ages. And, what is worse, Mankind may hereafter, from this unfortunate Instance, despair of establishing Government by human Wisdom, and leave it to Chance, War, and Conquest.

After this gloomy picture, Franklin moved that "henceforth Prayers, imploring the Assistance of Heaven and its Blessing on our Deliberations, be held in this Assembly every morning before we proceed to Business; and that one or more of the Clergy of this city be requested to officiate in that Service."[12]

In a sense it may seem inappropriate for a deist such as Franklin to sponsor public prayers. He probably did not

12. *Ibid.,* pp. 600–601.

believe that a sparrow cannot fall to the ground without being noticed by God. Indeed in his speech he did not make a positive affirmation, merely giving the impression that he believed it. True, he declared in his formal statements of his creed (in his autobiography and his letter to Stiles) that God governs the universe by his providence and that he ought to be worshiped, but he did not connect the two principles. In other words, even though believing that God controls the destiny of the United States and that he expects acknowledgment and worship from its citizens, Franklin could also believe, like most deists, that God would not necessarily take notice of prayers in the convention if they were held. As he wrote to Stiles, "I do not perceive, that the Supreme takes it amiss, by distinguishing the Unbelievers in his Government of the World with any peculiar Marks of his Displeasure."

Still, Franklin would have reason to propose public prayers. They make men mindful of their human deficiencies and inspire humility. And by imbuing independent spirits with a sense of common interest and identity of purpose, they prepare the ground for unity and co-operation. These qualities were needed by the constitution-makers in 1787 just as they had been necessary to all citizens of Pennsylvania when Franklin had proposed a day of fast in 1747 during the Indian wars. On neither occasion had Franklin been guilty of a hypocritical or pharisaical act. It is true that he used Christian symbols to arouse a sense of identity with the common cause among the predominant sects. But both appeals were consistent with the pragmatic side of his deism.

Franklin believed that private prayers also were efficacious chiefly in helping the individual to organize his thoughts. He condemned public confession or display of personal religious crises. Thomas Paine revealed in conversation that Franklin once commented with some asperity on "some religious posthumous anecdotes of Doctor Johnson, of resolves he had made and broken though he had prayed for power and strength to keep them."[13] According to Franklin, this showed that Johnson "had not much interest there. And such things had better be suppressed as nobody had anything to do betwixt God and man."

Despite popular belief, Franklin's proposal for public prayer was never adopted. He remarked in a note, "The convention except three or four persons, thought prayers unnecessary." And James Madison in his report on debates in the convention revealed that the motion was defeated solely because of lack of funds to pay a minister. Indeed, the convention was so little inclined to foster religious sentiments that one clergyman in the early nineteenth century complained that after solemn debate God was "not merely forgotten . . . he was absolutely and deliberately voted out of the Constitution."

Franklin's final speech at the convention, his plea for the unanimous adoption of the Constitution, epitomizes his pragmatic attitude toward religion as well as politics. In it, Franklin stressed experimentation and compromise and affirmed that for human beings truth must remain tentative. Men are like most religious sects, he concluded, since they "think themselves in possession of all truth, and that wherever others differ from them, it is so far error. Steele, a Protestant, in a dedication, tells the Pope, that the only difference between our two churches in their opinions of the certainty of their doctrine, is, the Romish Church is *infallible,* and the Church of England is *never in the wrong.*"[14]

Franklin opposed intolerance, intellectual authoritarianism, and the concept of infallibility in sects as well as in individuals. Because of his devotion to experiment as well as his distrust of metaphysical dogmatism, he consistently avoided positive assertion in both his public and private religion.

13. Journal of John Hall in Moncure D. Conway, *The Life of Thomas Paine* (New York, 1892) , II, 465–466.
14. Smyth (ed.) , *Writings,* IX, 607.

CHAPTER TWENTY

LAST WORDS

WHEN the Constitutional Convention came to an end, Franklin realized that his own public life had also terminated and that he would soon be entering upon the "sweet Sleep of Death," as he had expressed it in his youthful tract on necessity. Ernest Renan in the same context with his criticism of Franklin's money-getting philosophy had remarked that it is of no consequence whether a man achieves material success in life. "What matters is to have thought much, to have loved much, to have regarded life whole, and, in dying, to be able to criticize death itself." From this standard, Franklin's life must be considered one of the most noble and valuable on record. Throughout his entire career he had needed no *memento mori* or death's head to keep the end of life constantly in his mind, for he had seldom contemplated death in a gloomy or fearful mood. He was curious, but in general quite optimistic, about his own and others' demise. This is the place to record some of Franklin's remarks on death as distinguished from immortality.

In his youthful necessitarian tract he had insisted that the dissolution of life is a comfortable, satisfying experience. At the approach of the final moment, according to his notion, the senses become numb and " 'tis an exquisite Pleasure to behold the immediate Approaches of Rest." In this view, death resembles the moment of truth so raptly praised by the aficionados of bull fights.

Franklin probably felt himself quite remote from his own dissolution when he concocted this theory of exquisite pleasure. As we remember, he was driven to it by the forensic necessity of vindicating his psychological notion that all men experience pleasure and pain in absolutely equal amounts.

In later life Franklin gave up his theory of the balance of pleasure and pain but retained essentially the same optimism about the departure from life. He continued to picture it as an escape from the ills and pains of old age—but instead of merely a sweet sleep, he sometimes projected positive pleasures in immortality.

After the death of his brother John, Franklin wrote to a stepdaughter of the widow, February 22, 1756, condoling with her over the loss. Our mortal existence he described as an embryo state or a preparation for the real life. "A man is not completely born until he be dead: Why then should we grieve that a new child is born among the immortals? A new member added to their happy society?"[1]

Conceiving of the body as merely a practical instrument to "afford us pleasure, assist us in acquiring knowledge, or doing good to our fellow creatures," Franklin felt that we should be grateful to God for kindly providing a way to get rid of it when it becomes an encumbrance and fails to carry out these functions. Since we sometimes choose a partial death, by amputating a painfully mangled limb or extracting an aching tooth, we should relish total death when the time comes. "He that quits the whole body, parts at once with all pains and possibilities of pains and diseases it was liable to, or capable of making him suffer."

In conclusion, Franklin compared his brother to the first in the family who had accepted an invitation to go abroad "on a party of pleasure, that is to last forever." "We could not all conveniently start together, and why should you and I be grieved at this, since we are soon to follow and we know where to find him?" Long before Franklin's letters were collected in print, this epistle was well known in New England. The Reverend Mather Byles, who probably knew Franklin when they were boys in Boston, once wrote to him that many copies of his letter on his brother's death had been made, and in his old age Franklin continued to receive requests for the text.[2] Since it was written to give comfort to a

1. L. W. Labaree *et al.* (eds), *Papers of Benjamin Franklin*, VI (New Haven, 1963), 407.
2. Albert Henry Smyth (ed.), *Writings of Benjamin Franklin* (10 vols., New York, 1905–1907), IX, 684.

bereaved family, Franklin took care to disguise his private doubts of immortality.

Franklin's condolences, although cheerful, were never trite or conventional. Writing to his sister on another death in the family, he suggested that death should make the survivors all the more affectionate to each other. "Out of Seventeen Children that our Father had, thirteen liv'd to grow up and settle in the World. I remember these thirteen (some of us then very young) all at one Table, when an Entertainment was made in our House on Occasion of the Return of our Brother Josiah, who had been absent in the East-Indies, and unheard of for nine Years. Of these thirteen, there now remains but three. As our Number diminishes, let our Affection to each other rather increase: for besides its being our Duty, tis our Interest, since the more affectionate Relations are to one another, the more they are respected by the rest of the World."[3]

According to Mason Locke Weems, Franklin at one time was traveling with a group of young men who amused themselves at his expense by calling him "Parson" and asking for a sermon. Good-naturedly, he gave them an impromptu one in verse.

On Man

This entrance on life is naked & bare;
His progress through out, with trouble & care;
His exit therefrom, the Lord knows where;
And yet, to save us from gloomy despair,
If we do well here, we shall do well there:
I could tell you no more if I preached a whole Year.[4]

Six years before his own death, Franklin wrote (April 22, 1784) a cheerful poem on the coming event with the title "B. F.'s Adieu."

3. Labaree (ed.), *Papers*, IX (1966), 18.
4. Manuscripts of Rembrandt Peale in Library of the American Philosophical Society.

LAST WORDS

If Life's compared to a Feast,
Near Fourscore Years I've been a Guest:
I've been regaled with the best,
And feel quite satisfied.
'Tis time that I retire to Rest;
Landlord, I thank ye! Friends, Good Night.[5]

In the year before his own death, Franklin expressed to
Price a somewhat grim view of the loss of his friends. They
were dropping off one after another at a time when his age
and infirmities prevented him from making new ones. And
among the rising new generation there seemed to be few
individuals who measured up to the high standards of the
old. "So that the longer I live I must expect to be more
wretched. As we draw near the Conclusion of Life, Nature
furnishes us with more Helps to wean us from it, among
which one of the most powerful is the Loss of such dear
Friends."[6] Price's biographer considered this a "gloomy view
of the future race of mankind" and attributed it to the
"common failing of old age." It might just as well be interpreted, however, as an optimistic attempt to reconcile us to
the approach of death or even to cause us to view it with
anticipation.

Thomas Paine, who visited Franklin two years before this
letter, found that Franklin regarded the coming of his own
death with equanimity. He was at that moment making new
arrangements for the installing of books in the library of his
home, which he had ordered built especially to his require-
ments. "Mr. Paine," said the aged philosopher, "you may be
surprised at finding me thus busily occupied at my advanced
state of life. Many might think me an old fool to be thus
busied in the affairs of this life, while making such near
approach in the course of nature, to the grave. But it has
always been my maxim to live on as if I was to live always. It
is with such feeling only that we can be stimulated to the

5. Manuscripts of William Temple Franklin in Library of Congress.
6. Smyth (ed.), *Writings*, X, 8.

exertions necessary to effect any useful purpose. Death will one day lay hold of me, and put an end to all my labours; but, till then, it is my maxim to go on in the old way. I will not anticipate his coming."[7]

Franklin received public praise for this same attitude. The *Federal Gazette,* November 20, 1788, in pleading for one dollar yearly subscriptions to the free school of the Episcopal church, rendered homage to Franklin, who by paying in advance his subscriptions for the next four years had anticipated continued life for this period.

Deathbed conversions are notoriously unconvincing, and witnesses of death scenes are notoriously unreliable. Eighteenth-century writers of religious tracts customarily described such unbelievers as Hume, Voltaire, and Paine as suffering untold agonies, recanting their skepticism, and crying out for salvation. Franklin was more fortunate. All of the accounts of his last days have the ring of truth. And only two attempt to present Franklin as at all orthodox.

An English Quaker, Robert Sutcliff, who published an account of his travels in America, learned that a young man who had some doubts concerning the truth of the Scriptures, had questioned Franklin on the subject while he lay on his deathbed. Having great respect for Franklin's judgment and deeming "this awful period" an opportunity of receiving a solemn answer, he asked Franklin about his sentiments. Franklin replied, "Young man! my advice to you is, that you cultivate an acquaintance with, and a firm belief in the Holy Scriptures; this is your certain interest."[8]

Charles Thomson, former secretary of the Continental Congress, visited Franklin often during his illness and reported a similar remark. Shortly before the final moment, Franklin said in alluding to a prior conversation, "It is best to believe."[9]

7. John Epps, *Life of John Walker* (London, 1840), p. 145.
8. *Travels in Some Parts of North America* (York, 1811), p. 225.
9. Deborah Norris Logan, *Memoir of Dr. George Logan of Stenton* (Philadelphia, 1894), p. 39.

In neither anecdote does Franklin commit himself to Christian doctrine; yet he gives the impression that he was sympathetic to it. Although in the first anecdote he advises the young man to cultivate the Scriptures, he says nothing positive about his own belief. In the second his advice is so cryptic that it could mean almost anything. Perhaps he means a belief in God, perhaps immortality. Either would be consistent with his profession during the major part of his life.

A certain Nicholas Collin wrote to Franklin's grandson William Temple Franklin shortly after the death of the "immortal sage" to inform him of conversations he had had with Franklin during his illness.

> The Doctor had sublime and affecting sentiments of religion. He believed that, by the invariable laws of God in the moral world, all crimes are punished *either here or hereafter;* and that, consequently, an evil deed can never be profitable in any case whatever: He was equally persuaded that *every good action* has its reward. Under a painful disease he expressed a firm confidence, that all the sufferings of this life are but the *momentary pricking of a pin,* in comparison to the total happiness of our existence: He rejoiced in a speedy approach to the regions of bliss and life eternal: He dwelt with rapture on the felicity of beholding the Glorious Father of Spirits, whose essence is incomprehensible to the wisest mortals; of contemplating His works in the higher world; and of conversing there with good fellow creatures from every part of the Universe.[10]

Although the language of this account owes somewhat more to evangelical terminology than that which Franklin ordinarily used, even the faith in a future state may be confirmed in some passages from Franklin's own writings although others seem to deny it. It is hard to believe, however, that Franklin ever "dwelt with rapture" on his deathbed or anywhere else.

A more reliable witness was Franklin's young protégé, Mary Stevenson, who had married and gone to live in Phila-

10. Oct. 30, 1790. Manuscripts of William Temple Franklin in Library of Congress.

delphia. Although present at the closing scene of Franklin's career, April 17, 1790, "which he sustained with that calm fortitude which characterized him throughout life," she described in more detail a day she passed with him during the previous summer.

> I found him in bed in great agony; but, when that agony abated a little, I asked if I should read to him. He said, Yes; and the first book I met with was Johnson's "Lives of the Poets." I read the Life of Watts, who was a favorite author with Dr. Franklin; and, instead of lulling him to sleep, it roused him to a display of the powers of his memory and his reason. He repeated several of Watts's "Lyric Poems," and descanted upon their sublimity in a strain worthy of them and of their pious author. It is natural for us to wish that an attention to some ceremonies had accompanied that religion of the heart, which I am convinced Dr. Franklin always possessed; [the identical sentiment which she had expressed to Franklin himself almost thirty years previously] but let us, who feel the benefit of them, continue to practise them, without thinking lightly of that piety, which could support pain without a murmur, and meet death without terror.[11]

"Religion of the heart" rather than "religion of doctrine" certainly epitomizes Franklin's approach to God.

Franklin's physician reported that "when the severity of his pains drew forth a groan of complaint, he would observe, that he was afraid he did not bear them as he ought; acknowledging his grateful sense of the many blessings he had received from the Supreme Being, who had raised him, from small and low beginnings, to such high rank and consideration among men; and made no doubt but that his present afflictions were kindly intended to wean him from a world in which he was no longer fit to act the part assigned him."[12]

Another physician, Benjamin Rush, who had enjoyed something of a political acquaintance with Franklin, wrote two conflicting accounts of his religious beliefs. In the first, to Elias Boudinot, April 18, 1790, he confirmed Franklin's agnosticism. "He expired without a struggle. I have not

11. Jared Sparks (ed.), *Works of Benjamin Franklin* (Boston, 1840), I, 532.
12. *Ibid.*, p. 530.

heard of anything that fell from him which discovered what his expectations were beyond the grave. My dear Julia wished this day that he had left a short testimony in favor of Christianity. I told her that if he had, he would have overset much stronger evidences of its truth, for we are told 'that not many *wise* are called,' and that 'the world by *wisdom* knew not god' " (I Cor. 1:26,21).[13]

In his second account, to Richard Price, six days later, Rush tried to make Franklin into more of a Christian, perhaps out of consideration for Price's calling as a dissenting minister.

> His conversation with his family upon the subject of his dissolution was free and cheerful. A few days before he died, he rose from his bed and begged that it might be made up for him so that he might die "in a decent manner." His daughter told him that she hoped he would recover and live many years longer. He calmly replied, "He hoped not." Upon being advised to change his position in bed that he might breathe *easy,* he said, "A dying man can do nothing *easy.*" . . . I had like to have forgot to mention that he desired in his will that the elegant epitaph (suggested by his original occupation) which he composed for himself some years ago should be inscribed upon his tombstone. By this request he has declared his belief in the Christian doctrine of a resurrection.[14]

This statement concerning Franklin's printer's epitaph is not true. In his will, Franklin requested that only his name and that of his wife be inscribed on his tomb, and his wish was faithfully carried out.

The most affecting—and probably in spirit the most accurate—statement concerning Franklin's death appeared in a report from Louis Otto, French consul in New York, to his superior, the Count de Montmorin. "Dr. Franklin, after patiently supporting the weight of 85 years, successively passed in philosophic meditations and the whirlwind of affairs, has just finished his career with the serenity of a sage, who yearns

---

13. L. H. Butterfield (ed.), *Letters of Benjamin Rush* (Princeton, 1951), I, 563.
14. *Ibid.,* pp. 564–565.

after repose. A few moments before his dissolution he repeated these words that he had made for himself, *that a man is perfectly born only after his death.*"[15] Otto failed to state his source for Franklin's last words, but there is little doubt that they are genuine, essentially identical with his comments on his brother's death thirty-four years before: "A man is not completely born until he be dead."[16] Throughout his long life Franklin had contemplated death with tranquillity. He met it with the same calm.

Despite the care Franklin took throughout his life to associate himself with pious sentiments and external observances of worship, the public image he had created for himself was not that of a religious leader. Indeed, *The American Annual Register . . . for the Year 1796,* to take a single example, gloated that the federal Constitution "betrays as much indifference about religion, as if it had been exclusively penned by Benjamin Franklin himself. It is well known that the doctor believed *nothing*. He was by far the greatest philosopher of whom America can boast. Yet all the world knew that this great man disbelieved christianity."[17] In England ten years later, an opponent of the deists, David Simpson, in *A Plea for Religion,* classed Franklin with the Earl of Oxford and David Hume as men who never "gave *Christianity* a serious and conscientious investigation. They were all too busy in life, and had little inclination to religious pursuits. The carnal minds of a *Nobleman* and a *Philosopher* are equally at enmity against God."[18]

In contrast to these explicit assertions of Franklin's agnosticism, we have the opinion of the abbé Fauchet that Franklin was "the philosopher *par excellence* of protestantism." And the historian James Parton called Franklin "the consummate Christian of his time." The views of those who claim Franklin as a Christian and those who see him as a deist are not, however, completely incompatible. There is no

15. Translated from the original manuscript in Ministère des Affaires Etrangères: Etats Unis, Vol. 35, fols. 88–89.
16. Labaree (ed.), *Papers*, VI, 407.   18. (London, 1807), p. 221.
17. (Philadelphia, 1797), p. 222.

doubt whatsoever that Franklin was a deist. Whether he was a Christian as well depends entirely upon how much breadth one allows to the definition of Christianity. Franklin himself used the term with great latitude. In one of his letters he referred to "that excellent Christian David Hume," knowing full well that Hume was a professed atheist.[19] Parton's conception of a consummate Christian was also far from orthodox. He felt that Franklin "exhibited more of the spirit of Christ" than anyone he knew—that Franklin "was tolerant of every thing but intolerance, and made some charitable allowance even for that." For Fauchet also, the spirit of Protestantism consisted in toleration and social benevolence. Every one will admit that Franklin was indeed a consummate Christian in terms of doing good, tolerating the beliefs of others, and using his rational faculties in the service of God and man. But he did not believe in either the divinity of Christ or the divine inspiration of the Bible. If these beliefs are essential to Christianity, Franklin was not a Christian at all.

As we have seen, Franklin's religion had a solid theoretical foundation. Particularly in the early years of his life, he was fascinated by metaphysical problems. Even though he failed to solve the insolvable problem of free will and determinism or the relationship of spirit and matter, he gave them independent study, refusing to accept the easy generalizations of theologians. Although world famous for compiling maxims of prudential morality, his personal moral system was fundamentally altruistic. He understood the problems most widely debated by contemporary ethical theorists and carried on the discussion of virtue in his own writings. As he reached middle age, however, he abandoned formal philosophical speculation to rely upon the broad principles which he expressed in his autobiography and in his letter to Stiles.

Of equal importance in Franklin's religion with regular petition to God was "doing good to his other Children." Franklin's acts of benevolence may be considered a prag-

19. Smyth (ed.) , *Writings*, V, 344.

matic manifestation of his religious spirit along with his broad tolerance of every religious opinion and his support of every church in the city of Philadelphia. William Duane, on the basis of his intimate association with Franklin's descendants, affirmed that Franklin considered all religions as human rather than supernatural, "none having superiority, but as they promoted the greatest good; but the proper business of man in the world of which he forms a part, and the perfection of his nature, was the promotion of universal happiness, by the prevention or mitigation of evil."[20]

Unlike many deists and Anglicans, Franklin never spoke out publicly against religious enthusiasm—one of the reasons he was able to remain on affectionate terms with Whitefield. Speaking to Thomas Paine on the effects of animal magnetism in France, a type of hysteria similar to religious enthusiasm, Franklin said "that he thought the Government might as well have let it gone on, for that as imagination sometimes produces disorders it might also cure some."[21] And we have seen that the abbé de la Roche affirmed that Franklin believed in dream visions. But he once soberly warned Polly Stevenson against wishing herself an enthusiast. "They have, indeed," he wrote, "their imaginary Satisfactions and Pleasures, but these are often ballanc'd by imaginary Pains and Mortifications. You can continue to be a good Girl, and thereby lay a solid Foundation for expected future Happiness, without the Enthusiasm that may perhaps be necessary to some others."[22]

Throughout the greater part of his life Franklin was nominally an Anglican. Although intellectually rejecting practically the entire body of Anglican theology, he kept strict Lents, probably took communion, edited the Book of Common Prayer, and urged upon his family regular participation in liturgical devotions. The explanation for this apparent

20. *Memoirs of Benjamin Franklin* (New York, 1861), I, xxiv.
21. Philip S. Foner (ed.), *Complete Writings of Thomas Paine* (New York, 1945), II, 830.
22. Smyth (ed.), *Writings*, V, 225.

gross contradiction lies in Franklin's character. As Renan pointed out, Franklin was strongly attached to formulas of all kinds—in religion as in other interests. As a Frenchman would say, "Louis par la grâce de Dieu" as an empty stereotype, Franklin could repeat Anglican rubrics without attention to their literal meanings. He sought method in all he did—and, for him, the Anglican approach to God was expedient and methodical. In private he followed his own "Articles of Belief and Acts of Religion" (in *form* patterned on the Book of Common Prayer), but he felt that religion must be public as well as private. For him, the Anglican was the most compatible system of public worship. But it was the ritual, not the theology, that counted. That is why he could devote equal energy to helping Despencer revise the Book of Common Prayer and Williams compose his deistical liturgy.

As a public figure, Franklin used the power of religion to accomplish political ends. He proposed fast days in colonial Pennsylvania and posed as a Quaker in Paris. And he respected the influence of Christianity in inculcating ethical behavior—even though he criticized some sects for emphasizing doctrine over morality. Yet he did not take the supercilious view of some deists that men of culture should rise above the superstition of religion but still support it merely to keep the masses in order. Franklin believed in religion for himself as well as for everyone else. And he advocated religion for its spiritual or emotional values, not primarily for its moral functions. He held that morality is every man's responsibility on other than religious grounds although doing good is the primary obligation of religion.

Throughout his entire life he engaged in a continuous quest for spiritual satisfaction. His search, like most things he undertook, was methodical and rational. In fact, it would be quite appropriate to call him a methodical deist. In the spirit of his remark to the abbé Soulavie, "Superior beings smile at our theories, and at our presumption in making them," he viewed his entire theology as experimental or tentative.

INDEX

Adams, John, 74, 115, 181, 203, 204, 230, 231
Addison, Joseph, 66, 188; *Cato*, 48, 51
American Annual Register, 268
American Weekly Mercury, 84
Andrews, Rev. Jedediah, 85–98, 150
Annet, Peter, 134, 202
Antonelli, Cardinal Leonardo, 236, 238
Arianism, 99
Aristotle, 80
Arminianism, 41, 99, 247
atheism, 17, 22–23, 36, 43, 76, 107, 124, 144, 192, 218, 225, 226, 230, 231, 269

Bache, Benjamin Franklin, 193, 232–233
Bache, Sarah, 159–160, 161, 187, 212, 267
Bache, William, 159–160
Bacon, Francis, 60; "Of Atheism," 226
Banks, Sir Joseph, 32, 213, 215
Baptists, 144, 145, 153–157
Baynes, John, 140
Baxter, Andrew, *An Inquiry into the Nature of the Human Soul . . .*, 75–77
Bayle, Pierre, 84; *Pensées diverses . . .*, 89–90, 124
Beatty, Rev. Charles, 174
Beeston, Rev. Francis, 248
Beiser, Conrad, 150–151
Benezet, Anthony, 113, 145
Bentley, Thomas, 213, 214, 218
Bolton, Robert, 109
Boswell, James, 223
Boudinot, Elias, 266
Bowdoin, James, 77, 79–80
Bradford, Andrew, 97
Brillon de Jouy, Mme d'Hardancourt, 116–117, 231–233, 251
Browne, John, 198
Brun, abbé André, 230
Budé, John Francis, 246
Buffon, Georges Louis Leclerc, comte de, 42
Butler, Joseph, *The Analogy of Religion . . .*, 3
Byles, Rev. Mather, 261

Cabanis, Pierre Jean George, 49–50, 59, 225–226
capitalism and religion, 55
Carroll, Father John, 237–242
Catholics, 8, 145, 167–168, 181, 205, 222–249
Cerutti, Joseph Antoine, 116
chain of being, 27–29, 64–66
Chubb, Thomas, *An Enquiry into . . . Religion . . .*, 3
Church of England. *See* Episcopalians
Churchill, Charles, "The Candidate," 167–168
Cicero, 49, 193
Clarke, Rev. Samuel, 188, 211
Clay, Joseph, 163

INDEX

Cohen, I. Bernard, 29
Colden, Cadwallader, *An Explication of the First Causes* . . . , 75
Collas, Jane, 243
Collin, Nicholas, 265
Collins, Anthony, 13, 84
Collinson, Peter, 44
Condorcet, Marie Jean de Caritat, marquis de, 225, 231
Conduitt, John, 29
Confucius, 120–121
Congregational Church. *See* Presbyterians
Constitutions of the Publick Academy . . . , 119
Cook, Captain James, 140
Cooper, Rev. Samuel, 203
Le Courrier de l'Europe, 228
Crigan, Bishop Claudius, 184–185
Cumberland, Richard, 50
Cutler, Timothy, 14

Dashwood, Sir Francis, Lord Le Despenser, 166–170, 175, 187, 207, 209–210
Dawson, Col. Richard, 213
Day, Thomas, 213
de Cissé, Archbishop Jerôme M. C., 241
Declaration of Independence, 3
deism, 17, 34–46, 77, 81, 107, 134, 135–140, 144, 156, 168, 172, 187, 190–191, 211, 212–219, 224, 247, 253, 258, 269–271; and the Chinese, 120–121; and the Jews, 120–121, 175–176, 202, 205
de la Roche, abbé Pierre Louis Lefebvre, 225, 241, 270
de Neufville, John, 203–204
Denny, William, 167
Descartes, 80
Dickinson, Jonathan, *Vindication of the* . . . *Synod,* 94
Dictionnaire des athées anciens et modernes, 231
Dryden, John, 44
Duane, William, 193, 270
Dubourg, Dr. Jacques Barbeu, *Petit code de la raison humaine,* 224
Dunkards, 149–151, 220
Dupont de Nemours, Samuel Pierre, 31

Edwards, Jonathan: compared with Franklin, 4, 5, 14, 38, 45, 62, 78–79, 100–101, 107; *Freedom of the Will,* 5, 41, 62; *Some Thoughts concerning the present Revival* . . . , 100–101
Edwards, Timothy, 40
Emmons, Rev. Nathaniel, *The Dignity of Man,* 102
Enlightenment, defined, 5
Ephrata Cloister, 150–151, 169
Episcopalians, 8, 13, 14, 50–51, 144, 157–194, 209
Erasmus, *Colloquies,* 177
Evans, Rev. Nathaniel, 220
evil, problem of, 44–45, 67
existence of God, proofs, 34–37, 76–77

Fauchet, abbé Claude, 233–234, 262, 267
Federal Gazette, 142, 264
Francis, Tench, 110, 119
Franklin, Mass., 102
Franklin, Abiah. *See* Franklin, Josiah and Abiah
Franklin, Benjamin—activities: church attendance, 13, 161, 166, 207, 209, 214, 220, 223; as a communicant, 189–193; first essays on religion, 13–15; hoaxes, 67–68, 133–143; liturgies, 30–31, 174–175, 214–215; motion for

INDEX

prayer in Constitutional Convention, 32, 256–258; religious oaths, 190–194
—characteristics: eroticism, 22, 167–168; justifying means by end, 22, 89;
morality, 11, 47–74; personal character, 10; pragmatism, 99, 130, 132, 212,
252, 259; reaction against Puritanism, 12–13; a secularizing force, 131–132
—interests: atheism, 21–23, 43; biblical authority, 97, 190–192; biblical
exposition, 84–85, 148, 165–166; biblical language, 148, 195–203, parody of,
198, 202; outer space, 20, 20 n., 32; philoprogenitiveness, 133–134; polytheism, 25–33, 135, 137, 219, 250; vegetarianism, 16
—views concerning: apostolic succession, 182–183; death, 260–266; dream
visions, 227; end of the world, 40, 132; enthusiasm, 270; ethical relativism,
51–52, 63; finances in religion, 141, 192; heresy, 85; immortality, 21, 122,
211, 252–256; intellectual culture, 102; millennialism, 176; morality vs.
faith, 88–90, 124–132; plagiarism, 14, 95; problem of evil, 200; providence,
34–46, 128–129, 202, 254, 258; religion and society, 147, 228–230; Sabbatarianism, 161–162; science and morality, 121; slavery, 141–142; Spanish
Inquisition, 93–94, 95, 223, 242, 246–249; toleration, 195–196, 205–206,
233–234, 247
—writings:
    Abridgement of the Book of Common Prayer, 170–174
    "Advice to a Young Tradesman," 54, 56
    "An Arabian Tale" ["Belubel"], 66, 67
    "Art of Virtue," 48–51, 213, 216, 224
    "Articles of Belief and Acts of Religion," 25–31, 48, 59, 100, 137, 139,
        161, 173, 179, 188, 219, 228, 250, 271
    autobiography [*Memoirs*], 17, 42, 48, 51–52, 60, 85, 103–104, 112–113,
        117, 124, 147, 174, 198, 206, 220, 222, 226, 232, 250–251, 252
    "Caring for the Sick," 84–85
    "Character of a Whig," 208
    "Concerning the Savages of North America," 55, 135
    "The Conduct of the Ancient Jews . . . ," 201–202
    "Conte" ["Montresor"], 116
    Defence of the Rev. Mr. Hemphill's Observations, 94–97
    "Dialogue on Man of Sense," 60
    "Discourse on Self-denial," 60
    Dissertation on Liberty and Necessity . . . , 17–24, 44, 76, 89, 252,
        255, 260
    Dogood Letters, 13–15, 96, 234
    Experiments and Observations on Electricity, 121–122
    "Extract from an Account of the Captivity of William Henry," 134–140
    Idea of the English School, 159
    "Letter from China," 140
    "The Levee," 199–200
    "Necessary Hints to Those that would be Rich," 56
    Observations on . . . Proceedings against Hemphill, 92–93
    "Observations on Reading History," 68
    Œuvres de M. Franklin, 224
    "On the Providence of God," 34–46
    "Parable against Persecution," 195–196
    "Parody of a Religious Meditation," 67–68
    Political, Miscellaneous, and Philosophical Pieces, 244
    Poor Richard, 40 n., 52, 55, 70, 129, 132 n., 135
    "Printer's Epitaph," 252–253
    Proposals relating to the Education of Youth in Pennsylvania, 118
    "Revision of Lord's Prayer," 175–179
    "The Royal Academy of Brussels," 80–81
    The Speech of Polly Baker, 133–134
    "Way to Make Money Plenty," 56
    The Way to Wealth, 23, 57, 165
Franklin, Deborah, 189

Franklin, James, 13
Franklin, John, 113, 261
Franklin, Josiah and Abiah, 98–99, 132
Franklin, William, 222–223
Franklin, William Temple, 128, 192, 231–232, 265
freedom of will. *See* necessitarianism
free-thinkers, 9, 114, 144, 224
Frink, Rev. Samuel, 163

Gant, Rev. Edward, 181–184, 242–243, 248
General Advertiser, 134
George III, 119, 254
Goldsmith, Oliver, 66
Green, Ashbel, 86
Grew, Theophilus, 89

Hall, Max, 134
Harvard College, 13
Harwood, Edward, 201
Helvétius, Mme Anne Catherine, 225
Helvétius, Claude Adrien, 217, 225
Hemphill, Rev. Samuel, 86–98, 132 n., 155
Hoadly, Benjamin, 50
Hobbes, Thomas, 50, 51, 69
Hodgson, Dr. William, 217
Holcroft, Thomas, 215, 218
Hopkinson, Francis, 187
Huey, Joseph, 125–127, 132 n.
Hume, David, 268–269
Hutcheson, Francis, 60
hypocritical profession, 14

Ilive, Elizabeth, 71
Indians, 55–56
Ingenhousz, Jan, 255

Jackson, James, 141–142
Jefferson, Thomas, 5
Jenkins, Obadiah, 97–98
Jenney, Dr. Robert, 158
Jews, 120–121, 172, 195–206, 215
Job, 67, 173, 178, 195, 198–200
Johnson, Joseph, 209
Johnson, Dr. Samuel (lexicographer), 258–259, 266
Johnson, Rev. Samuel, 158–160
Jones, Rev. Jenkin, 153–156
Jones, Noble Wimberly, 163–164
Jones, Sir William, 193
Journal de Paris, 225
Junto, Franklin's, 34, 62–64, 69, 220

Kames, Henry Home, Lord, 196
Keimer, Samuel, 16
Kinnersley, Ebenezer, 153–156

La Luzerne, Chevalier Anne César, 240
La Mettrie, Julien de, 22
Lay, Benjamin, 146–147, 149
Le Despencer, Lord. *See* Dashwood

INDEX

Liberation, 205
Lincoln, Abraham, compared to Franklin, 9–10
Lindsey, Rev. Theophilus, 188, 208–211, 234
Locke, John, *Essay concerning Human Understanding,* 27
Logan, James, 145
London Chronicle, 134, 136, 196
London Journal, 84
Louis XVI, 235, 238
Lovell, Michael, 146
Luther, Martin, 91
Lutherans, 246

Madison, James, 130, 259
Magaw, Samuel, 188
Mallet du Pan, Jacques, 131–132
Mandeville, Bernard, 63, 69–70; *Fable of the Bees,* 23, 53, 61
Manning, Dr. James, 185, 186
Marbois, François Barbé de, 230
Maryland Gazette, 84
Masons, 156–157
materialism, 18–22
Mather, Cotton, *Essays to Do Good,* 62–63
Mecom, Jane, 42, 72–74, 82, 99–100, 127, 181, 244, 262
metaphysics, 75–80
Methodists, 103–123, 186
Miller, Johann Peter, 150–151, 220
Milton, John, *Areopagitica,* 83
ministerial profession, 13–14, 83, 141, 146, 164
Mirabeau, H. G. Riqueti, comte de, 225; *Considerations on the Order of Cincinnatus,* 152
Mohammedans, 117, 206, 215
Molière, *Dom Juan,* 114
Montaigne, Michel Eyquem de, 71
Montesquieu, Charles de Secondat de, 224
Moravians, 151–153
Morellet, abbé André, 5, 182, 194, 221, 223–228, 254
Morris, Robert, 203
Morris, Thomas, 213
Murray, Mrs. John, 212

Napoleon Bonaparte, 225
necessitarianism, 18–22, 34–44
New England Courant, 13
Newton, John, 29–30, 40 n., 76, 80, 218, 219
Noble, Abel, 146

original sin, 45
Orpheus, Priest of Nature, 219–220
Otto, Louis, 267–268
Owen, Robert Dale, 114

Paine, Thomas, 8, 145, 206, 211, 258, 263, 270; *The Age of Reason,* 3, 13, 128, 129–130; *Common Sense,* 203
Palmer, Samuel, 17, 18
Pamphili, Prince Doria, 238–243
Parton, James, 29, 268–269
Pemberton, Isaac, 145
Penn, Thomas, 109, 110
Pennsylvania Gazette, 60–61, 63, 67–68, 83–85, 104, 108–113, 121, 124, 133,

INDEX

144, 152–153, 153–154, 158, 198, 200, 223
Peters, Richard, 110, 159
Pinckney, Charles, 204
plagiarism, 196
Plowden, Rev. Charles, 242
Pope, Alexander, *An Essay on Man*, 27, 65
prayer and prayers, 13, 32, 40, 140, 148, 159–160, 166–179, 193, 256–259
pre-existence, 71–72
Presbyterians, 8, 82–102, 134, 144, 192–193, 236, 245
Price, Rev. Richard, 192, 207, 208, 263, 267
Priestley, Rev. Joseph, 31–32, 191, 195, 198, 208, 209, 211
Pringle, Sir John, 207
Proverbs, Book of, 49, 52, 226
Provoost, Dr. Samuel, 188

Quakers, 8, 76, 140–142, 144–149, 175, 192, 224–225, 233–234

Raynal, abbé Guillaume Thomas, 134
reason, 66–67, 73–74
Renan, Ernest, 23, 56, 260, 271
Rowland, Rev. John, 153–156
Ruiz de Padrón, Don Antonio José, 245–249
Rush, Dr. Benjamin, 211, 266–267

Sainte-Beuve, Charles A., 131–132, 173
Sandiford, Ralph, *The Mystery of Iniquity*, 146
Seabury, Rev. Samuel, 184, 188
Selden, John, 11
Seward, William, 108–112; *Journal of a Voyage . . .* , 108
Shaftesbury, Anthony Ashley Cooper, Third Earl of, 8, 24, 41, 51–53, 58, 60, 63, 68–70, 84, 133, 155, 202, 217, 226, 248; *Characteristics*, 13, 28, 38, 61, 95, 129; *Inquiry concerning Virtue*, 51; *Letter concerning Enthusiasm*, 16
Sharp, Granville, 185, 186, 188
Shelburne, William Petty-Fitzmaurice, Earl of, 223
Shipley, Catherine, 197
Shipley, Bishop Jonathan, 151, 162–163, 255
Simpson, David, *A Plea for Religion*, 268
Smith, Joshua, 67–68
Smith, Rev. William, 181, 187
Solander, Daniel Charles, 213, 215
Soulavie, abbé Jean Louis, 32, 228–229, 271
Steele, Sir Richard, 259
Sterne, Lawrence, *Tristram Shandy*, 162
Stevenson, Mary, 165–166, 265–266, 270
Stiles, Ezra, 125, 176, 190–191, 206, 251, 256, 258
Strahan, William, 43, 122, 164, 196
Stuart, James, 213, 214
Sutcliff, Robert, 264
Swift, Jonathan, 67, 96, 133; "The Day of Judgment," 256; *Gulliver's Travels*, 140, 142

Talleyrand-Périgord, Charles M., 240
Taylor, Jeremy, 196
Taylor, John, 41
Tennant, Gilbert, 154
Thayer, Rev. John, 243–245
Thomson, Charles, 264
Thomson, James, 49
Tillotson, John, 94, 108

INDEX

Tindal, Matthew, *Christianity as Old as the Creation*, 3
Tryon, Thomas, *Way to Health* . . . , 16

Unitarians, 114, 209–212
Universalists, 212, 256

Van Limborch, Philipp, 247
Vaughan, Benjamin, 131 n.
Vergennes, Charles Gravier, comte de, 238, 240
Voltaire, 35, 66, 202, 224, 230, 231, 233, 248; *Treatise on Toleration*, 149
von Zinzendorf, Count Nicholaus Ludwig, 152–153

Washington, George, 181, 189, 247, 256
Watts, Isaac, 266
Wedgwood, Josiah, 213
Weems, Rev. Mason Locke, 181–184, 242–243, 248, 262
Welfare, Michael, 149–150
Whatley, George, 209, 255
Whichcot, Benjamin, 50
White, Bishop William, 187
Whitefield, George, 39–40, 41, 83, 103–123, 125, 152, 153, 155, 163, 270; compared with Franklin, 106; his integrity, 113, 123; his orphanage, 105, 112–113
Wilkes, John, 151, 168, 169–170; *Essay on Women*, 170
Williams, David, 31, 212–219, 234; *Essays on Public Worship* . . . , 212–213
Williams, Jonathan, 245
Winter, Cornelius, 163–164
Wollaston, William, 41; *The Religion of Nature Delineated*, 3, 17–22, 35

Xenophon, 60

Yale College, 14, 251

Zoroaster, 190

DATE DUE

APR 2 2 '70			
OCT 26 '71			
FE 27 '77			
JE 13 '77			
OC 25 '77			
MR 30 '79			
OC 7 '79			
OC 14 '80			
OC 19 '81			
MR 3 '82			
AP 26 '83			
FEB 10 '85			
AUG 05 '86			
GAYLORD			PRINTED IN U.S.A.